IN THIS THEATRE OF MAN'S LIFE

IN THIS THEATRE OF MAN'S LIFE

The Biography of Carl Ebert

Peter Ebert

The Book Guild Ltd
Sussex, England

The Book Guild Ltd.
25 High Street,
Lewes, Sussex

First published 1999
© Peter Ebert, 1999
Set in Times
Typesetting by Raven Typesetters, Chester
Printed in Great Britain by
Bookcraft (Bath) Ltd, Avon

A catalogue record for this book is
available from the British Library

ISBN 1 85776 347 5

To Silvia

'In this theatre of man's life it is reserved only for God and angels to be lookers on.'

Francis Bacon

CONTENTS

ACKNOWLEDGEMENTS

I am very grateful to the following copyright owners for permission to use their material: Sir Hugh Casson; Dame Janet Baker; John Skelton; the Carl Ebert archive of the Akademie der Künste, Berlin; the archive of the Deutsche Oper, Berlin; the archive of the Glyndebourne Festival Opera; the archive of the Staatsoper, Wien; Deutsches Theatermuseum, München; Guy Gravett, and also acknowledge gratefully the work of the following photographers: Roger Wood, Anthony Armstrong Jones, DN Smith, Ilse Buhs, Kurt Eschen, John Skelton and the following publications: *News Chronicle*, *Weekly Illustrated*, *The Sketch*, *Picture Post*, *Sussex Review*, *The Observer*.

I am indebted for encouragement and guidance to Hilary Rubinstein, Gritta Weill, the directors and staff of my publishers, The Book Guild Ltd, to many knowledgeable friends and particularly to my wife, Silvia.

FOREWORD

Over the last few years I have occasionally been given the melancholy task of writing an obituary or speaking at the memorial service of people in the musical world whom I knew well. The research involved usually resulted in a feeling that one now knew one's friend better in death than in life and a longing to re-run our time together, armed with greater insight. When I finished reading this book, those feelings were stronger than ever before.

When my old friend and colleague Peter Ebert asked me if I would write an introduction to this biography of his father I was greatly honoured and surprised. Carl Ebert will always be, in today's terminology, a world-class figure in the history of theatre and opera production in all its aspects, and had he not forsaken his acting career for the more challenging task of *Intendant* and producer in the opera house, he might well have been one of the greatest actors that ever lived.

Had this book been written by Carl himself or by Peter soon after his death, the list of candidates he might have invited to write these few words would have been much longer. As it is, I, in my 79th year, am perhaps one of the few people left who was directed by Carl Ebert for a substantial period (1947–1961) in nine productions plus revivals, all but one of them at Glyndebourne or the Edinburgh Festival. It was a very small fraction of his extraordinary career. For me it was the greatest stroke of luck any young artist could have experienced.

Much that you will read in this book describes opera production from the producer's or director's point of view. Peter is, of course, a fine director as well. This is a glimpse of what it was like on the receiving end of a Carl Ebert opera production.

The memory of that time in my life is still green. I first met 'the professor', as we called him, in 1947 at the Cambridge Theatre in London, where the Russian impresario Jay Pomeroy had mounted a highly successful long-running season of Italian operas the previous year, and had invited Carl Ebert to produce *Rigoletto*.

Much to my chagrin I was given, before his arrival, the small part of the Count Ceprano. I had already sung much larger parts in the season like Dr Bartolo in *Il Barbiere di Siviglia* and I felt this was a humiliating reverse.

I was all of 27 and my operatic career was but a year old and had been preceded, not by vocal and musical training, but by reading law followed by army service, where I succumbed to tuberculosis of the spine, which kept me on my back in plaster from 1942–44. With that background I was obviously not in any position to show haughty disdain to a minor role. Thank God I was persuaded to take it by our splendid musical director, Alberto Erede.

Ebert made a great impression on us all. There was something of the lion about him. The large head with long silver grey hair, the shrewd, slightly pouched eyes, the smooth brow and cheeks which instantly crumpled into lines and furrows as all the different emotions he wanted us to express marched obediently across his countenance. He would stand on the stage at early rehearsals, his shoulders hunched and his eyes restlessly following the action until he would stop us and demonstrate, giving an arresting performance of one of our roles, even singing quietly in his rather unsteady but effective croon.

Today no director in theatre or opera house would dare to get on stage and demonstrate, thereby diluting the actor or singer's own interpretation; but for most singers in our day it was gratefully accepted. Ebert was such a good actor and had had years of teaching students, which enabled him to draw from us, without any embarrassment, acting performances that were beyond our most optimistic expectations. It was like a very intensive post graduate course, particularly for me as I'd only graduated in law!

As you will read later, he was capable at rehearsal of sudden bouts of rage which were frightening but short-lived. He would run his hands distractedly through his hair and then his seat in the stalls would be slammed up as he hurried to the stage to roar his displeasure at a cowering cast. The cause was nearly always the same – a feeling in his mind that someone wasn't working hard enough or paying attention. Someone, in fact, who had for the time being failed to have the same intensity of feeling about the production as he had.

Work hard and pay attention and he was a marvellous person to work with and kept an eye on the production throughout the season. 'My boy, you have been adding some business. It is funny but not in the character of Don Magnifico, please go back to what we rehearsed.'

If Peter has erred at all in this account of his father's extraordinary career it is in showing an understandable reticence; inevitable for a son writing about an adored and admired parent, and a refreshing change from recent scurrilous filial biographies; but it is sad that he could not bring himself to build on Carl's beginning of his life story until 15 years after his death. He suffered a writer's block, again understandable and anyway, how does one find the objectivity let alone the time to work on such a major book in the midst of one's own busy and peripatetic career, particularly when one is not getting any younger?

For all his flamboyance (he loved taking a curtain call in full evening dress beside the conductor at the end of every performance) Carl was not interested in self aggrandisement. He yearned for opportunities to create permanent artistic establishments for the performance of opera, supplied with singers and musicians by an academy, making an entity where only the highest standards of teaching and performance would be acceptable. This interested him far more than producing operas on a freelance basis for different opera houses, where they would be used for a couple of seasons and then be heard no more.

He had no agent nor anyone doing PR for him. He was bad at publicising or pushing himself. Peter has inherited that modesty and writes of Carl's extraordinary achievements without superlatives. Thus they come off the page rather quietly but startle the reader in the process.

For example, his incredible presence of mind when only 5; his huge talent for the theatre first shown by giving auditions after seeing only two dramatic performances in his life and being offered an unprecedented free scholarship to train with Max Reinhardt; the amazing creation of a national theatre, an opera company and teaching establishments in Turkey from a standing start, all achieved in only a few years. His vast contribution to Glyndebourne, and for those who crave a touch of scandal, his divorce with its unusual outcome. After both he and his wife had married again, the two couples became lifelong friends, even going on occasional family holidays together; but there was one sad family casualty.

Ebert had his critics, and his ideal of a repertory ensemble opera with no stars became less and less practical in the age of air travel, but this book triumphantly celebrates a great man. The Polish aristocrat and the Irish-American music student who produced him enriched the operatic world beyond belief.

Ian Wallace

AUTHOR'S NOTE

During the last two decades of his working life, whenever there was a serious discussion on the place of the theatre in society, opera's unique combination of the arts, on the capacity of all the arts to survive the changes in the public's perception of entertainment with their true value intact, my father would say: 'I shall write about these thoughts in my book.' He was resolved to start work as soon as he retired. He felt he had so much to communicate to future generations, drawing on his long experience as a man of many talents in the theatre: actor, producer, theatre director and teacher. He was convinced the human character needs theatrical expression to present ideas for discussion, to highlight conditions of society and to challenge the establishment. All this under the overriding aegis of entertainment.

When the time to retire had arrived, there were so many new experiences. It took a while to get started on writing. My father chose not to launch out on a continuous story, but to reminisce about various periods in his life, important episodes in his career or on the political scene. Eventually, in spite of increasing pressure from a publisher and the family, he became more reluctant to finish the job. It suddenly occurred to me one day what the reason might be. I asked him: 'Can you not bring yourself to finish the book because you feel that would be the end of your life?' He nodded. And so the book was never put together and large important tracts remained unwritten.

I have tried to finish the task because I had a close relationship with my father all my life and have worked with him for many years. I have used most of his material, occasionally verbatim. I have also drawn on the extensive correspondence and other documents which my stepmother had carefully preserved. All this material is now deposited in the Carl Ebert Archive of the Akademie der Künste in Berlin, where it is made available for research.

P.E.

1

Childhood

Carl Ebert, one of the most famous men of the theatre in his time, actor, opera producer, theatre director, co-founder of the Glyndebourne Festival, founder of the Turkish National Theatre, inspiring teacher, suffered all his life from the stigma of his illegitimate birth. But he did not discuss his problem with anyone (even his children were not told the facts until they approached adulthood). He certainly did not believe in seeking professional help from psychiatrists – not at any time. Carl Ebert was born on 20 February 1887. His birth was registered under the name of Charles Lawless. No mention of his father, who was Count Anton Potulicky (pronounced Potulitsky), the second son of a long line of Polish aristocrats, who had their estates in the province of Posznan (that part of Poland that was swallowed by Prussia in the carve-up of the country in the late eighteenth century).

His mother was Mary Collins, an Irish-American music student in Berlin. She was so frightened that her family would find out about the birth of her child that she persuaded a friend, probably a fellow student, to 'lend' her name for the birth certificate. As soon as Mary was able to leave hospital she turned her back on her baby and Berlin. Count Anton had no experience in dealing with week-old babies. He managed to persuade Herr and Frau Ebert, with whom he was lodging while he worked at the Berlin Foreign Office, to care for the child. Seven years later the boy was formally adopted, and 'Charles Lawless' became 'Charles Ebert'. At the outbreak of World War One he decided to change to the German version of his Christian name and was henceforth known as Carl Ebert.

My father did not become aware of his romantic beginnings until he was summoned to a hotel in Berlin – he was about 17. Mother Ebert had stipulated at the time of the adoption that the child must not be told about his real parents until he was old enough fully to understand the implications. At the hotel he was met by Anton Potulicky, known to him as 'Uncle Anton', and another man who introduced himself as Anton's elder brother, Sigismund, the head of the family. It was explained to him who his real parents were, but also made quite clear that he could not be accepted into the Potulicky family. When Charles said he would at least like to bear the family name, Sigismund replied that it was more exciting, surely, to be the root of a new family tree than a small insignificant branch of a very old one. My father did not like the patronising smile with which this homily was delivered – and determined to be just that: the beginning of a new family tree.

When he came home to the Eberts, still deeply disturbed by this shattering interview, Charles found two people suddenly aged and broken in spirit. They could not imagine that he would still look on them as father and mother. Especially Maria felt that life had lost all purpose. 'Now you will not love us any more, we'll just be acquaintances for you,' she said. Charles swore that he could not wish for better parents and that, as long as he lived, he would look on them as father and mother. The last years of Maria Ebert's life were made relatively happy because Charles was able to prove that his words had not been empty rhetoric. He had discovered through this experience that 'it is not blood alone which speaks the truth'. He often said

'I cannot believe that there could be any other mother, anywhere in the world, who could have brought up a completely strange little creature with such genuine and all-embracing mother-love as Maria had for me.'

The fact that his own mother had abandoned him immediately after the birth, and had even disowned him by borrowing another's name for the birth certificate, was a deep, lasting shock for my father. This strong hurt was all the more pronounced because, in contrast, Maria Ebert lavished an almost exorbitant amount of love on her foster-child. Some time before the birth of Charles she had a miscarriage and had been told she could never have children of her own. When Anton Potulicky asked her whether she would be prepared to look after his first-born child it seemed like a gift from heaven for her. This emotional coincidence was perhaps the reason for her devotion to the child. The resentment Charles felt towards his own mother and the real mother-love expended on him by a stranger was, in turn, probably responsible for the very intense love my father had for his own children. His admiration for Maria Ebert had become such an obsession that he used every opportunity, such as a family gathering for a special birthday, to make a little speech in which he invariably came to talk about the most amazing, loving mother who ever lived. I remember, as a boy, finding these eulogies rather embarrassing when delivered in the presence of my mother or my stepmother. Certainly my father seemed to feel the need to offer up this kind of prayer of thanksgiving to Maria Ebert because she had, so to speak, provided the right to life for him.

Charles grew up in a lower-middle-class household. His adopted father Ebert had tramped through Europe as a young man, finding jobs here and there as an apprentice carpenter – the normal start for an artisan's career. Finally the farmer's son from Stolp in Pomerania, one of the eastern provinces, came to settle in the capital Berlin, which fascinated him. By the time Charles was born he had worked his way up to the ownership of the first '*steam-fraise* (milling) works' in Berlin. He had a horse to pull the delivery van – which also served to take the family on country outings on Sundays. He had engaged several apprentices, business boomed, and with it the living standard of the family.

Mother Ebert appeared to Charles to be the driving force within this circle. She was a peasant girl from the village of Schippenbeil in East Prussia, short, fairly stout and blonde. She had wonderful blue eyes and a happy, lively disposition. In spite of her quite basic schooling, she was the centre of attention at any gathering where she appeared, because of the absorbing and sensitive way she spoke. Father Ebert was a quiet, withdrawn man. Tall, blue-eyed and with a prophet's beard, he had an aura of 'sovereignty'. He had built himself an amazing workshop in the loft of the house.

3

There he spent his happiest hours: he invented and developed all kinds of technical gadgets, from a new beer-bottle-stopper to a washing machine. Sometimes Charles slipped into the loft unnoticed, and stood there without saying a word and watched as Father Ebert worked away at his projects using his enormous range of tools and machines.

He had amassed a quite substantial amount of capital and dreamt of making the 'great breakthrough' with one of his inventions. This, he hoped, would allow him to retire to the country on a secure income and indulge in his hobby. He entered into a partnership with two business people who, he thought, would be capable of marketing his inventions. Instead they exploited his unsuspecting trust, provided faked securities and robbed him of most of his life savings.

The Eberts had moved out of Berlin meanwhile, to a small village where they hoped to spend the rest of their lives. The devastating blow of the partners' fraud had a profound effect on the lives of the whole family. Mother Ebert cried day and night. It was probably the beginning of her serious, steadily worsening heart condition. Father Ebert's hair turned white, and he began to drink. Through the brutal fact of seeing the fruit of his life's work destroyed and having to face an old age in poverty, he became apathetic, unable to do any further work. Charles never saw him laugh again. Coming home one night, totally drunk, he stepped off a moving tram and fell into the ditch beside the track, where he was found next morning, bleeding and unconscious.

'I was five or six at the time and obviously less affected by these catastrophes. I played and fought with the other boys of the village (witness a scar near one eye), went barefoot in summer, in wooden clogs in the winter. The first day at school made a devastating impression on me as it appeared to deprive me irrevocably of freedom, sun and air.'

However, as he was placed at the end of a row of desks, near a window, it was quite natural that he would sit there, looking out of the window at the trees and birds, daydreaming. His teacher decided to establish discipline from the start and, as an example to

4

the class, caned him for inattentiveness. It hurt; Father Ebert had never used such methods of education. He did not cry, but he hated school from that day on.

Village life provided other incidents that made a lasting impression.

'I committed my first, and I believe my only, theft in life, and it made me deeply unhappy. Although I had only taken a few pansies from the neighbour's garden to give to my mother, his dire prophecies led me to expect that I was destined to end life as a criminal. I have never forgotten the scene with the enraged neighbour; it must have been a foundation stone of my moral education.'

This experience was underlined by the tragic case of another pupil who was caught during a real burglary and who took his own life by drowning himself in a nearby lake. It was the first corpse Charles had ever seen. He was firmly convinced that such experiences in early childhood have a much greater influence on character and attitudes in later life than is generally accepted.

The darkest hours for Charles were the times when the parents quarrelled. And that happened frequently. He tried to be the mediator: Don't quarrel, please don't quarrel! Weeping, begging, in all the ways a child's terror can find he tried to persuade the parents to make it up. More and more Mother Ebert took the child into her confidence. She told him, all of seven years old, about many kinds of problems and worries – principally of a financial kind – she cried a great deal, but sometimes would even ask his advice on which course she should take. These sessions were mostly monologues which she apparently needed to concentrate her mind. Charles learned quickly that there was a harsher, more stressful life than his schoolboy existence. Photos from that period show a strangely serious child's face.

'One day mother said we would go into town to meet an aunt who had come from America specially to see me. I should call her Aunt Mary – which I paraphrased into Aunt Maryca. I had to put on my best suit. Aunt Maryca was staying in a big hotel near Friedrichstrasse station in the centre of Berlin. She overwhelmed me with embraces and kisses so that I felt awkward. I did not take to her at all, although she led me round the room to see all the presents she had brought. I was told later that I did not take to those either. There was, for instance, a clown, a so-called Pojaz, bigger than myself, in a white suit with red dots. He was decked out in white leather shoes and a pointed hat of white felt, and he could move his head and arms and legs. I never knew how to play with him. At home he later just stood in a corner. Then there was a picture book with movable figures, a magic lantern and boxes of mounted "*Spahis*", which were three times as big as my brave old toy soldiers at home whose elite had already lost their heads in battle. Somehow every detail of that visit remained engraved in my memory all my life. Possibly because of an incident which showed my gentle "Mutsch" as I called her, in a totally new light. Aunt Maryca wanted to show me the great flow of traffic in front of the hotel and lifted me up to stand on the sill of the open window. It was really a very confusing view from that height, as she let me lean far forward and I felt quite dizzy. Suddenly I was pulled back into the room. It was my Mutsch; with a white face she shouted at Aunt Maryca: "What are you doing?" That was the end of our visit. We gathered the exotic toys and travelled back to our village of Schmargendorf. Not till much later did Mutsch explain that she thought at the time that I was to be allowed to fall down into the street.

'About two years later we met Aunt Maryca again – under even more dramatic circumstances. This time we all went up to town: Father, Mutsch, myself and Grete, a niece of Mutsch who had come to live with us in order to help with the housework. Grete and I were told to wait on a bridge over the river Spree until the parents returned from one of the nearby houses. It was quite a long wait. Suddenly Aunt Maryca came rushing out, shouting something she took hold of my hand and tried to pull me along. I hung on to the railing, and a moment later Mutsch appeared, quite out of breath, and grabbed my other arm. This went on under much swearing and shouting, people stopped to look, and finally a policeman arrived. Aunt Maryca belaboured him in a wild jumble of English and German, from which it became clear that "the police should free the boy from the clutches of that woman."

'Two women, one tall, slim and dark, the other small, well-rounded and blonde pulling a small boy in opposite directions and arguing their rights to the boy in different languages, must have been a bizarre spectacle. No wonder it attracted a host of curious passers-by, who began to take sides. An open carriage also stopped because the cabby wanted to see what was happening. I used the opportunity to pull Mutsch into the carriage and told the driver the address of her sister, where he was to take us. Mutsch never got over her amazement about my presence of mind, at the age of five and a half. At the time nobody explained the strange happenings of the day to me. But I did hear the parents talking late into the night and Mutsch crying.'

Many years later Maria Ebert still enjoyed recalling Charles' quick action, which seemed to her to be the proof of his natural love for her and with that her definite right to regard him as her own child.

Not until Charles was told who his real parents were, did he also learn the background to the quarrel on the bridge. 'Aunt Maryca' had decided to claim him as her own and had come to negotiate with the Eberts, with the help of a solicitor. The Eberts stubbornly refused to hand Charles back. When they were threatened with a court case to establish the right of the natural mother to the child, Father Ebert said: 'How can you prove that you are his mother? The mother's name is given as "Eileen Lawless" on the birth certificate.' At that point Mary Collins tried to abduct Charles.

2

Theatre Dreams

One day Maria Ebert decided the family should move back into town to try to create a sounder economic basis for survival. Years ago, as the young wife of a master artisan, she had already found that housework alone did not satisfy her. She had provided some additional income for the family by letting a few rooms to suitable tenants, among whom was the young Count Anton. She now decided to try the same thing on a grander scale. With her enormous energy she invested the remainder of the family's capital, obtained some credit and with astonishing taste, furnished a rented apartment of 11 rooms which she had found in the very fashionable district of banks and government ministries. She had some cards printed and sent them round to various offices. The desperate gamble came off. Within days she had let all the rooms, mostly to young bank executives, who proceeded to enjoy their comfortable bachelor existence under the wings of Mother Ebert. Among them was Fritz Andreae, Junior Partner in the bank 'Hardy & Co'. He lodged with the Eberts until his marriage to the sister of Walther Rathenau (the future Foreign Secretary) and remained a true friend and support, particularly in later anxious years.

'I was seven when we moved back to Berlin, and the family council, consisting of the parents Ebert and Uncle Anton, decided that I should go to the Friedrich Werder Oberrealschule (roughly Secondary Modern school), which specialised in vocational training. In our financial situation it was out of the question to even think of going to university later. I soon displayed a frightening lack of talent for the mainstream subjects of this school: Maths, Physics and Chemistry, for which my interest in German and modern languages could not compensate. Unfortunately the director of the school, a famous mathematician, took our class himself. He soon developed a sadistic pleasure in calling me to the blackboard, in the certain knowledge that I would be incapable of solving the problem he had set. His acid comments made the class roar with laughter. The German lessons were my favourites, because our teacher believed in making classic literature more accessible by letting the class read all the plays on the curriculum by sharing out the roles among the boys. After a short time I was always given the lead role, male or female, in all the plays we read. Maybe this activity was the unrecognised seeding of an interest in the theatre.'

Uncle Anton was a tall good-looking man with impeccable behaviour. The Eberts treated him with respect and always called him 'Herr Graf', while he called them 'Muttchen' and 'Vater', but addressed them as 'Sie' not the familiar 'Du'.

'I always looked forward to Uncle Anton's visits. He now worked in Warsaw, but stayed in Berlin for a few days on his way to and from the South of France. They were usually wonderful days, particularly when Mutsch winked at me and said "It was another good harvest". Uncle Anton always bought me expensive new clothes, but I had to learn not to wear the most outlandishly modish garments to the Oberrealschule. My classmates' teasing was merciless. Uncle Anton enjoyed taking me out to lunch, invariably to the most fashionable restaurant in Unter den Linden, called Dressel. The very first time, I recall, I was almost frightened by a good half dozen waiters dashing about with "Herr Graf this" – "Herr Graf that". I was quite flustered and naturally at a loss what to do with the array of forks, knives and spoons in front of me. Uncle Anton helped out with whispered commands like: "Now take the other fork, the big one is for the meat course and the smallest one for the dessert", or "Don't cut the potatoes with a knife" (these were the days before stainless steel; indeed, in Germany, to this day, it is bad manners to cut potatoes with a knife). It was very exciting, even when it seemed more like torture.'

Sometimes when he stayed at the end of winter, on his way back from Monte Carlo, where he had gambled at the Casino, he was in a particularly good mood, but occasionally he was grumpy and stayed only for two days or so.

'Once I overheard the parents discuss by how much they could afford to subsidise his return trip to Warsaw. For me his visits were always sensational. Uncle Anton did not merely want to spoil me and teach me the finer points of etiquette. I was questioned regularly about my progress in school, my interests, what I had learned, what else I wanted to study, etc. Once he engaged a lady to give me English lessons, but since it was a grumpy year this novelty was cancelled on his return from the South.'

The Eberts' economic situation seemed to have stabilised, even though the redemption of their loans was a burden for them. Mother Ebert's heart condition worsened rapidly, however. Fritz Andreae sent her to a famous specialist and promised to finance a long rehabilitation visit to the renowned Bad Nauheim. But when Father Ebert asked the specialist whether he could risk sending his wife to the spa, he received the unhelpful reply: 'Consider yourself lucky, if you get her home alive.' With an ever-weaker body but bright intellect, she lived for another 20 years.

'The time had come to decide about my future, and I was asked what career I wanted to pursue. I was quite unsure at that point, I only knew it had to have something to do with the arts. On my way home from school I often stopped at the stage door entrance of the Royal Drama Theatre and watched the artists going in and coming out. They stood out from ordinary people through their clothes. The men always wore large cravats and wide-brimmed hats and carried elegant canes with silver knobs. One day a tall gentleman came up to me and asked, "Would you like to see the performance tonight?" I was a little confused for a moment and stepped back, shaking my head. He guessed my problem and said, "No no, I don't want to sell the ticket. I want to give it to you." I think I just grabbed the ticket out of his hand, ran home to announce, "I have a ticket for the Royal Drama Theatre", and ran off again not to miss the beginning of the performance. It was Shakespeare's *Richard III*, my first visit to a real theatre. From my wonderful seat in the Dress Circle I savoured the performance, which was probably terribly traditional and old fashioned. "Herr Hochstetter" was written on the back of the ticket, and I found the same name in the programme, playing, I think, the Third Courtier. Mother had to listen to a comprehensive account of my experience which had excited me immensely. She said: "We ought to thank the gentleman; let's invite him to coffee." And so we did. I wrote a few lines to Herr Hochstetter at the Royal Drama Theatre, Mother produced a lovely cake, and we had a really nice conversation with the kind actor.'

At the height of his career as an actor and later as *Intendant* (General Director) at the Berlin Opera, my father sometimes met the man again who, unwittingly, had had such a decisive influence on shaping the life of adolescent Charles. Herr Hochstetter received a standing invitation to any performances in which the actor Ebert appeared or which the producer Ebert had mounted.

This first encounter with the theatre affected my father's whole being, but as yet there was no thought of a career on the stage. He was so moved by the experience of his first drama performance that he spent long hours of the night closeted with text books, learning monologues. He bought a long-haired wig at a cheap store, which he put on to declaim his favourite speech: the entrance monologue of *Richard III*. He gave performances for Maria Ebert and selected schoolfriends in the kitchen of their apartment, with enormous success. He had caught the theatre virus.

At a further family council to decide on his future, he admitted, after much prodding, that he wanted to be an actor. The outright rejection of this idea did not surprise him. Charles knew that he would need to earn some money as soon as possible to help the precarious family finances. Therefore the offer of Fritz Andreae to find a post for him in the bank where he was a junior partner was accepted. He worked in that unloved establishment for four years after leaving school.

Starting as an apprentice banker and advancing to being a so-called 'Young Man' helped a little to alleviate the parents' worries. The area where their apartment was situated had become less sought-after as a residential district, and Mother Ebert had to take more short-term lets with less distinguished customers. To help out, Fritz Andreae asked my father to deal with his private correspondence, which was done after office hours and meant additional income.

At this stage Charles began to feel very conscious of his lack of general education. He went along to the local Evening Institute. It is not recorded whether he even looked at the list of business courses on offer. But he was intrigued by the wide range of subjects available. Strangely enough, there was nothing whatsoever on the theatre. On the spur of the moment he inscribed for 'Comparative Religion'. Although unlikely to improve his mastery of banking practice, it proved to be a lucky shot. The course was taught by two of the most famous professors in this field. In later years my father was often grateful for the insight into human behaviour and the human need to believe, to search for a faith, which these courses had given him. Coping with all this, plus the time spent learning more monologues in the classical drama repertory, meant that he became accustomed to having only six hours' sleep – excellent training for his later career.

'I found it hard to master those demands of my work which went beyond simple adding and subtracting. Even so all my colleagues and superiors were friendly and helpful. One of the senior clerks in my department, wishing to encourage the young newcomer, started to dictate his business correspondence to me. I was not up to it yet. I got flustered, and had to keep asking how to spell some technical terms and even to admit to not understanding some of the banking terminology. In my despair I pretended to be a little deaf, whereupon the kind man proceeded to yell his: "With reference to yours of the nth inst ..." into my ear. My ploy had misfired.'

My father acknowledged later that these four years at the bank had taught him the need for and the advantages of a sense of duty and responsibility. His hated work helped keep the family alive. The mental torture of this banker's existence was, however, heightened by the fact that the view from his Victorian stand-up desk was straight on to the stage door of the Royal Drama Theatre, the door which had already proved so important in his life.

'I tried to do my sums and to write, but often I found myself daydreaming. I could not rid myself of the idea that this house and that door could be part of my life one day.'

Finally he made up his mind that his future lay in the theatre, and that he would pursue that goal, whatever the consequences. He read a notice in the paper announcing entrance examinations for the school attached to the Royal Drama Theatre. There was no fee for the exam and, for the chosen ones, the one-year course was also free. It appeared to be a dream come true.

Almost 300 candidates turned up to battle for six available places – three men and three girls. Charles passed the first hurdle and went forward into the second and final round – one of 30.

'On the appointed day I walked out on to the hallowed boards of this famous theatre and delivered the speech which I had drummed into my brain: Fiesco's address to the citizens of Genoa, from Schiller's play *Fiesco*. When I had finished a voice called out from the dark auditorium: "A". The stage manager, shepherding the throng of candidates, translated: "A – *abgelehnt* (meaning 'rejected')" and called the next victim. I pulled his sleeve and said: "A could also mean *angenommen* – accepted." He just repeated: "Rejected." I don't know how I got to the door, where my girlfriend was waiting for me. I was too stunned to explain what had happened. I just broke my new imitation ebony walking stick with the imitation silver knob in half.

'My girl, Cissi was her nickname, tried a little realism by saying that, perhaps, there would be something else that I could do. May God forgive her – she knew nothing about the theatre. Then suddenly I remembered passing a fat young man on the way down from the stage. He had said: "My God, you look dreadful. I'm not going to worry myself silly. I'll go to Reinhardt." '

The name stuck. Charles discovered that this Max Reinhardt had taken over the Deutsche Theatre and there was a lot of talk about it in Berlin. It was said that it offered modern productions, quite different from the old conventional ways. The actors apparently behaved and spoke naturally, life-like, and even the classics were given in a totally new modern format.

Charles bought two tickets and took Cissi to a performance to find out more about this Reinhardt style of theatre. The production of Heinrich von Kleist's *Käthchen von Heilbronn* appeared very beautiful to both of them and so different to what my father had seen and described to Cissi before. There was none of that grand declamation and pathos, none of that prancing and striking of attitudes which he had seen and heard on the stage of the Royal Drama Theatre. He had gone to that, his first, performance in a state of high excitement and quite uncritically – and, of course, without any means of comparison. Naturally he had come to associate what he had experienced with the term 'acting'. In the performance at Reinhardt's theatre speech, gestures and movement were totally natural. What went on on stage seemed absolutely real – the most surprising effect was the smell of a pine forest which wafted through the auditorium as the curtain opened on the first scene – an innovation, which I am glad to say, soon died out. In his first two visits to the theatre my father had experienced two diametrically opposed styles of performance. Reinhardt's, by all accounts, was the new way, the modern approach. His mind was made up.

'Next morning I went to see the administrative director of the Reinhardt school, Dr Legband, and asked for an audition. He was businesslike-friendly and mentioned the fee required for the two-year course. I laughed and said: "No, no – I need a free place", whereupon Dr Legband laughed and said they were a private school and there were no free places. I jumped to my feet, banged the table and shouted: "But I want to audition." The director was apparently impressed by this dramatic outburst and gave me the place and time of the audition.'

Charles realised it would be all or nothing this time, there would not be another chance to gain entry into the theatrical profession. He prepared a number of speeches. They were all evil characters, which, oddly, he thought offered him the best opportunity to prove his talent. The tame ones did not interest him. The auditions were held in Max Reinhardt's private villa, to which he had attached a tiny theatre. Waiting for the ordeal with the other candidates, Charles overheard them discuss the panel of judges. They said that several of the greatest actors of the day, all members of Reinhardt's company, were present, at the audition, among them Eysoldt, Wrangel, Durieux, Winterstein and Kayssler.

'When I was called in, there they were, sitting in a row on a narrow platform. The whole place was brightly lit and friendly, in complete contrast to the atmosphere at the Drama Theatre. I started with Richard III's monologue which I had seen at the Royal Theatre, determined to give it my all. At one point I threw myself onto a table with such vehemence that a leg broke; later I smashed a chair into a corner. As I went through my piece I thought I was conscious of an air of happy appreciation emanating from the row of judges. I left the room in a state of intoxication. The wait until all candidates had been heard seemed endless. Finally Dr Legband called me into his office and said: "You are the first student to be granted a free place in the Reinhardt school." It was a miracle that I did not squeeze the man to death in my exuberance.'

And so my father came into the hands of Max Reinhardt, who was about to play such a vital part in his development as an artist, who later called him 'the son of the house' and who really seemed to have a feeling of love for him – something which was not easily recognisable through his pronounced defensive reserve.

A secret, distant dream had, after this audition, suddenly become tangible reality. And the drudgery of working in the bank would soon become just a memory. In hindsight it is really strange that my father, who must have had a very obvious talent for the stage, should have acquired his obsession for the theatre in such a casual, almost coincidental way. Reading classical plays at school, watching the traffic in and out of the stage door of the Drama Theatre from his office stool and witnessing two very divergent performances with enthusiasm, sound more like typical manifestations of being stage-struck than the firm knowledge that 'this is my profession'. It was probably his somewhat puritan upbringing and his awakened sense of duty which had stifled his imagination. The successful audition was the catalyst that finally cleared his mind.

On the half-hour walk home, however, he gradually returned to realistic thinking: how could their little family exist, how could the parents manage without the 120 Marks per month which he brought home as a 'Young Man' with Hardy & Co., plus the extra he earned through his work for Fritz Andreae? He was proud to have been an important prop of the family's finances from the age of 17. Maria Ebert's heart condition had worsened, she was confined to bed for a lot of the time and had to use an invalid chair to get about. Although her niece Grete was a great help in the house, she also was an extra mouth to feed. Charles seriously asked himself how he could find the courage to tell the parents what he had been up to behind their backs. A rather unhappy 'first scholarship student of the Reinhardt school of drama' faced his parents.

Father Ebert listened to his report silently and without any reaction, but Maria Ebert, crying and laughing simultaneously, embraced Charles and said: 'I knew it, I knew it all along that our little boy would become something quite special one day'. My father's doubts and worries turned back into determination in that instant. He decided he needed to act and not think about the family's problems any more. But the action he took was, as he recognised a few years later, totally unethical and professionally immoral: after his first few weeks at the Reinhardt school he put an advertisement in a local paper saying that a young actor was prepared to give private drama lessons at a low fee. It was a desperate action, of which he was ashamed all his life. In the course of his professional career my father taught thousands of students in different parts of the world. They would all agree, I am sure, that he had fully atoned for that early lapse.

One of them wrote on the occasion of his first 25 years in the theatre: 'I can see you clearly now, with your burning eyes, your thin, pale face walking along, leaning forward a little, always hurrying, wearing a tight, shiny suit. That's how we saw you in the Drama Academy, always alert, but with great warmth and kindness; you represented security, justice for all and authority. You always had time for everyone, however great the pressure and when you spoke to one, any one of those undiscovered geniuses, who were so timid and inhibited, he or she walked away happy, uplifted and stronger.'

3

Reinhardt: the School and the Deutsche Theater Berlin

'Fate held its protecting hand over me when I failed the
entrance exam to the Drama School of the Royal Theatre.'

That was Charles' assessment after only a short time at the
Reinhardt School. He had no knowledge of the theatre, no stage
experience of any kind. In Germany at that time there was no
amateur drama that would have been accessible to him. The sum
total of his knowledge was what he had read and the two very
diverse performances he had seen. The first few days at the
Reinhardt School opened up a new world to him.

'Only a few pupils of his school had the great fortune to be
taught by Reinhardt himself. I was one of the few. From the
first moment I was fascinated by the self-evident and authoritative logic of his teaching and, later, his productions. No
other man, I believe, could express so convincingly his
assessment of an actor's personality and how he wanted him
to build his role. With his searching, penetrating eyes he
could make actors tremble or give them a kind of inner
elation. He very rarely demonstrated his vision of a role by
acting it – instead he expressed everything he wanted to communicate through his voice. And his voice was unique:
slightly nasal, it somehow conveyed a feeling of giving an
order. When explaining a particular role, he never tried to
give his voice the required colour (which meant that imitat-
ing him would, inevitably, sound absurd). But the way he

18

used it was like the opening of a gate to something obvious, self-evident. Whether working on Gretchen's prayer, "*Ach neige, Du Schmerzensreiche...*" (in Goethe's *Faust*), or Karl Moor's vow of retribution, "Men – false, deceiving brood of crocodiles..." (in Schillers *Die Räuber*), he never gave the actor a line reading, instead he led him/her to the underlying spiritual content of the scene. This was solely done through the way he used his voice in explaining the essence of a scene and what he wanted to achieve in the interpretation. His method of hinting at the required vocal expression was so compelling that everything else, body language, movement, etc. fell into place naturally. Even as a student one was almost ashamed that one had not found the right road to what seemed the only possible interpretation, unaided.'

While at the school Charles was lucky enough to rehearse two very contrasting roles with Reinhardt, the mason Mattern in *Hanneles Himmelfahrt* (*Hannele's Entry into Heaven*) by Gerhart Hauptmann, and the vicar Hoppe in *Jugend* (*Youth*) by Halbe. It is easy to see the reason for Reinhardt's choice. He had witnessed my father's extravagantly wild interpretation of Richard III and wanted to test him in that contrasting range of roles to see whether there was genuine talent. He particularly wanted to see how his new recruit would fare with a more lyrical, perhaps weaker character. The mason Mattern, a work-shy drunkard, brutal and sadistic towards his stepdaughter Hannele, is a psychopathic beast. As a counterbalance he wanted to see him tackle the role of the very humane, well-educated vicar Hoppe in Halbe's play. He is an intensely religious man, who has taken into his house the two children of his sister after her sudden death. He is understanding and liberal in his attitude to young people's needs, within the confines of adhering strictly to Christian values. Both plays were very much products of their time: protests against the purely romantic tradition, attempts to show 'real' people and situations on stage. Although they were unbearably melodramatic post-romanticism, these plays heralded a new epoch in dramatic literature. Working with Max Reinhardt on these two roles literally laid the foundation of Charles' career as an actor.

'In those months I learned the craft of acting.'

The school, without any doubt, pioneered the most revolutionary training for the stage at the time – the end of the first decade of the twentieth century. Reinhardt was already a famous producer and theatre director. His new conception of drama production was completely unforced, untendentious. He had begun to demolish the traditional style of drama productions as practised by the Court Theatres for generations. He succeeded in scraping off layers of accumulated dust, senseless tradition, empty declamation of texts, antiquated stage designs which wrapped every play in band-box romanticism. His aim was to create real people on stage, in surroundings which were instantly recognisable and believable. Both speech and body movement were recreated in a modern idiom. In 1909, the year Charles joined the Reinhardt stable, these innovations were still in a process of development. A beautiful natural speaking voice was essential basic equipment for Reinhardt's productions. Alexander Moissi, one of the most prominent members of his company, was even allowed to retain a certain romantic mannerism in his vocal expression. The creation of the 'kitchen sink' type of modern stage delivery lay some years ahead still.

Apart from his creative talents Reinhardt was an astute businessman as well as a showman (the use of a pine essence spray in the auditorium for a forest scene). A decade later he applied his combined talents to a succession of super-productions in drama, operetta and films, which became legendary through their breathtaking extravagance. Those were the years of an explosion of creativity in all the arts in Germany after World War One.

The second most important factor in the moulding of my father's acting talents was the influence of Alexander Strakosh, whom Reinhardt had engaged as a sort of Professor Higgins for his Deutsche Theater in Berlin, including the Drama School. He was the undisputed best speaker on the German stage.

'He had not been present when I gave my memorable audition, resulting in the scholarship award. Strakosh wanted to get to know the new intake of students and asked them to perform something for him. I was already somewhat too cocky where auditions were concerned, and launched straight into my wild interpretation of Richard III. During the action I was occasionally conscious of a noise like the gurgling of a drain. With the flourish of my exit Strakosh released his barely suppressed amusement with a gale of laughter: "My dear boy, did you see X.Y. do this role at the Royal Theatre? Your caricature of it is pricelessly funny." I was stunned and humiliated; the exquisite dream of life in the theatre seemed to have been vandalised. I could not believe nor understand Strakosh's reaction.'

Alexander Strakosh was Hungarian. He had arrived in Vienna as a young man of 17 with only a basic knowledge of German and announced that he wanted to become an actor. He was very small, almost a dwarf, with a very large head and had a dreadful accent in German. People just laughed about his ambition to become an actor in the German-speaking theatre. With immense self-discipline he succeeded in learning fluent German – more than that, he learnt to understand and subsequently to demonstrate the most subtle nuances of which the language is capable. He became a teacher who, through merciless discipline, inculcated into his pupils the ability to give each vowel and consonant exactly the right expression within each word, commensurate with its meaning within the whole text. His teaching method was uncompromising: endless repetitions of sentences from the classics which, on the face of it, appeared to be of strictly secondary importance. One of his favourite exercises was Beaumarchais' line from Goethe's *Clavigo*: 'A French merchant, who called many children but only a small fortune his own, had a number of correspondents in Spain.'

That sentence, which the students would have been inclined to speak in a throwaway manner, was scraped clean and analysed like an important archeological find – until they mastered speaking it absolutely clearly, but with exactly the right lack of emphasis. Every vowel and every consonant had its correct measure. The students hated the, by now, old little man and his chicanery in making them work on these minute details of expression for hours and hours. At that point none of them yet understood what lay behind their teacher's method: to create complete mastery over the technique of using speech – the most valuable tool in the actor's trade.

Charles became one of the leaders of the protesters who considered this obsessive preoccupation with minutiae a waste of time. One day he regaled his fellow students with a persiflage of Strakosh's relentless method, speaking in a very affected manner. It brought the old man to tears. Throughout his life my father felt burning shame at the thought of that terrible, brutal parody. In his own long teaching career in different countries he always used Alexander Strakosh's method and hoped this would go some way towards atoning for his sin – his second since becoming a member of the acting profession. He had obviously been blinded by his hunger to get on in his new vocation.

The technical perfection in using the voice, which Strakosh taught, certainly bore within it the danger of superficiality and affectedness. A counterweight to the Strakosh method was required. Possibly with this in mind, Reinhardt had engaged Emil Milan for the school. He was the third of the three men who decisively influenced my father's development as an actor. Max Reinhardt had entrusted Milan with a number of productions in his theatres over the years, but that activity was, in fact, not his forte. He became, instead, an essential cog in the team which Reinhardt had collected for his crusade of renewal. The influence of Reinhardt and his predecessor Brahm created an almost cataclysmic upheaval in the German theatre round the turn of the century. They began to crank open a sluice which released streams of revolutionary ideas through the landscape of German-speaking theatre and finally washed away the whole edifice of the old regime, the Court Theatres. It was a turbulent time of experiments, of trial and error and an enormous investment in serious analysis of the whole basis of the theatre's *raison d'être*. Some of the exploratory paths inevitably led into no-man's-land. This process of change did not happen overnight – some theatrical innovations sometimes do so, only to disappear again just as quickly. This fundamental change took many years to develop fully, probing, retreating and feeling its way forward again. The common denominator under which this turning away from the old Court Theatre style took place, was 'simplicity'. Emil Milan was the principle architect of this new mode of expression.

Milan's teaching method was unusual. His lectures were really recitations. He spoke long texts, mostly by heart, to demonstrate his views on the use of speech. As the students could not acquire the teacher's virtuosity of expression by dint of repeating his phrasing and melodic line, his method required a learning process from them: it was an intellectual process of listening, absorbing and understanding the way Milan made his texts come alive – with the simplest possible means. He spoke his texts in a real, modern idiom, shorn of all 'theatrical' ballast. Understanding Milan's dramaturgical approach was, of course, only half the battle. The student had to integrate the 'simplicity' of the new order into his own personality and, so to speak, 'retune' his own speech to a completely new wavelength. In short, he had to make it his own. Only then could he hope to give the texts that freshness and conviction which had become such a rare quality in the old style of acting.

After only 18 months at the school Charles was entrusted with a few smallish roles with the company at the Deutsche Theater and on the occasional forays of the company 'guesting' at other theatres. This honour was a mark of his talent as well as the speed with which he was able to absorb what the teaching at the Reinhardt school offered. The roles he was allocated gave no hint of the career which was about to bloom. He usually played old men, an odd initiation into his profession for an actor in his late teens. The opportunity, however, of being part of 'real' productions, and as a partner of some of the most gifted and celebrated actors and actresses in Germany, amounted to an incalculable benefit to his progress. He could observe and analyse how these experienced professionals had mastered the tools of their craft and how they were able to make them into attributes of their stage personalities.

Charles performed his tasks well, but luck played a part in giving his career an early boost.

'It so happened that the Deutsche Theater had been invited to perform at a new small Festival theatre in Munich. Two days before the first performance Paul Wegener, who played the mason Mattern in *Hanneles Himmelfahrt*, fell ill. There was no understudy. Max Reinhardt had the courage to send for me, his student, who had never professionally walked on a stage before, and to let me play this role, replacing one of the most prominent members of the company. Through this chance I more or less stumbled directly into the senior squad of the theatre. There is always a very special bond between performing artists – the new baby in their midst was accepted and helped by all. Presumably it was obvious that I was nowhere near the same class as my partners Alexander Moissi and Lucie Höflich, but for me the important thing was that, without much ado, I had started my career as a professional.

'A few days later catastrophe almost overwhelmed me. Since I had to be in Munich anyway, Reinhardt gave me another role: the Archangel Michael in a new production of Goethe's *Faust*. The rehearsals were wonderful. When I was not "on", I hid in the stalls and listened to the master producing other scenes of the play. The day of the premiere arrived. It was an enormously important occasion for me. I stood on a very high platform like the other two archangels and had to speak the first lines. My whole body was shaking. "*Die Sonne tönt nach alter Weise…*" (untranslatable without the context). I was stuck. It was black in front of my eyes, my ears were drumming. Empty. Was my voice on strike? Did I really not know the next lines? The verses which I had spoken so often in all the rehearsals? There was a deathly stillness around me, but in my ears, in my head there was a thumping noise. The blood was pulsing through my body like hammer blows. Then I heard voices. It was my neighbour archangel, who prompted me: "*… in Bru-der-späh-ren Wett-ge-sang…*" It was also Alexander Moissi who, as Mephisto, was lying at our feet and who whispered the same words, and it was the prompter above all, who whispered, spoke, shouted – in whispers. I understood nothing. Finis. Go home, jump into the river or just fall off the platform and lie dead. Then my mouth spoke the lines which arrived at my place from all sides. My mouth spoke the lines and even spoke them to the end. My stage life had started with a short triumph as the stonemason Mattern and had ended with a fall into the abyss with the Archangel Michael.

'Afterwards I did not know how to meet the others' eyes. I can't remember how I got out of the theatre, how I survived the night, I only remember that Max, the great Max, held out his hand to me at the beginning of the rehearsal the following day, without saying a word. It was the greatest kindness which I have ever received in my professional life, which can be so unbelievably harsh and brutal and ugly.'

My father's Polish-Irish lineage was possibly responsible for sudden outbreaks of a quick temper through most of his life. While still in Munich he read an article in which the theatre critic had concocted a mean and nasty attack, trying to shred Reinhardt's genius and his achievements. This enraged the actors – particularly the younger ones, who had not yet acquired a healthy immunity to that kind of character assassination. The article was signed with a name which they knew from the drama school: it was an arrogant, young nobody who always hung about near the theatre, because he was having an affair with a middle-aged actress. As usual he stood outside the stage door the following night, waiting for his flame. Charles went up to him and asked whether he was the author of that article. He said, 'Yes,' and Charles slapped his face left and right without saying another word. Two days later the critic's *amour* complained, with an undertone of admiration: 'Charles, whatever did you do to the poor man, he still has your five fingers on each cheek?' The judge showed no mercy. Charles was find 300 Marks for 'grievous bodily harm'. In 1910 that was a fortune. But Albert Steinrück, a senior member of the company, came to tell him: 'It's all been taken care of.' The ensemble had passed the hat round – presumably because they approved of his action.

When he got back to Berlin he found a contract with the Deutsche Theater waiting for him. It was to run for five years, starting at 180 Marks per month, rising to 600 Marks. This did not represent immediate riches, but it was enough for a certain sense of security for the Eberts, even though they were now going to be two families. The five-year contract gave him the courage to marry. His girlfriend and he had waited seven long years for this moment.

When Charles had just started working at the bank, he sometimes saw a most beautiful young blonde at the tram stop. The frustrating thing was that he had no suitable opening gambits for such an occasion, being very shy by nature and totally lacking in experience in social contact outside the family. Eventually the weather came to his rescue. It started to rain while they were both waiting at the tram stop. The girl eagerly accepted my father's offer that they should share his umbrella. From there it was only a few steps to the question:'How old are you, if I may ask?' 'Fifteen,' she said, 'and you?' 'Not quite seventeen,' was his overoptimistic reply. He still had more than six months to go to his next birthday. Her name was Lucie Frederike Karoline Splisgarth. She came from a very normal bourgeois household. The father was a gifted craftsman, working for one of the giants in the emerging electrical industry, the mother a very warm and kind woman with a great sense of humour and a quizzical look. Both parents came from peasant stock with a strong Slavonic influence. In an area near Berlin, called the Mark Brandenburg, there were still small enclaves of people descended from Slavonic tribes who were swamped when the Germans slowly began to push eastwards some hundreds of years ago. Both parents had the high cheekbones typical of their ethnic origin. It is strange to observe that both sets of parents/foster parents of the young lovers shared so many features of their origins and personalities.

Charles and Cissi, for that was my mother's nickname all her life, developed a very close relationship quickly. But they were not lovers in the modern sense. Both had, of course, been brought up conventionally. Even after they decided to get engaged, it took another seven years of purely platonic relations before they reckoned they could afford to get married and become lovers physically. The reality of his own background had made my father constantly aware of the dangers of promiscuity or even of a physical relationship entered into too lightly. He was, one might

26

say, on the edge of being prudish. He could never bear smutty jokes or stories, which, so often, appear to be the psychological release for real prudes. There is a certain justification in the common belief that the theatre world is awash with love affairs. Charles was strikingly good-looking, tall, slim, dark, with intense blue eyes and an excellent bone structure. Hidden under his shyness was a warm, kind personality, grateful for and somehow in awe of all the beauty and pleasure which life could offer. This later grew into an unquenchable zest for life, and he became increasingly outgoing and positive in his relations with other people. I believe that Charles resisted the many amorous temptations which must have come his way in his stage career. After I had started to work in the theatre myself, he certainly repeatedly warned me and begged me to avoid all physical involvement with the members of the company. Apart from anything else, it could ruin a burgeoning career.

Although Charles could never forgive his real mother for having 'denied' him by using a borrowed name on the birth certificate and having abandoned him, ostensibly without a thought for his well-being, he was naturally curious to find out more about her personality, her background and her character. What had become of her since that fateful second meeting on the bridge over the river, when he was almost torn in half? Had he, perhaps, inherited her obviously dramatic temperament? Anton told him that he thought she lived in Paris, married to a businessman or banker, and had three daughters. When Charles was sent to Paris for performances with the Reinhardt company, he made enquiries through the police and set off, accompanied by Cissi, to find the address. In spite of his negative feelings towards his mother, he was certainly under emotional stress: he suddenly thought the elegant lady with her three children they had just passed in the street, must be his mother Mary. Only the suspicious look of the concierge, when he enquired whether Madame was at home, made him come to his senses. Quite plainly, if he had persisted, he might have ruined a human life. It is extraordinary that his curiosity had not been checked earlier by a rational assessment of the situation. Perhaps stubbornness, which often brought success for him in life, was also a quality inherited from Mary Collins. The idea of persuading a fellow student to 'lend' her name for the purpose of the birth certificate, he found quite grotesque. To him there was some kind of prophetic madness in the fact that the borrowed name was 'Lawless'. On the other hand he was intrigued by his mother's background, the mixture of modern, energetic USA and the mystic, mythological Ireland – both countries, one must remember, much more distant from Berlin than the Polish provinces of Prussia. His mother's elegant appearance had made an impression on him, and the memory of her dramatic behaviour in his childhood had made him curious.

My father was not a religious person in the sense of regular churchgoing. But he believed strongly in a Higher Being. The Christian God? Another? When, as a teenager, I had problems 'believing' as taught in class, he simply asked me whether I though the spirit of grandmother Splisgarth, who had died a little earlier, was still with us or had just vanished. His real parents were Catholics, of course. The Eberts were Protestants. He never joined the Catholic faith, but when visiting churches on holiday, for instance, one was bound to notice that he genuflected very slightly and made an almost surreptitious sign of the cross. He said his prayers every night throughout his life, and the spiritual bond with his family was clearly expressed through the ritual of kissing a number of photographs before going to bed. These ceremonies were enormously important to him, but he totally rejected the rituals of the normal church services, because he felt that they had become empty shells of their former emotional/spiritual meaning. The run-of-the-mill priests, supposedly shepherds of their flocks, were, in his view, hopelessly inadequate for their task, and their unconvincing verbosity was responsible for the gradual emptying of the churches. Through his study of comparative religion he became very interested in and knowledgeable about the subject. Whenever he met eminent theologians, such as Dr Barth, he grabbed the opportunity to discuss the future of Christian belief. He felt that the practice of contemporary Christian religion was no longer true to its origin and could not be of any help to his own spiritual needs.

Cissi, my mother, was fascinated by the strange new world which she began to glimpse, the theatre. She was an equally avid learner. Some of the more senior colleagues at the Deutsche Theater began to take an interest in the insatiable appetite for study of the young couple. Paul Wegener, one of the stars of the theatre, for instance, was an expert over a wide range of the arts and finally had become a connoisseur of Far Eastern art, with which he had filled his home. He himself was quite un-Germanic in looks. Hollywood might have typecast him as Genghis Khan, with his very pronounced high cheekbones and narrow eyes. With the help of such expert guidance from several sources, my parents learned more about the history of art than they could have filtered from years of evening classes. Both kept this enthusiasm for learning through inquisitive appraisal, rather than following trends, all their lives. Cissi retained a remarkable faculty for understanding and living with contemporary art, right until her death at the age of 92. She remained totally receptive, but not uncritically, towards all streams of new expression in the visual arts, music, theatre and literature – with the exception of the 'Painted by a chimp on a bicycle' variety. My father became slightly intolerant of modern art in his last years. He felt that a trend of lack of honesty was slowly permeating the international art world and that 'marketability' became the sole aim of some of the sensationally modernistic artists. This anxiety about the eroding standards of quality was probably fuelled by my stepmother's choice of Los Angeles as their home in retirement. LA has, arguably, the highest density of outstanding artistic brains in the world, and yet it gives the unmistakeable impression of being a cultural desert and, particularly, a breeding ground for phoney 'isms'. But these worries were far removed from the arts world of Berlin before and after World War One, which was brimming over with the most exhilarating developments in all fields. Charles became determined to be part of the revolutionary flood, and through his work soon met its most prominent leaders.

Towards the end of the first decade of the twentieth century, when Charles was initiated into the theatrical profession at the Reinhardt School, the arts world throughout Europe began to experiment with new modes of expression. Picasso and Braque developed the Cubist view of life and objects ('Paint not what you see, but what you know is there'), the German philosopher

Oswald Spengler wrote *The Demise of the Western World*, which aroused heated discussion. Diaghilev founded Les Ballets Russes and commissioned Stravinsky to compose the *Firebird* and *Rite of Spring*, which caused a massive scandal – just as Synge did with his *Playboy of the Western World*, and James Joyce and the poet W.B. Yeats. In Germany Gerhart Hauptmann, Hermann Loens and Ernst Barlach were in the forefront of experimenting with Expressionist drama. Kandinsky pioneered abstract painting. Kokoschka, Chagall and Modigliani made their own excursions into the unknown in sculpture and art as well as design. André Gide, H.G. Wells, Maeterlink, Claudel, D.H. Lawrence, Proust, the Sitwells, Kafka, T.S. Eliot and Ezra Pound are examples of the writers who exerted an enormous influence on modern literature and poetry, often against fierce opposition from the establishment and the general public. It was also the time of the introduction of 'blues', of Irving Berlin's 'Alexander's Ragtime Band', of Arthur Honegger and his 'Nouveaux Jeunes' group, of Richard Strauss' revolutionary operas *Salome* and *Elektra*, and of the growing influence of Arnold Schoenberg. And in 1917 (!) Reinhardt, R. Strauss and the writer Hugo von Hofmannsthal founded the Salzburg Festival.

All these names and incidents only serve to represent the host of artists in all fields, including film and architecture, sensing a common need to explore. Perhaps the first seeds of this revolution were sown by the Art Nouveau movement at the end of the nineteenth century. It was a long period of exuberant experiment, lasting into the early 1930s, which crushed the ossified frontiers of tradition. It was like opening a window, it created a 'hands-on' vision of the arts, banishing the elitist and precious attitude of the nineteenth century. This cauldron of striving for new expressions also produced many 'isms', naturally. They simply fell away when their essential leavening influence had been absorbed.

For everybody, 'Member of the Deutsche Theater, Berlin' was a proud title; more than that, it was the visiting card for a particular style of acting, just like 'Member of the Stanislavsky Theatre, Moscow'. Even so, for Charles it meant starting his career from the bottom, together with several other young actors whose later fame proved that Reinhardt had a special gift for recognising

30

talent early. Among his contemporaries in the ensemble were several actors whom Reinhardt brought to Berlin from the provinces, among them Werner Krauss, Emil Jannings, Mary Dietrich, Fritz Kortner, Paul Grätz, Josef Danninger et al. It was hoped that they would, in time, take over the mantle of the great protagonists who presently stood in the limelight. It was a very rare plethora of young talent at a single theatre, and they all started on level terms. Nobody ever asked whether they were going to get a bigger role in the next production or whether it was only 'The horses are saddled, sire'. Charles just wanted to be on stage, he wanted to be on stage every day – acting tall, small, fat, thin, old or young, it made no difference, just to be on stage, to breathe in that dust-laden air was to be where he belonged, and he savoured it. To be allowed to take over a leading role as second cast was a great distinction. At that point one had to show one's mettle.

After Charles' debut in Munich, Reinhardt felt he could entrust him with bigger roles. In 1911 he was allowed to play the title role in Stucken's *Gawan*, replacing Kayssler, and his confidence grew with every role. In his second year with the theatre he was very surprised to be asked to 'guest' at the prestigious Goethe Festival in Düsseldorf. Although he had, so to speak, only just begun to test his wings, he was invited to play Dunois in Schiller's *Joan of Arc*, Tellheim in Goethe's *Minna von Barnhelm*, Judas in Ludwig's *Makkabäer* and Leicester in Schiller's *Maria Stuart*, four decisive roles. The festival had a reputation of being a seat of the traditional style, but Charles accepted the challenge happily, perhaps a little cheekily. As the date came closer, however, a feeling of panic almost overwhelmed him, and

'when I boarded the train I prayed for a derailment – without casualties, of course – to save me from making a fool of myself. We were not derailed, I played all four roles.'

Ten minutes into the first session of rehearsals in Düsseldorf all was revealed: the confrontation with the old pathos-ridden style of acting of the Wilhelminian Court Theatre tradition. How could a second-year beginner of the Deutsche Theater stand his ground against such a phalanx of traditional actors? Charles also had the distinct feeling that his colleagues regarded him as a foreign body, which the press echoed: 'modern' and 'nervous' were the adjectives used to describe his speech and his acting, which 'did not gel with the rest of the ensemble'. 'Quite a strange, modern trend, without declamation' was another turn of phrase. Both words, modern and interesting, were always set off by inverted commas, but at least it was admitted that Charles' performance 'held the audience spellbound'. Only one, very brave, critic dared to praise 'Herr Ebert's ability to communicate the essence of a play, compared to the superficial intonations' of the traditional actors. It was his death warrant. He was never invited to the Goethe Festival again.

The romantic circumstances of his birth, the unusual Polish/American-Irish combination of parental background and the fulfilment of his dream of gaining entrance to the theatrical profession seemed like a fairytale to Charles Ebert, alias Lawless, alias Collins, alias Potulicky. He was now a member of the most prestigious German drama company and he played a range of young leads in the classical repertory, such as Horatio in *Hamlet* and Pylades in Goethe's *Iphygenia*. Even playing title roles as second cast was a wonderful experience and an incomparable training ground. Second casts were necessary in the German repertory system, a) in case of illness, and b) to release an actor from a role when he was required for too many new productions. Reinhardt did not make time to worry about second casts. Their rehearsals were usually left to Berthold Held, a trusted keeper of Reinhardt's production details, but, of course, he had neither Max's personality nor the strange fascination of his voice. The young, and still fairly raw, actors had to grope their way through the short, but pertinent production notes which were transmitted to them by the assistant. But they also had the wonderful chance of trying to find their own interpretation – severely within limits, to be sure, because Reinhardt's notes were so convincing and also let one feel the dictatorial weight of his genius. In those years Charles soaked up Reinhardt's mastery of the medium, but also had a certain freedom to work on his own ideas – and used it.

However, there was a total lack of resonance for the work of the second casts, either in-house or from the press. Reinhardt never went to see repertory performances, not even of his own productions, and the press were not invited either. He told Charles many years later that the performances did not interest him any more, because they very soon acquired a varnish: 'Theatre is only fully alive in rehearsals when all the nerve-ends of the actors are engaged in the act of giving birth, in the excitement of the process of creation.' Charles understood perfectly how Reinhardt felt: it is often too painful to see imperfections which one was unable to master or, in some cases, not to be able to discard a production and start all over again.

Charles was even given title roles and leads, as second cast, early in his career, including Faust and Tellheim (in *Minna von Barnhelm*). He and his colleagues were deeply hurt that Reinhardt completely ignored these performances. That their efforts had no echo in the press was tantamount to damaging their careers. One day, rather naively, Charles wrote to Reinhardt and invited him to one of these repertory performances in which he played the lead as second cast. He added, however, that it was of no value to him if Reinhardt simply sent one of his 'courtiers'. It was the measure of the bitterness they all felt that Charles used this disparaging expression and, at the time, he did not care that such excellent men of the theatre as Felix Hollaender, Arthur Kahane and Berthold Held were thus defamed. Among the recipients of his barb there was no perception of the overwhelming frustration which initiated the writing of the letter, only the insult was registered. Maybe Charles was still too much of a firebrand, but in this case his action stemmed from an incorruptible sense of justice, which he retained all his life, regardless of whether it was to his advantage or not.

A very serious discussion with Reinhardt followed, in which Charles pleaded the point of view of the younger actors playing major roles as second cast. He felt that, although Reinhardt showed only a cool reserve, he understood the actors' case. He thought he must have understood – he had been an actor himself, after all.

When Charles became a theatre director years later, he decided to do the opposite and to make it his duty to see as many performances of his productions as he possibly could. He was convinced of the artists' need to feel the director's physical presence, his interest in the continuing quality of their collective work.

Many years later still, my father came to my theatre and we both sat in my box to watch one of my productions. Within a minute word had gone round the whole theatre from the stage: 'The boss is out front – and the old boss as well.'

Still in pursuit of justice and reform, he made an attempt to break the class system at Reinhardt's theatre. Reinhardt's working method was a process of giving and taking when he was rehearsing the star actors, personalities like Wegener, Moissi, von Winterstein, Eysoldt, Höflich, Wrangel and Durieux. In this dialogue he contrived to let the ideas given to him fuse with his own, very clear, image of each role, thus allowing a tailor-made interpretation to develop, taking account of the characteristics of every actor. But actors in smaller roles had to follow his instructions in every nuance. To underpin the inequality of this system, the textbooks for smaller roles were given out only the night before the first rehearsal, while Reinhardt had, of course, discussed the conception of the bigger texts with the top actors long before. Charles made one or two desperate attempts, working through the night on the text of his minor role, to arrive at the first rehearsal with a conception of his own, but it was hopeless.

He loved Reinhardt and had the highest possible admiration for him, but after three or four years he felt thwarted in the attempt to find a way to fully develop his personality as an actor. He decided to leave the Deutsche Theater at the end of his five-year contract.

Chance took a hand again. Charles received an invitation from Frankfurt am Main to guest as 'Tellheim' with a view to a contract. Although he had not mentioned this fact, some of his colleagues guessed his plan and advised him not to leave Berlin because he had such excellent prospects with Reinhardt. The great, humane actor Wilhelm Diegelmann said to him: 'For heaven's sake, don't go to Frankfurt. I was there for years – it is the biggest cauldron of intrigues you can imagine.' His remark was soon confirmed. At the familiarisation rehearsal one of the actors came to Charles and said in his jovial, deep bass: 'Dear colleague, I advise you to use a lot of voice. The acoustics in this theatre are terrible.' He had hardly turned away when another

34

actor whispered: 'I don't know what Herr Pfeil said to you, but I warn you not to speak too loud, because the house is over-resonant.' My father thanked both colleagues equally politely and played 'Tellheim' according to his own judgment, because an actor or singer can normally gauge acoustics from the way his voice comes back to him/her on the stage. Charles was very lucky to be acting opposite Frau Sorma, with whom he had established such an excellent working partnership in their identical roles at the Goethe Festival the previous year. At the end of the performance he was given a five-year contract, to start in the autumn of 1915. In August 1914 war broke out.

4

'Romantic and Heroic Lead' in Frankfurt and Berlin

Germany declared war on Russia and France in August 1914.
Charles witnessed the historic moment with his friend Alfred Else,
stuck in a solid mass of people filling the huge square in front of the
Royal Palace in Berlin. They waited to hear the result of the conference which was to decide on war or peace, staring at the Palace as if
hypnotised. After hours of waiting, the enormous main door slowly
swung open. A car drove out, in which stood a young officer. The
crowd parted as the car sped towards Unter den Linden, with the
officer shouting just the one word 'War' again and again. The
release of tension and the cry of 'War' transfixed the crowd. Then a
few voices started a call, which was soon taken up by the whole
mass in the square: 'We want the Emperor'. It was repeated more
and more aggressively, rhythmically. What has become a common-
place of demonstrations seen on TV today, was then a novel, very
exciting herd reaction. After a while the balcony doors on the first
floor opened, and the Emperor with his entourage came out. His
words to the crowd: 'I do not recognise parties any longer, I only
know Germans', became an effective rallying cry for the people of
Germany. My father could not realise it at the time, but these words
later played an important part in his political awakening.

He had been brought up as a good Prussian, under the motto
'With God for Emperor and Country', and he was deeply moved
by the unfathomable implications of the declaration of war. Every
emotion, from near-panic to patriotic exuberance, could be read in
the faces of the people assembled in front of the palace. They
dispersed very slowly.

As a little boy Charles was a conforming patriot. He and his friends often played in the fashionable Unter den Linden, the tree-lined avenue of embassies, banks and big business, linking the centre of the city with the western suburbs via the Brandenburg Gate. Whenever the Emperor and his adjutants came riding past on their way to the Tiergarten, the Hyde Park of Berlin, the boys made it a competitive event by racing the horses to the Brandenburg Gate, cheering all the way. Many years later my father amused us children with a fully staged imitation of the military ceremonies that went with the Emperor's ride, such as the calling-out of the guard at the Brandenburg Gate, with all the thumping of boots and smacking of rifles and the guttural barks of commands.

When the call to arms came Carl, as he now called himself, like most young men across Europe at that time, volunteered. There was such a flood, he was told he would be called up later. Maria Ebert often said she would not survive the call-up of her boy and she did, indeed, die on the day the call-up papers came – before she had been given the news. The time which elapsed before Mother Ebert was buried saved my father from joining a regiment which was annihilated on the Eastern Front by the Russian offensive. His eventual call-up put him into the Pioneer Corps.

Outbreak of war is a catastrophe for every country and individual, and yet is taken as an immutable misfortune, presumably because it induces a sense of inevitability, almost apathy in people. When Carl's turn came to report to barracks, he went along in the same frame of mind: there is no alternative. Several hundred young men lined up in the square. One by one they had to step forward, shout name and profession and step back into line. Proudly he called out: 'Actor'. There was some whispering: 'You're an actor? Come off it!' When they were dismissed to collect their kit, he was surrounded by a throng of men. Out of the babble of voices he made out: 'Mach mal einen' (act something). Carl had decided not to let himself be questioned about the theatre, because he thought the men would not understand. Their open curiosity and persistence made him change his mind suddenly. He jumped on to a big table and, like a busker, asked for requests. In an instant he had a few dozen men around him, calling out what came into their heads first. He had never, so far, encountered such

37

an unusual, but exhilarating audience. He had to 'perform' everything, from a clown pulling funny faces to a man dying with a dagger in his chest. From then on he had a mildly privileged position in his troop.

The Pioneers' task, particularly at the beginning of World War One, was to build a network of defensive trenches. It was a boring routine and not at all heroic; in fact, it had a touch of prison life about it. Everything went 'on command', including breaking into song every time the troop marched past the house of the battalion CO. Carl worked hard – his unit set up a speed record for digging trenches – but military routine irked him. His lifelong inclination to get up late and be unpunctual for appointments created problems in the barracks. His fellow 'diggers' were coached by him to cope. At the morning roll-call, for instance, during the 'One, two, one, two' count, his neighbour always bellowed the 'Two' as well as his own 'One'. The battalion was first deployed at the Eastern Front, then moved to the West, to the beautiful valley of the Mosel – where sampling the inherent benefits of the location combined well with digging – and ended up in front of Verdun. Many of his comrades were later killed there.

Once more my father was saved by good luck. Standing in a puddle, scrubbing the mud off his boots, he heard the call of a colleague: 'Carl, Carl, the Lance Corporal wants to see you at once.' The 'Vice', as he was called, received him with a sweet and sour expression: 'You are demobbed. Get yourself ready. A car is leaving for the station in an hour.' Only when he got home to Cissi and their two-and-a-half-year-old daughter Hidde did he discover what had happened. His contract with the Frankfurt Theatre was, of course, held in abeyance through the outbreak of war. Through some bureaucratic error, the actor who was playing the roles which Carl had been signed to take over in the autumn of 1915, had himself been called up. The Frankfurt Theatre, which would have been unable to mount the demanding repertory on which it had embarked, managed to get Carl demobilised.

The famous saying: 'Any person under 25 who is not a communist is an imbecile, and any person over 50 who is still a communist is a fool' did not apply to Carl. His political awareness was triggered by his experiences during World War One, both in the field and in the theatre. The sudden realisation that neither the mass of German people nor even Parliament had any say in the decision over war or peace; the fact that hundreds of thousands of people died in mammoth battles while the political parties in the Reichstag quarrelled at length over whether universal suffrage should be granted to the people; these nagging thoughts made Carl question his traditional upbringing and made him aware of the existing lack of social justice for the first time.

He became a convinced Social Democrat and remained so all his life. But he was never a party apparatchik, perhaps not even a subscribing member of the party. As a natural leader he could easily have reached high rank in political office, but I do not think he would have made a successful politician. He was never a wheeler-dealer, was too much of an individualist and far too scrupulous for the political 'game'. It is often said that a successful *Intendant*, the general director of a theatre, has to have considerable political skills, but I believe diplomatic flair would be a more accurate job specification. The only ruthless streak Carl possessed was his artistic integrity. To the artists and staff at his theatres he was a charismatic leader as well as a father figure; for the ministry officials and politicians with whom he had to deal, he was a respected, even feared duellist.

Within six years of his first stage appearance as 'Reinhold, (in English Reynaldo), servant of Polonius' in Max Reinhardt's *Hamlet* production at the Deutsche Theater in Berlin, Carl had reached the pinnacle of his profession. He was one of the elite of outstanding actors in Germany. Straight from drama school he had joined the Deutsche Theater and now, after his short war service, he was able to take up his contract in Frankfurt, regarded as the best ensemble theatre in the whole of Germany. He had leapfrogged the normal slog for aspiring stars through tiny, small and middling provincial theatres to the top houses.

The German theatre is organised differently from the Anglo-Saxon pattern. There are a number of privately owned theatres, in the bigger towns at least, but the majority of theatres are run by the State or by the municipalities (sometimes by both of them together). There are no boards of directors. The responsible authority appoints a General Director (called *Intendant*) who has a free hand from there on to run his theatre as he thinks fit, without any political or commercial interference, but within the budget which the authority has given him. The *Intendant* is usually contracted for three or five years. He is chosen by the state or municipal authority from a short list of candidates, who have to develop their ideas on the aims and purpose of the theatre in general and the house they hope to take over in particular.

The majority of theatres in the German-speaking world (Germany, Austria and German-speaking Switzerland) produce opera, operetta and musicals, ballet and drama, and symphony and chamber music concerts in one (or frequently two) houses. The *Intendant* is ultimately responsible for the programme of works he puts before the public, as well as the engagement of all the artists he chooses for his programme – conductors, producers, designers, singers, actors, dancers, dramaturgical staff, public relations, etc. etc. A modern *Intendant* will consult continuously with a close circle of colleagues on every aspect of the theatre's work, but it is he alone who is responsible to the public and to the authority for the quality of the output. He normally appears before a committee of the authority once a year, to announce and explain his plans for the following season.

The committee can debate and criticise the *Intendant*'s proposals or the current season's record, but they cannot force him to change his plans, let alone sack him for being too modern or too traditional. If he has not reached the budgeted 'box office takings' he gets a mild rebuke at the most, because it is generally accepted that the budget position can only be regarded as a guesstimate. Ticket receipts depend on all kinds of factors outside the theatre's control, and it is also accepted that an important part of the theatre's work is to present new operas, plays, etc. for discussion. The *Intendant* is, therefore, a kind of 'Czar of all the Russians', a dictator, a last vestige of absolutism. If he turns out to be a benevolent dictator, all the better, but I am afraid they come in all shapes and sizes. To run a complex theatre of that kind according to one's own beliefs of what life and theatre is all about, is the most wonderful job imaginable, but it is also a lonely one.

The Frankfurt *Intendant* had assembled a formidable array of actors and directors, had demolished conventional frontiers in the

40

classics by mounting modern, challenging productions and given great weight to new writing. It was this aspect which particularly interested Carl, because he had not been exposed to it before.

Here he had the chance to *find* himself as a person and as an actor as well as exploring new dramatic literature, with which he would never have been confronted in such a direct way in Berlin. The new *Intendant*, Zeiss, felt instinctively that the Frankfurt Theatre, held in high esteem by its loyal audience, had become dangerously comfortable and set in its ways. By mounting carefully selected new writing in exemplary productions he honoured his dictum: 'Theatre of the highest standard will convince even the most staid reactionary audience.'

Frankfurt became the pathfinder for renewal of the theatrical scene when Reinhardt's tremendous achievement in Berlin was beginning to flounder, to get stuck in a groove of lavish naturalism. Ludwig Berger, a man of wide artistic talent as actor, director and film maker, wrote to my father 20 years later: 'For how long was Naturalism fertile? For exactly as long as it served as a straitjacket to cleanse us of false court theatre melodies, rid us of "tenors" on the legitimate stage who concentrated more on the declamation of classical verses than the portrayal of the inner person. But now we want to build anew, want to flee from the straitjacket, to search for purer fields of poetry ... You always strove for fresh air, opening doors and windows, always learning – and growing as an artist.'

Carl felt that Frankfurt gave him the food for which he had been yearning. In seven years he played all the leading roles in the repertory in the range for which he had been engaged. It is perhaps opportune to explain that the German ensemble theatre, playing a year-round repertory system, had devised categories or 'spheres of influence' for the actors' long-term contracts. Thus my father's contract was for the position of *Erster Held* which might be translated as 'Romantic and heroic leads'. In practice it meant that he had a certain right – and also obligation – to play Peer Gynt, Faust, Karl Moor, Guiscard, Egmont, Wetter vom Strahl, Tellheim, Leicester, Posa, Dunois, Richard II, Henry IV, Henry V and many others, while Richard III, Franz Moor, Mephisto, etc. would normally be the domain of the 'First character actor'. Over the years these hard and fast categories gradually became more blurred – to the benefit of everybody, particularly actors and audiences.

The name of Carl Ebert became synonymous with exciting – and satisfying – theatre. Some people like to divide actors into intellectuals and those that function 'from the stomach', a crude way of saying intuitively. Carl was not an anaemic intellectual, instead he gave the impression of somebody following his intuitive instincts on stage. But in the portrayal of every role he played – so natural, so inevitable – lay the intense study of the inner character, the background to the outer manifestations which the bare text provided. Nowadays it is called motivation. Having learnt to become such an expert in eliciting deeper meanings, it seems strange that my father harboured such disdain for psychologists all his life.

The training he received at the Reinhardt school and working with Max himself, were a decisive influence and preparation for his career. This he acknowledged gratefully all his life. After about four years, however, he had felt that the Reinhardt stable was holding him back in his development. Here in Frankfurt from 1915–22, followed by five years at the State Theatre in Berlin (until 1927), he was able to play his part in building the foundations of modern German theatre art – and was indeed encouraged to experiment with new projects.

'The wind of adventure blowing about my head seduced me into an extension of my activities. The Frankfurt bookseller Tiedemann and the painter/writer Ottomar Starke came to me in 1917 with the idea of organising poetry-reading evenings. The theatre was already playing an important part in familiarising audiences with the new wave of dramatic writing, but there were other strands which remained inaccessible to the public. The aim was to offer the public a chance to get to know the bubbling, fermenting process in poetry which began worldwide in the second half of the war. Two complimentary thoughts came together in this venture: my desire for direct political activity and my friends' realisation that, to be totally immodest, my unusual popularity with

Frankfurt audiences would guarantee the widest possible interest.

'The poetry evenings became famous instantly because of the adventurous and exciting subject matter. We had reached the third year of the war. The initial mood of imminent victory had slowly changed to worried estimates about the chances of success. In the ballroom of the most prestigious hotel I read, once a month, wartime poetry – meaning anti-war literature from France, England and Russia. One evening ended with Albert Ehrenreich's *Der Mensch schreit* ("Man screams"). It is the story of a waiter who suddenly runs out into the middle of the road, repeatedly shouting: "Peace". He shouts as if his heart would break. People stop, look out of their windows, come out of their houses and finally form a long procession, of all ages, poor and rich – walking through the streets with heads held high, shouting just the one word: "Peace". At the end of my reading, the audience stayed in their seats for a while, silently. I myself felt stunned, as if I had been struck a blow, and totally drained by the emotional intensity of the poem. I found it difficult to rise from my chair.'

Carl got a shock next day when he was ordered to cancel these poetry readings instantly, otherwise he would be sent to the Front at Verdun. The readings were cancelled, and the advance bookings were refunded. Three months later he started a new cycle at the same venue, entitled 'European Literature'. The war was nearing its end and no-one in authority bothered any more about the obscure dissenter.

'Working in Frankfurt confronted me with social problems in the theatre world for the first time. As the leading actor in the ensemble, I took part in auditions of young people who wanted to enter the theatrical profession and were seeking a contract as a "Beginner". This is the way, under the system, to make sure the theatre has enough people on its roster to cover all the minor roles, but for the individual actor it can mean a fairly quick rise to a full contract, depending on talent

43

and development. After my own privileged, sheltered start in the theatre I was horrified to see in these auditions how the system normally worked. I came to realise why so many of the smaller theatres in the provinces were so bad. Most of the young people who came to us had saved for many years and then spent considerable amounts of money on so-called drama tuition, usually dispensed by clapped-out, retired "father" or "comic" actors. The second, shattering revelation was that unscrupulous *Intendants* engaged these young hopefuls at wages below the poverty line so that they could boast how skilled they were at negotiating contracts. I felt that these two problems — professional education and contractual conditions — needed urgent attention. I became active in the work of the artists' union, the *Bühnengenossenschaft*, which succeeded, over the years, in transforming the working conditions and the status of theatre people from the level of "untouchables" to a highly respected profession. [This was also true in Britain: rental agreements before World War Two often contained the clause: "No actors, children or dogs."] My love of teaching made me pursue the idea of founding a new academy that finally led to the establishment of the Frankfurt Drama School, staffed entirely by active theatre artists and offering subsidised tuition.'

During this time in Frankfurt Carl must have worked almost round the clock, because everything he did involving speeches, meetings, interviews, correspondence, etc. was always meticulously prepared (witness the reams of rough drafts which exist), although he managed to give the impression that he was speaking spontaneously, improvising. And beside all these activities he was totally immersed in his main job, preparing and acting in an extremely demanding repertory of leading roles at the theatre, and sometimes performing in other theatres as a guest.

I was born in 1918, seven months before the end of the war, by all accounts a very placid, uncomplicated child. Somebody said of me as a baby: 'He awoke in this world roundly contented.' I don't remember much of my father in Frankfurt (I was only four and a half when he moved on, to a contract at the State Theatre in

Berlin). What stays in my mind is the only beating I ever got. It was not very fierce and arose out of an uncharacteristic moment of truculence on my part: I refused to hand back to my adored grandmother the scissors she needed and, instead, threw them from the balcony into the garden. I must have felt the punishment just, since I harboured no resentment against my father. Presumably I did not see all that much of him in those years, but festivities like Christmas and Easter were always beautiful, impressive occasions – not just eating and drinking – and we had wonderful summer holidays on the wild, unspoilt island of Sylt in the North Sea, which was only just becoming a popular resort. Building sandcastles featured prominently, of course, as well as hide and seek and Trappers and Indians over the endless expanse of sand dunes. My father's shock of dark hair was always visible through the tufts of grass behind which he was hiding. When his name was called, he could never believe that he had been spotted.

Carl's extreme workload, coupled with his built-in lack of time-keeping, made him always rush to his next appointment, but once there he never gave the impression of being in a hurry. Whether it was a meeting, a rehearsal or an interview, he imposed on the proceedings the speed which he considered right for the occasion. Apparently many people remember seeing him running across the bridge over the river Main from our apartment towards the theatre, coattails flying. I am not sure whether he was unable to combat this strange disability of permanent unpunctuality or whether he did not care. I don't think I ever heard him apologise for being late. In a sense, it seemed to amuse him. He later told the story of his dresser at the theatre standing outside the stage door before every performance, peering down the street to see whether he was approaching – while the stage manager telephoned the apartment to ask my mother whether and when he had left home. As often as not he was still at home, but he expected my mother to say that he would surely arrive at the theatre any moment. When the dresser did see Carl turn the corner at the end of the street, he rushed upstairs to his dressing room and held out the costume for Act I ready for Carl to dive into. He liked to do his make-up, go down to stage level and more or less straight onto the scene.

Possibly his method of concentrating did not allow for any hanging about or small talk backstage, but it must have made the stage managers prematurely grey.

Every performing artist has his own recipe for preparing for 'curtain up'. Some people need space to walk up and down backstage undisturbed, others like to be sociable and chat, to steady their nerves. The famous Wagnerian tenor Windgassen is said to have needed no more than singing three or four scales in the gent's loo to warm up his voice before a five-hour-stint as 'Siegfried'. But I have known a baritone who insisted on arriving at the theatre four hours before 'curtain up' to warm up his voice and adjust his mental attitude to the coming performance. My wife, who was a dancer, waiting in the wings just before her cue for her entrance, always cleared her throat! The wonderful singer-actress Elisabeth Söderström always concentrated on her nail varnish, to stop people from talking to her.

Carl was hailed, by critics and public alike, as the epitome of all that is best in a German artist: his manly figure, his strong features, his good looks, his sensitive portrayal of every role he played, his intellectual grasp of the various characters, his carefully gauged body language and his outstandingly beautiful voice, which he had learned to control so that he could express every possible subtlety demanded by the role. He had, in fact become something of an icon as well as a matinee idol to the Frankfurt theatregoers. It must have amused him to be called the incarnation of what is best in a German, when he had not a single drop of German blood in him. But, of course, he could not – or rather would not – share the joke with anyone. In later years, as an opera director, he was needled by the very occasional review calling his production 'Germanic' or even 'Teutonic', but refrained from replying. Perhaps my father did have some German traits, it is difficult for me to judge.

Janet Baker, one of the most sensitive British artists, must have had a traumatic experience watching Carl at work. She felt he totally destroyed a fellow artist at a rehearsal at Glyndebourne. I can only think that Carl was so harsh because, rightly or wrongly, he felt that the singer was deliberately not cooperating or was guilty of not taking his work seriously. Certainly, these were the two things which could rouse his anger. If my father did show German traits, it would be grist to the mill of the argument: genes versus environment.

In her diary of her last year as an opera singer, *Full Circle*, Janet Baker talks of watching Carl work when she was a member of the Glyndebourne chorus in 1956/57:

'Carl Ebert, whom we chorus members thought of as god, dominated Glyndebourne in my first year there. He looked like a god too! Incredibly handsome, power sat very well on him. I wish so much that I had eventually reached the stage of working with him as a principal; I think he must have been pleased as the years went by, to see the change in opera singers as they gradually rose to the challenge of ever higher expectations ... Today, a completely rounded performance, visually and histrionically, is the norm. Carl Ebert must have been one of the great innovators in this respect ... Even watching him, as I tried to do whenever possible, I felt his passionate concern, his delight when a singer succeeded in the demands made, his displeasure when things did not go right.'

An actress colleague of my father in Frankfurt and Berlin, Gerda Müller, wrote to him on the occasion of the twenty-fifth anniversary of his stage debut, with this appreciation of his personality:

'... In the penultimate year of the war, 1917, I came straight from the Reinhardt School in Berlin to the Frankfurt Theatre, a young nobody. The director made it abundantly clear that I had to work exceptionally hard to measure up to his marvellous ensemble. My first rehearsal was for Ibsen's *Peer Gynt*, in which I had to act the role of "Ingrid" to the "Peer" (you) of a great man, called Carl Ebert. My heart had sunk very low. But this famous man CE was such a good comrade, so friendly, ready to help and so appreciative of my efforts without being superior, that my courage returned. The rehearsal was a great joy artistically – and personally a decisive revelation. I understood then what real comradeship meant and promised myself to treat my colleagues always the way you treated me, who was a stranger to you. After that we acted in many plays together, classics and modern, and we probed many -isms of literature together. We enjoyed our acting partnership and artistically we fed on each other's qualities. In your wonderful creation, the Frankfurt Drama School, we tried to pass on what we had learnt at the Reinhardt School and on stage. But above all we fought for a cleaner, fairer artistic comradeship in the theatre. With the help of some colleagues we attempted to rid the ensemble of jealousy and intrigue. Many people told us that it would be impossible, because these things were part of life in the theatre. But it was possible and we achieved it. That we succeeded was, above all, due to you, your unblemished character, your strong will and your human understanding, never sentimental goodness...'

These two qualities, his comprehensive art as an actor and his great humanity, were remarked upon by almost everyone who 'experienced' Carl as his career blossomed. He was recognised everywhere and besieged at the stage door. Whether he first met the stage-struck young woman, who later became his second wife, at the theatre entrance, I do not know, but it is quite possible.

There must have been a gradual build-up of tension in our family, which I was perhaps too young to notice or from which my mother skilfully shielded me. My sister Hidde, approaching her teens, felt the impact of the increasing problems intensely and, in fact, never got over the eventual divorce. Our mother had a strong character herself and was probably not inclined to give my father the undivided attention and, indeed, adulation to which he had become accustomed. In the meantime Carl had come to know and to work with a young musician, Hans Oppenheim, who became a friend of the family. He was the exact opposite of Carl in many ways, quietly spoken, retiring and ascetic, where Carl was outgoing, even theatrical at times, and simply enjoying life. Oppenheim was, however, possessed of the same ruthless pursuit of artistic integrity. I must have felt that there was something special about his personality, because I was reported to have said

48

to him one day: 'Hans, you are a big flower.' After the divorce, my mother, Cissi, married Hans Oppenheim and my father married Gertrud Eck, always called Gertie. She bore him three more children, my sisters Renata and Christiane and my brother Michael. The two couples remained friends, often saw each other and even shared holidays on occasion. This rather unusual arrangement was, no doubt, designed to make the divorce more bearable for Hidde and myself. The two of us lived with one set of parents for two or three years and then with the other pair. My sister found this exercise too much of a strain and she was sent to a girls' boarding school, an hour or so from Berlin. I took the changes of regime and abode in my stride, without any apparent effect on my equilibrium. I did once ask Gertie, without malice, whether she and my father had been married in church, and when she said: 'Not actually', I pronounced my judgement: 'Then you are not properly married.' Had the remarriages in 1924 disturbed me, after all?

In July 1925 Hans and Cissi (the 'Oppis') with Hidde and myself were on holiday in Switzerland, in a little village called Majola in the Engadin. The 'Eberts' i.e. Carl and Gertie, had announced they would join us after a short climbing tour near Lucerne. Gertie recorded in her diary:

'19 July. When we arrived at the Hotel Post the Oppis had gone out for a walk. At 6pm they come sauntering along the road. Carl puts on his sunglasses and woolly hat and stands by the window pointing at the mountain top with his ice-axe. Cissi recognises him first. Tumultuous greeting all round. 20 July. Combined walks along the Engadin lakes morning and afternoon. Idyllic landscape. Lunch all together at Hotel Post. 21 July. All together climb to mountain lake "Carloccio". Lunch together. Pm Carl, Gertie with Hidde and Peter sail to Sils Maria. Gorgeous trip. Splendid Coffee and cakes. Back along lake on foot. 22 July. Lying in the sun by the lake. Carl & children build harbour. After lunch Hans & Cissi play tennis. Again coffee and cakes, this time with music. A Frankfurt family recognises us together! Very agitated/non-plussed. Play with children by stream. After dinner sit on verandah with Hans & Cissi discussing artists and their friends' attitude to them and their development. Good wine. Late to bed. 23 July. Grown-ups attempt assault on Piz Lunghino (2700 metres). Lovely picnic-breakfast by lake. On way to top run into rain, hail, thunder storm and finally thick fog. Give up. P.M. sleep. After dinner long discussion with Hans & Cissi about our views on foreign countries and "their" views on Germany. Hans: if he could find the same appreciation for his music-making abroad, he would leave Germany at once; he hates its politics and despises the people for their stupidity, their lack of character etc more than he can express in words. Cissi is horrified. 28 July. Lovely family outing into Fextal with picnic. Then Carl, Cissi, Hidde & Peter climb across glaciers. Hans & Gertie on strike, eventually go ahead to Fex Hotel. Finally proud glacier conquerors, former Ebert family, arrive safely. Exuberant reunion, to the astonishment of another Frankfurt family.'

While Frankfurt was blazing the trail of modern theatre in the provinces, there was turmoil in Berlin. Max Reinhardt, having helped to wipe the Court Theatre style off the map, failed to develop further from his original revolutionary phase of 'naturalism'. Meanwhile other theatres were experimenting with Dadaism and other ism-visions which are needed from time to time to allow live theatre to progress. However mad and wrong-headed such excursions may seem, they are essential for cleansing the blood-stream. Expressionism was the strongest force in this quiver of try-outs. Reinhardt felt the tide running against him and retreated to Vienna – usually a little slower in embracing new trends – where he was very successful. He appointed some of his closest adjutants to run his Berlin theatres, while he occasionally brought one of his most acclaimed productions from Austria to Berlin. The Berlin State Theatre, formerly the bastion of the old order, had by this time been entrusted to a new *Intendant* from the provinces, Leopold Jessner. He was a gifted man of the theatre who assembled another remarkably talented ensemble.

In 1922 Jessner headhunted five of the most prominent members of the Frankfurt Theatre for his Berlin State Theatre, a

C.E. at 19 'To my beloved in faithful memory, dedicated with love Charles'

Count Anton Potulicky, C.E.'s father

Lucie ('Cissi') Splisgarth, at 17

C.E. with his first born Hidde 1916.

C.E. and Cissi: *The Young Lovers*. Portrait by expressionist painter E. Betzler 1921

C.E. as soldier, 1915
(centre behind comrades)

On holiday in 'Theo' 1927

C.E. with his five children 1936

Five Ebert men: the new family
tree! C.E. with Michael and Peter
and the first two grandsons Tobias
and Charles 1953

Photo: Gravett

Top Team:
Peter and Family, Silvia holding
Susanna, Ades House, Sussex
Photo: Gravett

C.E., P.E. and Judith with
Dr. Tom Walsh.
Wexford Festival 1965
Photo: D.N. Smith, *Observer*

C.E. and Gertie, Los Angeles 1953

C.E. on 70th birthday with Gertie,
P.E. and Silvia, 20 February 1957

daring act of highjack. They were Carl Ebert, Gerda Müller, Heinrich George, Renee Strobawa and Theo Lingen. From other provincial stages Walter Frank, Elisabeth Bergner, Heinz Rühmann, Erich Ponto and Gustav Gründgens were drawn to Berlin. They all became stars, some overnight. By this time Berlin had become the New York of Europe. Commerce, the arts, advertising and publicity, politics and social life were all transformed as if nourished on champagne. In every field there was innovation, experiment, excitement. A whole new generation of writers and dramatists achieved their breakthrough, including Berthold Brecht, who had a drawer full of plays which had never been performed before. Paul Hindemith was the brightest comet on the musical horizon, the *enfant terrible* of the time, who dared to bring jazz rhythms to the concert platform in his serious music. The film makers led the way in adventurous techniques as well as treatment. The theatre experienced the last explosions of Expressionism and experimented with 'Theatre of Brutality'. Guenther Rühle writes in his book *Theatre for the Republic*:

'What the early Brecht, Bronnen, Weiss and Jahnn accomplish in their plays is the destruction of idealism, of faith in modern man; instead they dwell on his urges and his sadism. These plays are brimming over with sexuality and lust, with murders and perversion. Everything is driven to extremes. The light, spiritual expressionism has turned into what we must call *black* expressionism. Although it manifests itself as a monstrosity, demanding our attention, it calls itself *new realism*. It is an attempt to blow bourgeois attitudes to art and the aesthetics of the theatre sky high. The scandals caused by performances of *black expressionism* are instant proof of successful aggression and the successful demolition of the bourgeois horizon.'

These were the 1920s. Theatre fashions seem to work in recurring cycles.

Any number of new theatres sprang up, including some actor co-operatives, each one with its own 'mission' in this maelstrom of theatrical activity. Jessner, at the State Theatre, was a fertile,

51

very modern play director and had engaged even more avant-garde directors as his staff. His theatre, doyen of all Berlin's drama houses, easily held its own in this competitive striving for new ways. One could say that Jessner fell into the trap that eventually stifles so many artists: he became a prisoner of his innovative style, unable to develop his ideas further. An outward sign was that he filled his stage space for almost every production with enormous swathes of steps in a variety of arrangements. As *Intendant*, Jessner was finally not so successful either. Carl felt that:

'the first years with Jessner were marvellous, exciting, fluid, active, carried by a very homogeneous feeling among the actors. The atmosphere changed when Jessner appeared to become more and more dependent on – even subservient to – Fritz Kortner, one of the most prominent members of the ensemble. It is difficult for me to talk about Kortner. Our pronounced physical and intellectual divergence made us into natural antipodes within the company. If our attitude towards each other never led to conflict on a professional level, it was probably due to mutual acceptance of fair play spiced with a dash of respect for the quality of the adversary. And the actor Kortner was an adversary for me in almost all departments of the craft of acting. His nasal voice, which commanded enormous vocal volume but no warmth at all, provoked caricature. His gestures were calculated, pointed, but never spontaneous or emotional, his walk was never elastic or driven by excitement, but – even as a young actor – always lurking, suspicious and shuffling, his "effects" were ambush, surprise and confrontation. If Kortner made a pause in the dialogue and moved upstage (away from the audience), one could almost count the seconds before he would sharply turn back to his partner and deliver his next line with an explosion of nasal vehemence. All who were familiar with his "technique", smiled about it, but had to admit its effectiveness. Kortner is reputed to have judged my acting as: "Ebert acts like a director, who demonstrates, how it should be played." At the time the remark seemed insulting to me – on reflection it may not have been all that wrong.

'After the initial sensational successes of Jessner's productions, audiences seemed to tire of exclusively intellectual theatre. The ensemble felt the theatre was drifting into a crisis. In the end the actors decided to send a delegation of four representatives to Jessner to air their views. Naturally, he knew about the feelings within the ensemble and received the delegation rather nervously. To have to confront him with our criticism was no great pleasure, it had an element of tragedy, for Jessner had assiduously worked his way up the ladder of smaller and bigger theatres until he gained the prize of the most prominent position in German drama. We explained to him how we viewed the situation, namely approaching a crisis, and what dangers we saw for the future development of the State Theatre. We told him that the ensemble hoped an honest, open discussion would counteract the present artistic and organisational weaknesses of the theatre. Jessner was very tense and excited when he began his reply. He feared a revolution was brewing in the ensemble, but he did not seem to have any idea how to answer our complaints. He spoke at length, talked about a secret conspiracy and finally said: "You know what you are doing? You are thwarting my planless ideas." Without realising what he was saying, he repeated the same phrase a minute later. We were speechless.'

Carl became more and more frustrated with his situation at the State Theatre. During these years the cinema had suddenly become an important player in the arts world. Carl was fascinated by the new medium and participated in a whole series of productions being made in the new Berlin Studios. He was also invited to play the detective in an action thriller which involved, among other hazards, jumping from a police launch on to the boat of the 'baddy' as they were tearing across the Bay of Naples at top speed. Stunt men had not been invented at that point. To do justice to the role, Carl had gone through a crash course of fitness training, including boxing and distance running. The police and Carl wanted to do the thing properly, realistically, unlike the glamorisation of the usual detective film. Detective Inspector Wernicke and my father were, so to speak, seconded to each other: Carl had to agree to accompany Wernicke at any time of the night to real-life calls. Wernicke watched over every foot of the shooting of the film.

One night the inspector invited Carl to accompany him to a rather special event: 'We will visit the Floral Halls, where lesbians hold their weekly, as they call it, family evening.'

'The large hall was full of women from all sections of society, which surprised me. In my innocence I thought at that time that, what I then considered a perversion, would not reach down to the ranks of maids and cooks. Everybody was already in high spirits, our entrance was hardly noticed. We took a table from which we overlooked the whole hall and watched the dancing, which was very "proper" to begin with. In time things hotted up, the dancing became more erotic, there were arguments and even some pretty brutal fights when suddenly there was a shout: The Queen is here, and everybody turned towards the door. An incredibly beautiful woman entered, tall and slim, surrounded by several young men. They came past our table, and I must say I was stunned. I forgot wife and child at home; I had the feeling I must talk to this creature. Wernicke must have been watching me. He leaned across and whispered, "That is a man, a homosexual, and the court of young men round him are part of his clique." We left soon after.'

The strain of his continual overwork, combined with his growing unhappiness at the way the State Theatre was run, began to tell on my father. He developed internal bleeding. He was so rundown that the doctors ordered a complete rest and, if possible, a holiday in a hot climate to recuperate. Carl grabbed the chance of a lengthy stay in – Egypt was the choice. He and Gertie set off, determined to see everything and to enjoy themselves. They clambered up a Pyramid, rode on camels, travelled on the Nile, lounged on the hotel lawn at Luxor, saw any number of temples. They were also invited to a three-day trip into the desert. Their host was a super-rich German industrialist who had a whole retinue of servants plus his own doctor, masseur, etc. The days and nights among the sand dunes were magic. They explored Egypt for several weeks with my father's typical zest for new experiences. The cost was astronomical and, since he and Gertie had no capital to fall back on, they had to reduce their life-style sharply for many years to pay back the bank loan, but Carl was restored to full health.

However, he had tired, as he put it, of smearing greasepaint on his face every night. The problems – and the opportunities – of being in overall charge of the operations of a theatre began to attract him. He felt he had learned enough about the art of total responsibility to make a move as soon as the chance appeared. The *Intendant*ship of the State Theatre in Darmstadt fell vacant in 1927. He applied.

5

Generalintendant Carl Ebert

With his appointment to the post of *Generalintendant* of the Darmstadt Theatre from the autumn of 1927, my father's most fervent wish had been fulfilled. He was glad to be rid of the *diktat* of highly gifted, but obsessively one-track-minded producers. The excitement of discovering new 'isms' was beginning to wear thin. He felt that the German theatre, in its search for the 'new truth', was getting bogged down in artistic polemics and barely disguised ego trips. The search for more relevant methods of communication with modern audiences had run into a dense fog. Although immensely popular with the public and gaining a foothold in the new medium of film, Carl had also become sensitive to the satirical and destructive style of writing which began to be fashionable among theatre critics just at that time. He felt these critics were rather self-indulgent in their 'clever' barbs at the expense of the artists. It is a problem which recurs periodically. Carl never lost this resentment of 'unjust' criticism – as he perceived it – even during the many peaks in his career. At times he was even triggered to write to critics, arguing how misconceived their pronouncements were – no artist should ever allow himself to be provoked to such an action.

Thus, at the age of 40, Carl achieved the big jump from membership of a team of actors to being in complete charge of the complex apparatus of a German repertory theatre. So much for being 'a late starter', as he always claimed. In 1927 it was unique for an actor, however distinguished, to be chosen for the post of *Intendant*, which was perceived to require proven ability as an

56

administrator, a good deal of financial acumen, diplomatic skills, as well as, of course, outstanding qualities as an artist. There could be no doubt about the latter: the name Carl Ebert was well-known in the theatre world as one of the pillars of the most prestigious drama theatre in the land. Whether he would be able to extract the greatest artistic benefit from a sizeable budget, governed by anti-quated rules of bureaucracy, was an unknown quantity. Luckily nobody knew about his permanent struggle to square his family finances – a problem arising, quite simply, from his exuberance for life. His administrative experience was at +/– zero; however, his flair for diplomacy must have been in his genes. Since his student days he had always been chosen as the spokesman for any group to which he belonged, and in his work for the executive of the actors' union he successfully argued for innovative reform. So, why was he preferred for the post of *Generalintendant* of the *Darmstadt Landestheater*? Primarily for his reputation as an artist and his known integrity. And then for his undoubted leadership qualities which he had demonstrated, not least in the establish-ment of two new Academies of Drama (in Frankfurt and Berlin).

The theatre in Darmstadt was already the subject of envy and admiration among its peers for its successful progressive policies, and it had won the applause of its subscriber audience, normally a notoriously conservative body. The *Darmstadt Landestheater*, had been run since the war by two or three very gifted *Intendants* who had ventured to introduce audiences to more than the normal quota of modern playwrights and composers. Productions ranged from the unconventional to highly experimental.

Darmstadt, a town of just under 100,000 inhabitants at that time, had been the residence of the Grand Dukes of Hesse until the revolution at the end of the war, and had become a focus for much artistic enterprise under their enlightened regime. Indeed, by the mid-1920s a whole lot of writers, artists, philosophers, musicians, craftsmen and theatre people had been drawn to this not particu-larly beautiful town. There was a feeling of intellectual adventure about the place, and the theatre was an important spotlight in the overall picture. Carl was tremendously excited to have become the Czar of that particular little empire. His last years in Berlin as an actor had been fruitful for his development, working with extremely modern producers, taking part in the avant-garde search for dramatic innovation. But the tyrannical relationship between producer and actors had provoked him into formulating his own ideas on production and a more positive approach to bringing the best out of the actors. He longed to be in total charge of that complicated being, the theatre, to realise his own conceptions of the dramatic and music literature.

It came as a surprise to most people that my father had had a love affair with music for many years. He had never worked on operas and had no musical training whatsoever, but he had felt instinctively that music would, perhaps one ought to say should, give dramatic relationships an added dimension, greater depth. 'Should' is the operative word. By 1927 the upheaval which had modernised drama productions after the war, had only brought forth rather timid, fragile shoots in music theatre. The pioneering work for drama by Reinhardt and his colleagues still had to be applied, in its own 'language' of course, to opera. Singers are notoriously more conservative, slower to adapt to new concepts of production, not only in acting, but even in vocal expression. To this day, when a singer starts to rehearse a scene, one can occasionally pinpoint from which recording he or she has taken their interpretation. Carl's great strength as an actor was his sincerity, coupled with his capacity to analyse and enter into the characters he was portraying. There were no superficial trappings to his art. Now he was ready to apply his knowledge and his artistic beliefs to the medium of opera.

Carl was often asked why he had changed from drama to opera.

'The short answer is: because I was appointed *Intendant* of the Darmstadt State Theatre. But it was more subtle than that, of course. I had had a secret love affair with music theatre – opera – for a long time. In my relatively short, but if I may say so, successful career as an actor I was lucky enough to be part of the great reformation which cleansed the drama stage of discredited traditions. In Darmstadt I had my first chance to work in opera. The question why I changed from drama to opera assumes that they are two different media. I believe the contrary: they are two expressions of the living theatre which complement each other and are indeed indivisible. And in the music theatre I found an even bigger and more satisfying field for reform. Opera was asphyxiating in routine and convention. Individual singers were almost always left to their own devices, mostly miming what their singing teacher had described as "effective": Sarastro is arms crossed on chest, Osmin is ... etc. More important than ridding opera of these ludicrous mannerisms was the task of demonstrating to the audience that the musical form of drama or comedy, far from being a hindrance to understanding, gave the viewer/listener a deeper insight into the emotional content of the plot. I ignored the old argument, *"prima la musica o prima le parole"*, and have always sought to find a convincing unity. How far I have succeeded in Darmstadt and my later career is not for me to say. I have always looked to the music for the more profound realisation of the right expression.

'Many years before my first *Intendanz* I had written an article on the "Work of the Actor". I explained the worrying phenomenon I experienced when studying a new role. I was never able to concentrate on my own role, but all the other characters in the piece became so vividly real that my natural and healthy egotism as "just one of the actors" was undermined. I also wrote that my spontaneous feeling during the initial conception of a role was more often a rhythmic-musical one and not a realistic-emotional one. To explain this discovery I quoted the first *Faust* monologue. The agitation in this speech lay, for me, much more in the alternating, thundering, precipitate rhythms than in the reality of the words. In the same way the protest, restlessness and longing-for-freedom in Egmont's prison monologue will be expressed more forcefully through the musical treatment of the impatiently galloping prose than through "acting" the words.

'When I wrote that article in 1917 (eight years into my career as an actor), I did not think of the possibility that my spontaneous vision of the "multiplicity of characters" on reading a play would lead me one day to directing and that my strong feeling for the formal elements of speech, melody

and rhythm, would lead me to seek gratification in directing
opera – music theatre.'

From the outset Carl was clear about his approach to opera: his
former professional base, the text, had to find its true meaning and
therefore the subtleties of its expression from the music. He
appointed a young composer/conductor, Berthold Goldschmidt, to
be his musical ear, perhaps one should say musical ferret. Carl
could not read a full score or vocal score well enough to hear the
music. However Goldschmidt, a discerning musician and an outgoing personality, had a singular capacity for playing an opera
score on the piano suggesting the moods and colours of the music,
at the same time singing all the roles with the appropriate expression, as he felt it. To prepare a new production Carl closeted himself with Goldschmidt for days on end. While Goldschmidt
performed at the piano, playing through the opera again and again,
my father stretched out on a kind of psychologist's couch, first just
listening, then making notes while following the music in the
score as well as, for the first time, reading the text and, finally,
questioning and arguing with Goldschmidt about the interpretation of each section.

After this thorough musical preparation Carl was ready to turn
to the visual aspect of a production before working with the
singers and chorus on stage. From his earliest days in music
theatre Carl strove to achieve the ideal situation – namely, complete accord with conductor and designer. He felt strongly that
worthwhile opera performances could be created only if the three
threads, music, design and direction, were totally at one with each
other in conception.

'It may not be possible to reach a consensus without a fight,
and maybe feathers will fly, but the eventual agreement will
always produce the best results.'

It sounds obvious and simple, but was often difficult to achieve
(the situation is even worse in today's jet-set age) because of the
enormous workload carried by leading staff members (today such
attempts at corporate decision-making are more often ship-

wrecked by the preoccupation with personal image-building).

Carl was both lucky and well advised in the choice of senior staff, those he decided to take over from his predecessor and the ones he had to find himself. His new music director was the Austrian Karl Böhm, who went on to become one of the most famous conductors in Germany and later internationally; Wilhelm Reinking was a gifted modern designer, one of a triumvirate of artists, whom my stepfather Hans Oppenheim recommended to my father for Darmstadt. Reinking, the producer Rabenalt and the choreographer Claire Eckstein, in collaboration with the music director Oppenheim, had made the theatre in Würzburg famous throughout Germany for its adventurous style of productions. However, the city had severe financial difficulties and could not guarantee the continuation of the theatre subsidy. Hence Oppenheim's recommendation to Carl which allowed the team to stay together. Many actors and producers were happy to come to Darmstadt, even at a cut in salary, because of the exciting prospect of working under Carl Ebert. Perhaps the luckiest factor in the constellation was the finance director, a civil servant who had become a great theatre fan and expert – a rare breed indeed. This splendid man, Dr Sander, had the dissecting brain of a born organiser, knew every thread of the complicated workings of a theatre which put on 60 new [!] productions every season, and ruled the financial maze like a benevolent hardliner.

Even with all this goodwill surrounding him and the eagerness of the artists to be part of his team, my father sometimes felt the giant waves of problems were about to overwhelm him. Many years later he confessed to me that he sat at his desk one night and shed some tears because he thought he would be unable to cope. 60 productions a year seems an impossible number, but it was the norm, at that time, for every theatre, which offered opera, operetta, plays, ballet, and a Christmas fairy tale for children – quite apart from concerts and special events. Since everything required for these productions, sets, costumes, props, even mediaeval armour, were made in the theatre's own workshops, the logistics had to work like a quartz watch. To keep that side of the business under rigorous control while giving the artists as much freedom and support as they need to do original work, requires a sort of schizophrenic balancing act on the part of the *Intendant*. If he is an artist in his own right within that structure, he has the added problem of having to be seen to be even-handed in the apportioning of stage time, workshop time, casting, publicity and all other resources.

An unexpected problem arose from my father's unusual leap straight from the ranks of actors to the top slot. It was compounded by the fact that the theatre unions, in their justifiable pride, hailed the arrival of the 'Peoples' Emperor' (*Volkskaiser*) on the throne of the *Intendant*. Carl noticed quite soon after his arrival in Darmstadt that this unfortunate phrase, coupled with the fact that he was a well-known socialist, encouraged the technical staff to regard him as one of them, metaphorically slapping him on the back and calling him 'Du'. When this euphoria led to unreasonable demands for extra payments for services previously covered by salaries, a strike was threatened. Carl warned that he would be forced to lay off the whole technical staff. The technicians did not budge. Carl issued dismissal notices after a further warning, in spite of pleas from many sides, including the State President, who feared an uncontrollable escalation. The technicians gave in and were re-contracted, with the exception of the three most prominent agitators. At their interviews one of them fell on his knees, begging to be taken on again. My father's resolution to stick to his decision was 'one of the worst moments' of his life. He offered the sacked man help to find a new job. Years later he heard that this character had become one of the most prominent Nazis in the town.

Not all his disciplinary measures took such a dramatic course. An excellent character actor and brilliant comic, Hermann Gallinger, recalls:

'a matinee for children before Christmas. My role is the villain, who does not even appear on stage but shouts his nasty threats through a megaphone from backstage. My colleague, Paryla, whispers a funny story in my ear just before my first bit. I am doubled up with suppressed laughter and have to speak my lines under this irreparable handicap. Very soon everybody laughs, the actors on stage, the orchestra and the whole audience. Only Professor Ebert does not laugh, he comes backstage, looking for me. My nerves have made me hysterical, I am still laughing. He is extremely angry and says to me brusquely: "Gallinger, you can pack your things and leave tomorrow. Come to my office after the performance." I obey, of course. When I enter, I think I can feel a smile behind his dark mien. He wants to find out at all costs who made me laugh. But I remain steadfast, I won't say. No more mention of packing bags. However, he says my indiscipline was so horrific, that he would have to fine me 50 Marks, much as he regretted it. [In 1927 that was a sizeable chunk of a monthly salary.] Shattered, I leave. He calls me back and says: "Listen, Gallinger, 50 Marks is perhaps a little much, and it's almost Christmas. I'll reduce the fine to 2 Marks." I thank him profusely and go quickly. But he calls me back again: "You know, 2 Marks is really ridiculous. I'll let you off with a warning this time." And now we both laugh. He makes me promise not to tell my colleagues any of this, in case they think it is easy to wind the new boss round one's little finger. I promise, but I can't keep it. The story is too good.'

The first season of the new *Intendant* began with a sequence of great successes and an incredibly tight programme of first-night dates: 11.9. Handel's *Julius Caesar*; 14.9. Shakespeare's *A Winter's Tale*; 25.9. Wolf-Ferrari's *School for Fathers*; 28.9. Gerhard Hauptmann's *Und Pippa Tanzt*; 1.10. Sternheim's *Die Hose*; 12.10. Strauss' *Salome*; 18.10 Kleist's *Käthchen von Heilbronn*, and thus it continued throughout the season, with the dates very carefully distributed between the large and the small house, with works chosen from the classical repertory and many examples of new writing, including a number of world premieres.

The distinguishing feature of the new era was the complete commitment to modern interpretations without embracing experiment for experiment's sake. My father felt strongly that the twin task of the modern theatre was to present every work in terms of a modern audience's understanding, and to respect absolutely the authors' intentions. Every production was a revelation, even for the fairly sophisticated audiences of Darmstadt. The opening night of the season, *Julius Caesar*, acted as a fanfare, a call to arms for all believers in the *raison d'être* of the theatre: to entertain, to question, to excite discussion, to highlight contemporary problems, to criticise society itself. Theatre of Illusion was out. Theatre of Rationale was in. It was a long way forward from Reinhardt's naturalism. No more pine scent, spiders' webs and all the other paraphernalia. Realism of action was the slogan of the moment. The trio of Reinking (designer), Rabenalt (producer) and Eckstein (choreographer) had stripped Handel's opera of all superficial scenic trappings, there was not a speck of oriental decor. Reinking had devised a multi-level stage constructed of open undisguised rostra, highly functional but dramatic in scale; the costumes were timeless; masked dancers were used to emphasise dramaturgical connections. From having languished as a musically florid costume piece, the opera became an exciting drama with contemporary relevance.

During the rest of the season, the attempt was made to give every work its just treatment within these goals. Naturally, the results had no 'sameness' about them, they varied enormously according to the personalities and accomplishments of the theatre's conductors, producers and designers working on the wide repertory of productions. Equally naturally, the Darmstadt crusade in favour of modern theatre did not meet with universal approval. Some sections of the audience were ill-prepared for this uncompromising wave of modernisation. For some critics this revolution did not go far enough. [When I came to Britain, it was strange to realise that German audiences were, on the whole, more conservative than the critics, while in Britain, anyway until well after World War Two, the critics were much more conservative than audiences.] However, most of the citizens of Darmstadt, not only the regular theatregoers, were engaged in, usually, heated discussion. The theatre had again become the focus of interest. And that is where it belongs.

I lived in Würzburg at that time, with my mother and stepfather, but of course visited Darmstadt frequently. I was nine years old, not particularly encouraged to go to the theatre, but allowed to do so. To this day I can remember every detail of about ten productions of my father's Darmstadt years. For his *Egmont*, Reinking had devised a large construction of many levels and steps. Within this structure were hidden several interior scenes, which opened out like dolls' houses. With this device, the many different scenes of the play could run like a musical, without interruption for scene changes. It seemed to double the speed of the action. The costumes were stylised period and the backdrop a beautiful architectural drawing of a stylised mediaeval town. Action, speech and body language were totally modern, and since the play has a timeless theme, it was as riveting as a thriller.

I saw my first *Threepenny Opera* in Darmstadt, which I thought very effective as well as moving, and also my first *Carmen*. Perhaps the latter stuck in my mind particularly, because of the sequence of ghastly tourist-Spain Carmens I saw later. In my father's *Carmen*, with decor and costumes by Reinking, there were no blouses falling off shoulders and no wiggling hips. The cigarette girls, including Carmen, of course, were dressed in factory overalls. Everything depended on intensity and personality. There is an excellent German word: *Ausstrahlung*, which means the vibes emanating from a human being's personality as from a pulsar in space. In the little scene between Carmen and Don José towards the end of the first act, when they are alone on stage in the midday sun, just after José had tied Carmen's wrists behind her back, she sings a ditty as if to herself, the so-called *Seguidilla*. Often the Carmen is made to perform a kind of snake- or belly-dance round José or take up poses like a prostitute. In the Darmstadt version she was motionless, near Don José but half turned away from him, and almost inaudible. José stood like a ramrod, head slightly tilted up, like somebody tied to a stake in a river with the water rising. As she continued her song Carmen's voice became more intense and expressive. His interjections grew more hoarse and desperate as he realised he could not escape the sensual web she was spinning. One could see José's nerves snapping and feel the sweat on his forehead. Still practically no movement from either. The audience were breathless through the whole scene. It was brilliant theatre.

The success of the innovative Darmstadt style of productions depended on the personal quality of the cast and the production team, since the stage was shorn of its former 'supportive' scenery, costumes and props. This modern stage had the function of creating the right space for each work, to be a participant rather than a background. Darmstadt's influence on the further development of the German theatre was felt well into the 1950s – interrupted, though, by the return to 'naturalism', during the Hitler years. It is strange that dictators are always conservative in the artistic sphere.

Carl was particularly lucky that the Darmstadt theatre was in such excellent shape technically. The workshops were well equipped, the technical staff very competent. The head of lighting was especially good, inventing his own novel and very powerful system of projection which was not improved for 50 years and which added another string to the designers' bow. In addition to running the whole complicated apparatus and dealing with the politicians, Carl also produced a number of the most important works in opera and drama, and acted in several of them.

In his fourth season at Darmstadt he began to feel that he had served his apprenticeship as an *Intendant* and was looking round for a larger theatre that could serve as the next step up the ladder. He was thinking of Dresden, for example, where a change of leadership was on the cards. One evening he read an article in a Berlin newspaper, discussing the fact that Heinz Tietjen would soon be leaving the *Städtische Oper* – the second Berlin Opera House. The article alleged that Tietjen was promoting the choice of a nonentity to succeed him, so as not to challenge his record at that theatre. And, it continued, that man had already been found in the person of Carl Ebert.

My father was horrified by the venom of this attack, and considered his career to be fatally damaged. After agonising through the night, he decided attack was the best defence and sent a telegram to the head of the selection committee to announce his candidature. He informed Tietjen, who, of course, swore he knew nothing about the authorship of the article, sent off his application and, very soon afterwards, made frequent journeys to Berlin to interview members of the committee. He invested a lot of energy and tried to mobilise all his connections. A few weeks later he was watching a performance from his box in the theatre in Darmstadt, when he was called away to the telephone. A Berlin newspaper was on the line to congratulate him on his appointment as the new *Intendant* of the *Städtische Oper* from the autumn of 1931.

6

Städtische Oper, Berlin – Autumn 1931–March 1933

The *Städtische Oper* was a giant leap for my father, who had
set his sights on gaining more experience by advancing from
Darmstadt to a larger, but not a top-flight house. The *Städtische
Oper* had had a chequered career since its inception in 1912, but
had been led by many eminent artists, among them Bruno Walter
and Leo Blech. The *Städtische*, or Municipal, Opera had almost
always played second fiddle to the venerable Court Opera House
in Unter den Linden, renamed State Opera after the 1918 revolution. But it is interesting that the *Städtische Oper* arose out of a
Citizens' Initiative before World War One. The increasingly self-
assured bourgeoisie wanted to have an opera house in which they
determined policy, repertory, etc.

The Initiative succeeded in establishing a committee in 1907
charged with organising support, raising the necessary funds, setting up a proper constitution and building a new theatre. 'This new
house should be open to all citizens and not, like the Court Opera,
be reserved for the aristocratic classes, and should be funded by
the citizens themselves. To be able to offer seats at reasonable
prices the new building will have 2,300 seats, no boxes and there
must be a clear view of the stage from all seats.' The reaction of
the citizens to the Committee's appeal was phenomenal. Long
before a proper legal and administrative framework had been set
up, and years before the theatre could be ready, an amazing
number of series bookings for the still far-away performances
had already been sold. The new opera house was opened on
7 November 1912 with Beethoven's *Fidelio*, and the citizens of

Berlin had pulled off a remarkable example of people power.

The year 1931 was the height of the (worldwide) recession in Germany, and the political situation was very tense. There were frequent Government changes, Parliament was increasingly impotent, the various Chancellors were forced to govern by decree and Hitler's Brownshirts were actively provoking street violence.

Although Carl was passionately involved intellectually, he simply could not spare the time to play a political role. But he noted articles in the Nazi organ, the *Völkische Beobachter* critical of his socialist background as well as his artistic direction, i.e. modern theatre.

Nor did he have time to apply himself to countering the Byzantine machinations of his predecessor, Heinz Tietjen, who had vacated the *Städtische Oper* post to become *Generalintendant* of the Prussian State Theatres. There were two of these in Berlin and at least three more scattered over this large province. At the same time Tietjen got himself appointed Consultant to the Ministry of Education and Arts for Theatre Affairs.

Obviously this would have been considered an irreconcilable clash of interests under normal conditions. But Tietjen persuaded the Ministry that it was a rational solution. He was, in fact, a passable producer, in the conventional tradition, and a conductor of some talent. But acquisition of power and devious diplomacy were his greatest talents. He was the archetype of a successful wheeler-dealer.

Carl was more amused than angry when he discovered that his new office was extensively bugged. It had hidden microphones in strategic places and hidden buttons to enable the *Intendant* to activate a recording machine placed in the room below (this was 20 years before the Cold War, and privately owned recording machines were still a novelty). There was also a battery of telephones for direct access to the Ministry, the Lord Mayor etc plus one dead line. Carl was told that Tietjen sometimes found it convenient, during strenuous negotiations, to activate this phone by pressing another hidden knob if, for instance, he needed a breather to collect his own thoughts. Tietjen also used the device to put his opposite number off his stride. He would feign a telephone conversation, monosyllabic on his part, until he was ready to continue the discussion.

Luckily Carl inherited a fine ensemble of soloists, two good conductors and a well-functioning technical apparatus. His late appointment to the Berlin post left him little time to prepare his first season. Under the prevailing conditions of political and economic uncertainty he considered it essential to start his era with a novelty instead of the usual *Fidelio* or *Mastersingers*. For his all-important opening production he finally decided on *Macbeth* by Verdi, which Berthold Goldschmidt had recommended to him.

An added incentive for this choice was the fact that the opera was practically unknown in Germany and would therefore arouse a lot of interest among public and press. He started his usual ritual of working on the opera with Goldschmidt. When he asked Fritz Stiedry to conduct *Macbeth*, Stiedry was horrified at such an inauspicious choice, tried to persuade him to change his mind and, finally, said he would rather not be involved. Carl used a little ruse to change Stiedry's mind. He told Rudolf Bing, his office manager, to send a telegram to Toscanini asking him 'to do me a great favour at a decisive point in my career by conducting my opening production of *Macbeth* in Berlin'. He told Bing the telegram did not have to remain a secret. This little trick – worthy of Tietjen? – had instant success. Two hours later Stiedry appeared and remonstrated with my father that he was about to ruin his career by inviting Toscanini, etc. All was well in the end: Toscanini regretfully had to decline – he said it was quite impossible to rearrange his busy schedule at such short notice, but hoped he would be able to do this wonderful opera with my father at another date. Stiedry conducted. Caspar Neher, a modern designer and librettist with a highly individual style, was invited to design sets and costumes. Everything was set for work to start in the pre-season rehearsal period in August.

My father was literally a tireless worker on the job. I recall an occasion when, after a full day's rehearsals and various meetings, he was still dictating letters to my sister at two in the morning. She remarked that it was getting fairly late, which brought forth the astonished question: 'Are you so tired already?' But Carl had always had an infectious zest for life and was able to switch off and relax into holiday mode in an instant.

My father, Gertie and myself spent the summer of 1931 at a small hotel in a secluded bay on the Yugoslav Island of Rab in the Adriatic. Even before our steamer anchored outside the harbour we could hear the phenomenal noise made by hundreds of millions of crickets across the water. This penetrating sound was with us 24 hours a day for the whole of our visit, but after about 10 minutes we no longer noticed it. It was incredibly hot, the sea was so salty that we astonished people in passing sailing boats by 'standing' in the water, just – and only by raising our lower lip a little. It was a wonderfully lazy holiday, swimming and sailing being interspersed by occasional forays to the picturesque old town of Rab for ice cream and cakes or a beauty contest in the garden of the biggest hotel. Carl had to send a telegram to Berlin now and then; apart from that we might have been in another world.

There were quite a few Germans in the neighbourhood. One morning, while swimming in the beautifully clear water, a stranger called out to Carl: 'Did you hear what happened at home?' 'No.' 'All the banks have closed their doors.' Carl almost drowned. He was expecting another tranche of his holiday pay and had practically no cash left. From that day, everything we spent at the hotel or in town had to be on credit. Soon there were hardly any places left where we could still dare to go. Our predicament did not worry the owner of the hotel. Carl called him Herr Ribaric. Whether that was his real name or the wine he served us I don't know – my father had a history of inventing names for people whose real names escaped him. For a couple of weeks he called the landlady of a small hotel/restaurant in Switzerland 'Frau Veltliner', because there was a sign over the door with that name. It was a brand of Swiss table wine. Ribaric was always particularly attentive in serving our table, in fact when he took our orders he seemed to give a faint impression of military posture. His country had, of course, been part of the Austro-Hungarian Empire until the end of World War One, and Ribaric spoke reasonable German. It was only when he returned our passports at the end of our stay that we stumbled on the reason for his military bearing.

71

Carl's profession was given as *Generalintendant*.

Our departure from Rab was a cliffhanger. Carl had a number of urgent appointments in Berlin. No money had yet arrived. In case it came with the boat on which we were leaving, the parents had made three lists so that we could separately rush about the town to pay our debts while the boat did its turn-round. The money did arrive. My stepmother and I were efficient and got back to the steamer in good time. My father was nowhere to be seen at the second blast of the siren. As the third blast sounded and the crew began to loosen the ropes holding the gangway in place, Carl rounded the corner of the large square adjoining the landing stage at a trot, weighed down by various parcels and free-swinging bottles of Prosecco wine he was trying to control. In spite of our frantic signals to the bridge, the gangway was pulled off and the steamer started to ease away from the quay. Carl leapt over the gap into our arms. The rest of the journey home was uneventful.

Within days of taking up his new appointment in Berlin, the atmosphere at the *Städtische Oper* changed dramatically. Carl's apprenticeship in Darmstadt was paying off. He inspired the whole staff of artists and technicians to adopt a new work ethic. Theodore Front, a resident assistant producer, summarised the transformation: 'It was an ensemble of stars, in the sense that eminent artists were suddenly fused into a real ensemble, which means an artistic community with a tangible common goal.' The quality of repertory performances, dating from before Carl's arrival and which had been severely criticised in the past, suddenly reached new heights of excellence. One paper wrote: 'The expression of the public's enthusiasm, such as we have not witnessed at the *Städtische Oper* for years, must be due to the spiritual impetus that Ebert has given to the whole house after only a few weeks.'

Press and public alike were eagerly awaiting the highly unconventional choice of his first offering, the first-night of *Macbeth*. Carl had chosen the opera, in part, because he felt that he had a near-perfect ensemble in-house. The choice of Neher as designer, whom he knew but with whom he had never worked before, proved to be inspired. He was a strange, highly sensitive intellectual, difficult to get to know, but his designs for dramatic works

72

had an earthy, passionate quality. Neher was, in some way, a withdrawn person, with an occasional shy smile. Sometimes, in the middle of a working session, he would suddenly feel the need to do something quite else and would simply abscond.

His designs for *Macbeth* made no concessions to historical correctness, but they evoked mist swirling over Scottish hills, the dour darkness of the castle – with a hint of baroque shapes – and the mysticism of the apparitions' scene. For me, as a 14-year-old, the long line of Banquo's descendants appearing from nowhere, looking at the terrified and ranting Macbeth while walking diagonally across the stage and disappearing mid-stage at the moment Macbeth lunged at them with his sword, was spine-chilling. It was all done, not with mirrors, but with gauzes and clever lighting. For the two witches' scenes Neher had devised an enormous gnarled old tree for their meeting place. Verdi had enhanced Shakespeare's three witches into three groups of women's chorus. These were deployed in clusters in front and on the tree and either side of the stage, and they were really totally invisible except for their masked faces and their arms. Verdi had not only increased their numbers, but wrote their lines in a tarantella rhythm – not normally associated with witchery. The conductor succeeded in making the chorus ladies sing in nasty, cackling voices for these scenes.

Middle Verdi had been looked down upon for many years in Germany – considered to contain too much primitive rum-ta-ta accompaniment. Lack of perception or just boring routine performances? The Berlin *Macbeth* changed all that. The performance was hailed as a revelation, a miracle, devastating, thanks to the fusion of music and stage which Carl Ebert had achieved – for many discerning people for the first time in their experience. There was nothing 'operatic' about this performance. As an actor Carl had himself achieved totally credible characters, and he had now done the same in the much more difficult medium of opera – for generations weighed down by clichés and superficial routine.

After the first two or three amazingly successful premieres at Carl's opera house, Tietjen, at the State Opera, felt uncomfortable about the growing competition. Ebert had not turned out to be the genial, laid-back colleague at the other end of town, whom he had secretly helped to engineer into his post. As the press sounded more euphoric about the *Städtische Oper* with every first night, it became increasingly scathing about the standard of ensemble work and the generally slipshod performances at the State Opera. While Tietjen was intriguing at the Ministry to widen his own powers, he apparently lacked the time to evaluate a new opera by Kurt Weill with text by Caspar Neher, which the publisher had offered him for a world premiere. He was probably hesitating because of its possible political impact. Thereupon the publisher offered the opera *Die Bürgschaft* (*The Pledge*) to my father, who accepted it immediately. Tietjen felt himself provoked, and threatened to hit back 'without scruples', as he called it.

Carl's next production was *The Seraglio* by Mozart, with designs by Reinking. Reinking wrote: 'I have never experienced an opera producer managing to characterise all the roles of a work so convincingly and to imbue the action with so much real life as Ebert did in this production. He had excelled himself. He had achieved the complete synthesis of music, action and design.' The two following premieres were in the hands of famous drama producers whom Carl had engaged as guests. Again they were enormously successful with press and public – and at the box office. Tietjen felt the artistic dominance of the *Städtische Oper* was endangering his own throne. He started to argue at the Ministry for the closure of my father's opera, on the grounds that Berlin could not afford three opera houses.

This ploy backfired badly, partly because the *Städtische Oper* was on an uninterrupted artistic high as well as beating the prevailing recession at the box office, and also because the two Berlin State Operas, under Tietjen's direction, seemed to lack a definable artistic policy. Indeed, the Kroll Opera was perceived to have forsaken its intended main function: to act as a progressive younger partner to the more representative house in Unter den Linden. Its audiences and takings were shrinking long before the Ministry decided to close the Kroll Opera.

Although the system of two co-ordinated music directors – which Carl had inherited – worked well enough in practice, he was keen to find an outstanding personality to be the sole music director of his opera house. He approached Fritz Busch, renowned music director of the first-rank Dresden Opera House. Busch was naturally reluctant to leave Dresden, where he had earned many laurels for the overall standard of performances and the interesting repertory, including several world premieres of Richard Strauss' operas. However, Busch agreed to test the much more turbulent waters of the Berlin artistic scene.

The invitation was specifically to conduct a new production of Verdi's *Ballo in Maschera* – a work which had never been particularly popular in Germany, but which Carl had chosen as the second opera of a planned new Verdi cycle. The opera must be difficult to produce, since it is only rarely an outstanding success. Based on a historic event at the Swedish Court, it contains five scenes of wholly different atmosphere and location, starting with a court scene of an almost eerie suppressed tension, a visit to a fortune-teller at the edge of a harbour, a love scene under the gallows, a conspiracy sealed in the house of the King's chief minister, and the assassination of the King at a masked ball. Verdi's score is an amazing display of atmospheric colour and intense emotion. With its very unconventional features, such as the air of foreboding at curtain rise, to the immensely moving, forgiving farewell of the dying King, it is far removed from the usual pattern of construction.

Perhaps these unusual features of the *Masked Ball* have misled producers – particularly in Italy – to introduce melodramatic signals, destroying the opera's subtle characterisations. I remember the Dress Rehearsal of the Glyndebourne production in 1949, when Paolo Silveri, singing Renato, in the middle of the 'conspiracy' scene, suddenly shouted: 'Where is the red spotlight that must be on me?' and stumped off the stage. That was probably the true measure of prevailing standards of production – in Italy at least.

Busch and Ebert were just as unconventional a pair of working partners as the opera they had decided to tackle. Busch, a workaholic, who had no interest in anything outside his music; Carl, a continual seeker after new knowledge, new experiences and thoughts, a connoisseur of debate and devoted to life. From the outset they found a common denominator: their incorruptible striving for honesty in artistic matters. They hit it off from the first moment and established a collaboration which is very rare in the world of opera. Their productive partnership lasted until Busch's death in 1951, through all tribulations and triumphs.

The premiere of *Masked Ball* at the *Städtische Oper* was an epoch-making event. It is still, after 65 years, written and talked about as the production which marked a new era in opera interpretation. It was also the second high point of Carl's crusade to rid opera of all accretions of stilted poses, bombastic gestures, primitive deployment of the chorus, etc. In only four years – since his first attempt in this unfamiliar medium in Darmstadt – he had perfected his individual technique of production. The success of the Berlin *Masked Ball* made waves around the world and resulted in an invitation to inaugurate a new music festival in Florence, the *Maggio Musicale* with two productions in 1933.

In retrospect, it is almost incomprehensible that this unrelieved success story developed in the 18 months between September 1931 and March 1933 against the background of political turmoil, violence on the streets and in the press, the strangling of the young German democracy and great economic hardship. Carl was attacked frequently in the Nazi-owned *Völkischer Beobachter* and *Der Angriff* (*The Assault* or *Attack*) for employing too many foreigners, Jews and Communists. It seemed bizarre that the music critics of these papers agreed with their competitors about the artistic qualities of Carl's productions while the political pages were openly threatening. More worrying and, of course, much more time-consuming, were the attacks in the City Parliament and elsewhere by delegates of the right-wing parties. The convoluted attempts by these intellectually stunted gentlemen to construct a case against the *Intendant* Carl Ebert sometimes provoked laughter among other delegates. But not for long. The Nazis were coming to power inexorably – but many people still tried to make themselves believe it could never happen. The mayor of Berlin, Herr Sahm, was a political opportunist, like Tietjen, and had no wish to compromise his own position – in case the parties of the extreme right should succeed in gaining power. The deteriorating political outlook was an enormous additional strain for Carl.

In a much less dangerous environment, 45 years later, I was

drawn into a similar, politically motivated, situation which included an offer of half a million German Marks from rightwing groups, if I resigned my post of *Intendant* in Wiesbaden. The ridiculous accusation was that my theatre promoted Marxist ideology. Carl decided to rely on artistic success rather than political infighting to silence the critics, but the German general election of 5 March 1933 made further discussion of the pros and cons redundant. Hitler's National Socialist Party became by far the strongest in the Reichstag, although it did not reach its goal of an absolute majority. Hitler had been appointed Chancellor by the aged President von Hindenburg on 30 January – because there was no-one else left among the traditional political parties who could muster sufficient backing and had the essential charisma for the job. The success of the 5 March election enabled Hitler to usurp absolute power by entering into a coalition with the right-wing Conservative Party and then railroading it into submission. Meanwhile rank-and-file Nazis went on the rampage, ousting Social Democrats and Communists from their jobs and positions.

On 9 March 1933 the 'Motorized unit No. 13' of the SA ('Stormtroopers' or Brownshirts) occupied the *Städtische Oper* and hoisted the swastika flag on the roof. Carl was at that time attending a premiere at the State Opera Unter den Linden, unaware of what had happened at his own theatre. He had arranged to meet Fritz Busch at a hotel for supper after the performance. Busch had phoned earlier to say he had important news and wanted to talk to him. When they met, Busch and his wife were very shaken. He told how he had entered the orchestra pit in Dresden the previous night, shaken hands with the leader, greeted the orchestra and turned to the audience to acknowledge the applause, when a storm of barracking, booing and shouting began, drowning out the applause. He signalled that he wanted to start the performance and turned to the orchestra again to raise his baton, when he saw that all the musicians had meanwhile fixed swastikas in their lapels and sat staring at him without raising their instruments. The cacophony in the house continued unabated with shouts of 'Get out' and more booing. After a few moments Busch had left the pit and the theatre and decided to go to Berlin to consult my father.

Halfway through supper Rudolf Bing, Carl's administrative secretary, appeared at the door of the restaurant, signalling to Carl to come outside. Bing told him that the SA had occupied the opera house and advised him not to go back to his office that night. Next day Carl received a summons from the office of Hermann Goering, who was Prime Minister of Prussia as well as Minister for the Interior in Hitler's 'Reich' cabinet. Goering was one of Hitler's closest allies. He loved flamboyant showmanship, always wearing innumerable decorations on fanciful operetta-like uniforms. He was by far the most colourful personality in the Nazi hierarchy. He was not the typical image of a political henchman at all, and people looked on him with a certain benevolent indulgence. When Carl presented himself at the Ministry he found Goering's anteroom buzzing with the coming and going of a crowd of immaculately groomed young adjutants. Goering's office was a copy of the well-tried model: a large desk at the far end of a vast room. Goering was very down to earth, saying: 'Stormtroopers in the opera house? What total nonsense! But these things happen in all revolutions. Stupid. Senseless. Little nitwits getting uppity, wanting to carve out a position for themselves. All these undisciplined excesses will soon have run their course.'

Goering had firm opinions about artistic standards, saying how much he had enjoyed performances at the *Städtische Oper* and how scandalously bad the last premiere at the State Opera had been. He was also well informed: 'I know you are about to start your first foreign leave to inaugurate the new Florence Music Festival. That is very convenient. When you return in six weeks I will reorganise the whole of the Berlin theatre scene with your help.' No response was required, Carl was graciously dismissed.

He went straight home to assess the situation with my stepmother. They decided to pack all their personal belongings and clothes and leave Germany at once. Their furniture and household chattels could be sent for storage. My father was clear that, as an artist, he was not prepared to make any concessions nor take orders from political masters. Beyond that he felt the need to set an example: if a number of prominent Germans in the arts and sciences were to leave their country voluntarily because they

78

disagreed with Nazi philosophy, it would send a strong signal to the world.

On their way into a totally unpredictable life as emigrants Carl and Gertie visited me at my boarding school in the Black Forest. My father explained to me that he could not contemplate working under a Nazi regime, but that I had to make an independent decision. It was my own life and my career which I had to think about and assess; German was my mother tongue, it would be a grave decision to leave my country. But there was absolutely no hurry, he said, I should watch developments and decide in my own good time. I was young, I had just turned 15. Two days later my father crossed the border into Switzerland – not to return until 1946, after the devastating end of Hitler's 'Thousand-year Reich'.

7

Emigration

The decision to emigrate from Hitler's Germany was the equivalent of jumping into a deep hole in the dark. Carl had never worked abroad; his pioneering achievements in the theatre were known only to a very small circle outside Germany. He had a family of five to support, plus two parents-in-law. Switzerland was the obvious place for a temporary home, but thousands of refugees were already pouring into that liberal, democratic haven of central Europe. Austria, the only other German-speaking country, was suspect for many refugees because there existed a strong right-wing political party. The great majority of asylum seekers were Jews or what the Nazis called 'non-Aryans', which they, ridiculously, defined as anybody with a Jewish grandmother. There were very few people like Carl Ebert or Fritz Busch who decided to leave Germany voluntarily out of antipathy to the regime. But it was sad and disturbing to see how many highly intelligent Jews could not bring themselves to leave while the opportunity still existed. Their emotional ties to the country of their birth and their mother tongue were so strong, and many of them could not contemplate living in any foreign country; others thought the Nazi nightmare would only last a few years at most, and the German nation would then find the way back to sanity. They did not understand Hitler's brutality, nor did they believe the comprehensive and explicit programme which he had set out in *Mein Kampf*.

Switzerland soon felt obliged to restrict the number of Germans allowed to settle in their country. Luckily Gertie's parents had Swiss nationality, even though their family had lived in Frankfurt for two or three generations. They were, of course, free to own or rent property in Switzerland. A charming little country villa was found in Cureglia, a village north of Lugano, and rented at a reasonable price in the name of Rudolf Eck. This house became the family headquarters from 1933 until after the end of the war. Although it was a time of adjustment, insecurity and worry, we all retain a great feeling of love and gratitude for this simple house in the Italianate, sleepy village, with its beautiful church tower and gorgeous views of the surrounding mountains. Whenever any of us have cause to be in Switzerland, a visit to Cureglia in the Ticino is a *sine qua non*.

While living in this semi-paradise it was unreal, almost uncanny, to hear Hitler's ranting voice on the radio. And not that far away, after all. For many refugees the idea that Hitler might one day swallow Switzerland, out of greed or, later, out of despair, was always present. Whatever the worries and speculations of his peers, my father always retained his capacity to enjoy the tangible pleasures of the moment. There were many excursions on foot or by car exploring our new surroundings, the picturesque, rather posh villages along the shores of Lake Lugano, and lonely valleys with dilapidated hamlets stuck to the steep hillsides, the houses looking like the gnarled faces of their hard-working inhabitants. On one of these occasions we found a village with a reputation for the excellence of its fresh, i.e. young, Parmesan. The parents decided to buy a substantial chunk for the larder and a bottle of the local red to go with it. Since there were no opportunities for a tea or coffee break on the way home, we started to enjoy slivers of the cheese and an occasional swig of the bottle. By the time we reached home there was no cheese left.

It all appeared to be our normal carefree family life. How my father managed to provide the necessary finance is still a mystery to me. He had no capital to fall back on. His Berlin salary was stopped from one day to the next, although his contract still had several years to run. He tried to agree a settlement with the authorities. There were, as yet, no follow-on engagements after the spectacular success of the Florence Festival. Carl had been a prominent figure of the German-speaking theatre scene. He knew the directors and leading members of most theatres personally, and was highly respected as an artist. The results of interviews at cities like Basle, Zurich and Bern came as a sobering shock. His admirers suddenly appeared defensive and cool. It was a new experience for Carl to have to ask for work, anyway, but it was even harder to come to terms with the lack of enthusiastic response. Hundreds, if not thousands, of German refugees were in the same position, learning to lower their sights to that of mere survival. In some countries highly-qualified doctors and lawyers had to sit exams, like students, before they were allowed to practise.

It is fair to say that the directors of the few large theatres in German-speaking Switzerland had to perform a balancing act. To safeguard the stability of their ensembles and, of course, their own positions, they felt the need to ration the number of foreigners they could employ. There was public interest in seeing eminent artists from abroad on Swiss stages, on the other hand the spectre of rising xenophobia leading to political agitation among native per-formers remained a permanent danger. The owner/director of the Zurich Drama Theatre, for instance, secured the services of several excellent German refugee artists. When he wished to retire from running the theatre himself he found an interested local lessee candidate, Dr Oprecht, a bookseller/publisher by profes-sion. The deal became common knowledge when Dr Oprecht applied to the city council for the necessary licence etc. An impas-sionately worded flysheet appeared with the banner headline:

'Marxist-Bolshevik Drama Theatre?
'[If the council should grant a licence to Dr Oprecht] our theatre will continue to serve tendentious policies and remain the playground of emigrants consumed by hatred ... Dr Oprecht has managed to swamp Zurich for years with Marxist-Bolshevik propaganda literature and the outpourings of rootless emigrants ... [citizens] fight to make your drama theatre once again the guardian of uncontaminated art.

[signed] Action for Switzerland'

In spite of such strong right-wing agitation, a workable formula

C.E. as 'Florian Geyer'
in Frankfurt 1917

As 'Secretary' in *Maria Magdalena*
in Berlin 1912

As 'Fernando' in Goethe's *Stella*
in Frankfurt 1916

C.E. in 1917

 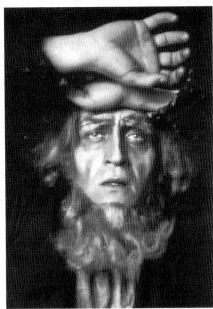

As the young 'Peer Gynt' in Frankfurt 1919   As the old 'Peer Gynt' Frankfurt

Napoleon play by Grabbe, directed by C.E., Darmstadt 1929   Photo: Collmann

Hamlet directed by C.E., Darmstadt 1930

Photo: Collmann

Portugalesische Schlacht play by Pentzoldt, directed by C.E., Darmstadt 1931

Photo: Collmann

was found for the sensible utilisation of foreign talent – without hindering native development.

The refugees soon established a grapevine of information, even though everyone was on his own, and they did help each other unquestioningly when asked. My father received a letter one week from an old friend, a gifted producer, actor and *Intendant*, asking for a loan of 100 Swiss Francs until the following Monday. It was a measure of the financial juggling in which everyone had to become an expert to avoid disaster.

In this time of turbulence a great number of new projects were initiated all over free Europe, on paper at least, and Carl was invited to join quite a few of them, ranging from a try-out of a new festival in Monaco, with Otto Klemperer as conductor, to a regular link with the Vienna State Opera under Bruno Walter. Some of these initiatives soon arrived at the stage of detailed planning, like casting, working with designers, even rehearsal schedules, etc., generating a great deal of preparatory work before the financial backing for the project had been fully secured. Everything was handled under pressure, telegrams and express letters were chasing each other across Europe. Plans always seemed to be on the point of realisation. At the same time everyone tried to keep alternative options open in case the first preference came to nothing, which was usually the case. All this required a voluminous correspondence with individuals, institutions and entrepreneurs, dependent on immediate replies – never my father's forte. In our age of ever-accelerating communications it appears quite unbelievable how much tedious writing in longhand, correcting and then typing was involved in keeping pace with all these developments – and without the benefit of a well-oiled office. Gertie was, in fact, the office, which involved acres of typing on her old portable typewriter – beside all her other duties.

Naturally the new breed of 'providers' felt they could utilise so much underemployed talent to start new ventures with world-class artists at a viable cost. However, Hitler's rise to power created an unfavourable climate for new financial commitments by governments or arts trusts in most European countries. Business sponsorship of the theatre was practically unknown on the Continent at that time. Inevitably most of the promising new schemes foundered sometime during the planning stage.

Over the same period Carl received a number of offers from the Nazi authorities – via go-betweens, of course, such as former colleagues who had decided to stay in Germany after the Nazi takeover. Some of them had even become friends of ministers like Goebbels and Goering. Carl received coded messages from both Ministers and, although he would have liked to reply with robust rejections, he was obliged to resort to diplomatic ruses – weasel words, which he hated – to delay things, because he still hoped to succeed in his legal wrangle with the *Städtische Oper*, from which he was demanding compensation for his broken contract.

In the midst of all this hectic, but not lucrative activity, my father drove to the bank in Lugano to draw the last 100 Francs from his account. When he arrived back home, Gertie told him that the director of the Basle drama theatre had phoned but would not say what it was about. He would ring again. It could be anything of course, the offer of a production or some advice about an actor or a recommendation for a hotel in the Ticino. Finally the call came through. After pleasantries and enquiries about the health of the whole family, the director at last came to the point, or tried to. There was much humming and hawing: he knew of course that the esteemed ex-colleague, he said, had switched to opera entirely, but he thought he might sound him out – and hoped it would not cause any offence that he broached the subject – he would quite understand if the answer was negative, etc., etc. Carl was thinking all the time: Come on, come on, *coraggio*! Finally the director came out with it. He wanted to put on a new play, *Tovaritch*, a comedy, which had already had great success in one or two theatres. It was charming and lively and needed a great personality for the protagonist. Would my father possibly consider going back to acting after several years as a director? Carl did not want to sound like somebody drowning, clutching at anything, while he was really jumping through the roof. Yes, he said, he would gladly have a look at it. The Basle director was overjoyed and promised to put the play on the next train. As soon as Carl had received the script, he retired to his bedroom, asking the whole family to be as quiet as possible, so that he could concentrate. After five minutes he reappeared and announced that he would do the play. Gertie was shocked: 'You can't possibly have assessed the whole piece in a few minutes!' 'No, but it begins with an exiled Russian Grand-Duke in Paris, going to the bank to draw his last hundred Francs.'

Carl enjoyed putting on a costume and smearing greasepaint on his face again. Not surprisingly, he was a totally convincing Grand-Duke in looks and bearing, he was elegant, charming and very funny. Over the following three years he played many of the great classical roles for which he had become famous, both in Basle and Zurich, and had the chance to play his first King Lear and direct several operas. This activity boosted his morale, after the strain of the first few months of voluntary exile. Carl had never wavered in his determination to have no truck with the Nazi regime; but for a time the total lack of income and the failure of all the high-flying schemes to materialise, had a debilitating effect. Apart from professional and financial worries, there was the anxiety about my sister's decision to stay in Germany, and also a certain nagging doubt about my eventual preference. I stuck to my father's wish to bide my time and find out for myself whether the Nazi way of life would appeal to me. It did not take me long to size up the Nazi creed. Even in the sheltered atmosphere of my boarding school in the Black Forest, it became evident quite quickly how deep the changes were going to be. My fundamental revulsion against any manifestation of jingoistic nationalism, which I acquired at the age of six, made me reject all the marching, flag-waving and playing of 'war games'. I was not a political animal at the time, just before my fifteenth birthday, but I thought I could see even then the direction in which the Nazis' antisemitic phobia would take the party eventually. I asked my father to send me to a school abroad.

The problem for my sister was a little different. By the time Hitler took over – later satirically called *Ausbruch der Rettung*, meaning 'outbreak of salvation' (the play on incompatible words does not work as easily in English) – my sister had just secured her first contract as an actress. This engagement was at the theatre of an almost wholly working-class coal town in the Ruhr area, Bochum, headed by an innovative *Intendant*. He saw his mission as weaning his regular audience away from pure light entertainment to appreciation of the classics. With that in mind, he went out in front of the curtain every single night on which a Shakespeare, Goethe, Schiller, etc. was performed, to introduce the audience to the play, its contents and the author's message. This bizarre notion was hugely successful. The theatre blossomed, became famous throughout Germany – and has remained a progressive theatre ever since. My sister felt she had done very well to gain entry into this hallowed temple, and was afraid of her chosen career evaporating into thin air in a foreign land – quite apart from the handicap of the language barrier. These were reasonable considerations, but the family worried about the tone of the letters Hidde sent from Germany. There was, of course, strict postal censorship, but Hidde's letters sounded rather too positive.

Hidde was a romantic girl, wanting to see only the good side in everything and every person. Her judgement often seemed naive. She could shut her eyes to the ruthless way the Nazis succeeded in demolishing the democratic institutions and, indeed, the constitution of the Weimar Republic. Initially the Nazis protested that the measures were necessary to prevent the collapse of the State. After the years of worsening economic conditions, deprivation and increasingly violent political confrontation in Parliament, in the press and on the streets, these arguments carried a good deal of plausibility for many people. They were so relieved to be free of the anxiety and insecurity of the immediate past that they felt entitled to half-close their eyes, in order not to know about the things that were going on. For instance, the humiliating order that all Jews had to wear a yellow star of David on their sleeves and all Jewish men had to add 'Israel' to existing first names, while women had to call themselves 'Sarah', was shrugged off.

The Nazis set up an all-embracing scheme of spying-on-your-neighbours, in the shape of neighbourhood or block 'wardens'. Everybody soon realised that any kind of nonconformism would be severely punished. Listening to foreign broadcasts was declared un-German, even subversive. The number of Germans prepared to lie on their beds with one ear glued to a radio set and a blanket over their heads, in order to hear the BBC news without being discovered, dwindled rapidly. Thus the Germans soon learnt to keep themselves to themselves as the best way of staying out of trouble, while making sure that they always used the 'Heil Hitler' greeting in public and didn't forget to display the Nazi flag from their balconies whenever required.

'I did not know' was the recurring excuse of Germans after the fall of the regime, if you engaged them in a discussion about the Nazi period and mentioned concentration camps, gas chambers, summary executions or war atrocities. And this was still true, unfortunately, 30 years after the war, even though the younger generation persistently challenged their elders with the question: 'And what did you do during the Nazi time?'

Hidde's letters were worrying in the way she sometimes mentioned 'the Fuehrer' and 'the enemies of Germany', citing phrases from Dr Goebbels' propaganda output as fact. There was no indication that she was merely pandering to the censor. On one occasion she reported that she had been invited to attend a grand function in Munich at which Hitler was present. It was, of course, impossible to engage in correspondence about her attitude to the regime. However, even when she was free of Nazi surveillance, as when she visited the families' homes in Switzerland and England – which continued right up to the outbreak of war – Hidde always broke off discussions that threatened to dig deep into political beliefs and attitudes. The parents sensed her agony of divided loyalties, and avoided a confrontation. It was not until after the end of the war that she referred to the Nazis as 'these criminals'.

Our parents, real and step-, had always been friends, and had stayed in each others' houses; the men had sometimes worked together, so that there was, in fact, a feeling of an extended family. The pressures of emigration brought them even closer together, judging by their open and loving correspondence, which dealt extensively with us two children, the political scene and, of course, the aspirations and anxieties of work initiatives. Their attempts to build new lives out of the void created by emigration are moving to read, whether they concerned the creation of an ideal opera company based solely on artistic integrity or the disgust at having to accept a job, out of sheer economic necessity, offering no hope of artistic satisfaction.

After his first spell as a re-born actor in Switzerland, Carl was lucky to receive an offer of joint direction of the Buenos Aires

German season at the Teatro Colon, together with Fritz Busch, the conductor. On paper the working conditions were terrible – a new production every 10 to 12 days – but the lure of encountering a new culture and the high salary were irresistible. The journey by boat from a Mediterranean summer to a South American winter was a fascinating new experience. It started from Naples and progressed via Moroccan and West African ports, Rio de Janeiro and Montevideo. My father, true to his nature, used every opportunity to go ashore, invariably leaving on the first tender and returning on the last. He savoured the architecture, the atmosphere, the smells, the colours and, with the eyes of the theatre director, the people, their facial features, their behaviour, the way they walked and carried themselves, their body language and their voices. It was a mine of valuable impressions for him, like finding a treasure trove of old coins. The leisurely progress of the journey gave him time to catch up with accumulated paperwork as well as recharging the batteries by relaxing on the sun deck. Some time was also spent on learning basic Spanish.

When the boat called at Montevideo a flock of journalists pounced on Fritz Busch and Carl. They were the Uruguay correspondents of the Buenos Aires papers and wanted a story for next morning's editions to coincide with the ship's arrival at BA. Such multiple press conference/interviews are hazardous at the best of times. Busch's and my father's halting replies in pidgin Spanish, interspersed with unmotivated 'Yes's seemed to encourage the journalists' enthusiasm. After their arrival in Buenos Aires next day, they read in the papers that Fritz Busch was a Jew and that Carl was the son of Friedrich Ebert, the first President of the German Republic – which he did not bother to deny.

Buenos Aires struck Carl and Gertie as ugly and noisy, but interesting. She did not dare to go out unescorted, so she spent most of her days sitting in her hotel room. Carl's work was worse than expected. He had to produce a string of operas in quick succession, with rehearsals overlapping. The singers were the cream of the world's artists specialising in the German repertory. They had all sung their roles many times at different theatres and were not in the least interested in 'new conceptions' of production. It was frustrating and hard work and required all Carl's diplomatic skills, because he was certainly not prepared to let things slide, but determined to get a measure of coherent thought into an ensemble of self-seekers. The nadir of his rehearsals was reached when his *Siegfried* tenor arrived in his dinner jacket, explaining that he had to go on to an important social function. He was obviously not in a mental or physical condition to rehearse *con tutta forza* or to forge his sword 'Nothung' on the anvil. The repertory of the stagione consisted inevitably of several Wagner operas plus works like *Fidelio*, Weber's *Freischütz* or *Oberon* and other operas of the nineteenth century Romantic period. There were no modern works in the schedule. Richard Strauss was as far as the management dared to push its plush audience.

The worst ingredient of the Buenos Aires scene was perhaps this audience. The opera had become incidental to the social function of the evening. It was normal for the auditorium lights to remain on for the first half hour or so of the performance, to give the numerous latecomers among the rich ticket holders of the Stalls and Grand Circle seats a chance to find their places. They walked down the centre aisle showing off their designer clothes and flashy jewellery, and greeting their friends. Many patrons, if that is the right word, used to leave the theatre soon after the last interval. For Carl the Buenos Aires German *stagione* was a dreadful burden, a negation of his artistic principles, but it formed the financial basis for survival for the whole year. For this reason, he and Busch continued to lead the German season in Buenos Aires for years. Full artistic satisfaction was never achieved in those six years, but since the artists were all world-class, many performances were good. They never achieved the accolade of being modern opera productions. The critical success was highly satisfactory, but that is no compensation for a producer who knows that the result of his work is nowhere near what it should have been. So the critical success tasted rather stale; the critics had no inkling of what a modern production should look and feel like, after all.

The one element of the Buenos Aires contract which could be relied upon to be an unqualified success was the boat trip – luckily there were no transatlantic flights in those days. Like modern railway timetable freaks, my father brought the planning of the trip to a fine art. In time he came to know every single port on the

West African and South American coasts. He always brought back with him a few trophies, ranging from a whole bunch of bananas (176 seems to stick in the mind), via beautiful and extremely useful textiles, to strange woodcarvings. He really enjoyed the subtle game of bargaining, without which one is not taken seriously as a person in the marketplaces of those regions.

He was distressed that most of the artists who happened to be on his boat were too lazy or unimaginative to go ashore and savour these colourful places. On one trip he persuaded a Wagner tenor from Saxony to take the risk and go ashore at Dakar. When he returned his only comment, in his ghastly Saxon accent, was 'Hm, weird – but very run-down.' He was not cut out to be an explorer. The 1936 trip coincided with the Abyssinian crisis. A famous Italian coach/conductor, called Ricci, happened to be on board. Carl knew him well from his work at Florence. One day an important speech by Mussolini was broadcast all over the ship, in which he issued an ultimatum to the Abyssinians and called on all Italians to stand by him. Ricci was seen to scribble a note, then he rushed up to the telegraph office. When he came back he proudly told Carl: 'I have sent a telegram – *"Il Duce, Roma. Pronto* [Ready], *Ricci".*'

It was strange that the German authorities who supported this annual *stagione* in Buenos Aires did not object to Busch and my father being in charge of it. They may have had an ulterior motive, such as making it a plank in their efforts to persuade the two to return to Germany. Or did the authorities perhaps realise that the Busch/Ebert leadership was the finest that Germany could muster?

The search for a school for me outside Germany revealed that the headmaster of the Salem Schools was engaged in setting up a new school in Morayshire, Scotland in 1934. Dr Kurt Hahn knew Britain very well, having studied at Oxford as well as Continental universities. He had made many friends in Britain, and at one time had worked for the Archbishop of York, Dr Temple, as one of his secretaries. The school he set up at Salem owed much to the age-old format of the traditional British Public School – hitherto totally unknown in Germany. But he introduced new ideas. There was a lot of emphasis on self-reliance and responsibility towards the community.

By Easter 1934 Hahn had succeeded in establishing his new school at a house, almost a castle, near Elgin in Morayshire, called Gordonstoun. When I arrived there, together with one or two other former Salem pupils, Hahn met us at the station. On the drive to the school, nervous and eager to see the location of our new life, I was quite shocked to hear him say: 'When we go back to Germany. . .' He was obviously deeply offended by the way he had been hounded out of his school in Germany. For me, having decided to leave Germany of my own free will, the future looked quite different. I came to love Britain and the people very quickly. We were 13 boys at Gordonstoun in that first summer term, roughly an equal mix of British and German-speaking.

Hahn was a brilliant headmaster, with exactly the right notion of what motivates youngsters. We respected him tremendously, even though we made fun of him for his occasional quirky behaviour. My father had met Hahn only once – before I was sent to Salem. The two men respected each other very much.

The first 18 months of emigration were the most disheartening. But by late 1934 Carl had built up a certain pattern of recurring assignments. They included the annual German season in Buenos Aires, artistically just as unsatisfying as the first time, and renewed invitations to the Florence Festival. Working with Italian artists was a pure joy for him. They responded immediately, and mostly with panache, to the merest suggestion of a direction. Quite a change from the more serious, thoughtful approach during rehearsals in Germany at that time. However, the Italians could not always be relied upon to repeat exactly what they had fixed at rehearsal the day before. It was stimulating for artists and director to fire their imagination, but one had to know exactly when to apply the brake, or the whole conception would degenerate into chaos.

Italian opera productions were hopelessly antiquated in the 1930s. Everything more or less carried on as decreed by tradition, so it was no surprise that Carl's productions at the Florence *Maggio Musicale* caused a great stir. All the Italian papers singled out the production as the outstanding feature of the performance. One critic went further:

'Every Italian opera producer should be obliged to make a pilgrimage to Florence to learn from Signor Ebert's work what opera production is all about.'

The main obstacle to achieving modern productions was, I think, that Italian opera houses had no permanent company of artists. They worked on the *stagione* system, which meant that all the artists, conductors, singers, producers, designers, etc. were contracted for rehearsals and performances of a particular work. Each opera was normally played only five to eight times in fairly close sequence, overlapping by two or three performances with the works brought out before and after. So if you stayed in a town for a week you could rarely see more than two different operas. The system has certain organisational, financial and artistic advantages compared to a permanent company, but it also has severe drawbacks. The *stagione* allows you to cast each role with the most suitable individual artist in the land, provided he/she is free and terms can be agreed for the relatively short period of employment. If, on the other hand, a theatre has a permanent company, all the artists are on salary, whether they are cast for a new production or not. The audience will see the same artists again and again in different roles, which can be interesting, but can also lead to boredom if the artists do not possess a high profile of character and versatility. The advantages are that you have the singers available for a much longer rehearsal time, and they are used to working as a team. Potentially you are set up for a better result than working with an *ad hoc* team, which needs time to gel and is available for a shorter period only. With a permanent company you can also give a far greater number of performances and spread them out over a longer period. That, in turn, means that the production costs, such as scenery and costumes, wigs and props and all, are spread over a wider output. Basically, it all boils down to whether your opera house plays a year-round season with hundreds of performances or bursts of shorter seasons spread over the year. The Italian way of *stagione* probably developed out of the *ad hoc* requirements of the princes' courts in the eighteenth and nineteenth centuries, and remained fixed in that format. It is still used today, although the seasons have acquired a more regular pattern. It has also been widely adopted in the United States and all other countries without a year-round season.

I am sure this Italian scheme of short bursts of performances created a dangerous 'tradition', in the sense that every opera was always done in the same way, wherever it was performed. Every time I worked in Italy there would always be one or two singers who came to apologise privately, that they had never done their role before. When I said I much preferred it that way, they were amazed. Young American singers often said they would be so grateful if I could show them how the role of Carmen, or Don Giovanni, or Lucia was 'done'. The perception obviously was that every role is done in a certain way – and that would be that.

The idea that a geographic or choreographic pattern of people on stage – and their redeployment into a different juxtaposition – were important dramatic elements in a production, was totally new in Italian performances. When Carl asked the chorus at a rehearsal to create a very tight mass of bodies to make a special effect for a particular scene, they all moved two inches nearer to each other. He had to use drastic symbols to get his meaning across. 'I want you to be as tightly packed together as sardines in a tin,' he said. Henceforth he was known as '*Maestro Sardine*'. Carl also had the chance to grapple with operas which he would never have experienced in Germany, such as Spontini's *La Vestale* and Rossini's *Moses*.

The opportunity to widen his repertory and the need to adapt to different cultures came just at the right moment – when he had almost reached the top of his profession in Berlin. In that sense, the upheaval and disappointment of emigration was a boon to his career and also his personality. He had always been keen to learn. Now he was soaking up – and filtering for his own use – the lazy mañana of the South Americans, the quick responses and the sunshine-happy eagerness of the Italians, the reliable solidity of the Swiss. He was lucky in his gift for languages. Before his first foreign production, in Florence 1933, Carl had taken a crash course in Italian – but needed the help of a German-speaking assistant for his production. He was not satisfied with his own performance, because he practised what he had admired so much in his first teacher, Max Reinhardt: the suggestive, almost hypnotic use of his voice in 'setting the scene' for the artists. Being obliged to work in a new language is the best way of learning the inflexions, the melody and the idiom, as well as vocabulary and grammar. With every further visit to Italy, my father made considerable strides forward in mastering the language.

He was soon to be given an opportunity of improving his fairly basic, heavily accented English as well. At the turn of the year 1933/34 a strange inquiry reached him via Fritz Busch. An English gentleman, John Christie, wanted to start an opera festival in the theatre he had built next to his country house. He needed advice and/or help from experts to set this up. Carl and Busch, both looking for artistically worthwhile and secure employment, did not give this unusual idea much chance, but decided that Carl should go to England, meet John and Audrey Christie and assess the viability of their plans.

8

Glyndebourne Pre-war

Carl had been brought up in his professional life in Germany on the concept that theatre is subsidised, with permanent companies playing all the year round in all cities of any size (roughly, those above 80,000 inhabitants). The few festivals which existed at that time, in the 1920s and early 1930s, were subsidised even more heavily. To him it seemed quite bizarre that a private person, a Mr John Christie, should want to start a summer opera festival in a theatre he had built next to his country mansion in the South of England. Carl had received a letter from Fritz Busch one day in the winter of 33/34, explaining that his brother, the famous violinist Adolf Busch, had been invited by Mr Christie through a mutual friend, to help set up an opera festival. Adolf had said that he knew absolutely nothing about setting up opera companies, but he would pass the invitation to his brother Fritz, who had been *Generalmusikdirektor* in Dresden before the Nazi take-over.

Now Fritz felt that such a task needed somebody who had been in total charge of a theatre, and not only the musical side. He thought the obvious person to approach was his friend Carl Ebert, who had been *Intendant* in Berlin before the Nazis and with whom he had collaborated on a new production of *Ballo in Maschera* there in 1932. The two men, although they were totally different in character, had established a rare empathy in their work, ethical and practical. They had exiled themselves voluntarily from Germany, and they were invited together to lead the German season in Buenos Aires. Since then each had gone his own way. They both had a handful of people to look after, and therefore needed to find work. Busch had established his base camp in Scandinavia, and did a certain amount of work there with the Radio Symphony Orchestras. He and Carl thought Mr Christie's scheme sounded like pie in the sky; on the other hand, they could not afford to turn down any offers out of hand. Having reached almost the top of the ladder at home, they now found it hard to build a new career abroad from the lowest rung. So, with much shaking of heads, they decided that Carl should go to Britain and see for himself.

He travelled to Sussex early in 1934, really with the intention of convincing the Christies of the folly of their plans. He had never heard of anyone achieving their goal before, and quite a number of fortunes had been lost in attempts to create private opera companies. My father did not know England at all. He was bowled over by the calm beauty of the countryside and the family mansion Glyndebourne. There was no time to savour the atmosphere. John Christie was a down-to-earth man with a kind of open, quizzical smile. He met Carl at the door and took him straight through the house to see the theatre. It was a disastrous beginning. As far as production facilities were concerned, the new theatre was a non-event. John owned a building firm, and being a festival aficionado, he dispensed with the services of an architect. He must have thought he knew what was required. The auditorium was simple, almost severe, panelled in oak, and held about 350 seats. Nothing wrong with that at all. The orchestra pit was rather small, even for small-scale operas. The stage was no bigger than a medium-sized village hall. It had no fly-tower (for hanging scenery and speed up scene changes), and the proscenium was narrow in real terms although right for the width of the auditorium at that time. The access door to the stage for scenery was not much bigger than a large house door. There were no side stages or backstage, indeed on one side the theatre had been built to join on to the back wall of the 'organ room', a beautiful high-ceilinged hall which John Christie had already added to his house a few years earlier. There were only two dressing rooms, one for men and one for women.

Carl did not get a chance to deliver his expert advice, based on harsh realism. He was soon enmeshed in the enthusiastic determination of the Christies to realise their plans. John was by nature friendly and warm, very direct and completely fearless. He was not bothered with obstacles in the way. You did something because you believed in the idea or you left it alone. He had been a teacher at Eton, eventually inheriting great wealth and much land in Sussex and Devonshire. He had also become a successful businessman because he possessed a certain flair for finding the right people to turn his hunches into profitable enterprises. One of these was a local company, Ringmer Building Works, and another was a firm of organ-builders which, reputedly, he bought because he could not find a firm willing or able to build the right instrument for the hall he had added to his mansion. An unkind story has it that John built his theatre to atone for the fact that his organ-building firm was responsible for many of the ghastly but fashionable cinema organs in the country. I think it most unlikely; atonement did not enter into his philosophy. John was very keen on amateur opera performances and using the organ room for these, with estate workers and friends as audience. It is recorded that he played Beckmesser in a performance of part of Wagner's *Mastersingers*, a role to which he must have brought suitably eccentric accents.

At one of his organ room operas he met Audrey Mildmay, a young singer of great charm and talent who was working with the Carl Rosa Company, doing sterling work touring the whole of Britain with the standard repertory. John fell for this fascinating creature and pursued her far and wide on her operatic travels, proposing marriage, until she finally consented. John obviously built his theatre with Audrey and many future productions of a much higher standard in mind. Now it would be possible to have proper scenery and a complete orchestra, without the need to fill in the missing instruments on the organ. But John could not quite throw off his inherent thinking along semi-amateur lines. While they were still talking about their new theatre, Audrey woke up one morning to the noise of builder's machinery. She saw workmen excavating for the foundations of the building and was inspired by that sight to say to her husband: 'If we are going to do this thing, John, for God's sake, let's do it properly.'

And that set the wires buzzing, which resulted in my father's journey to Sussex. The Christies, that is to say Audrey, had decided that there was no point in achieving a hybrid, there should be no room for compromise. They wanted a totally professional festival. Audrey was a beautiful woman, with a willpower to match John's. She was high-spirited and possessed a quick wit, capable, when necessary, of delivering a sharp barb with great charm. She had a smallish, not outstandingly beautiful, but expressive voice, and she was an excellent musician.

Serious discussions now ensued about what exactly the Christies wanted to achieve and how they envisaged the realisation, with Carl listing the requirements of the operation and the backing that would have to be provided. But the first thing to be decided was the choice of opera for the inauguration of a new festival. John had already asked tentatively whether it might be possible to mount a production of *Parsifal*. Carl replied, perhaps a little brutally: 'If you put the singers and the orchestra in the auditorium and the audience on stage, it might.' To John's question, which works he would consider suitable, he said: 'This intimate theatre simply asks for Mozart's operas.' John countered: 'English audiences don't like Mozart very much,' to which Carl replied: 'Then we must try to help them to like Mozart.' And thus the foundation stone for Glyndebourne's later fame was laid.

My father felt an immediate rapport with the Christies. All four of them, John and Audrey, he himself and Busch – for whom he could speak without hesitation – had the same incorruptible approach to their work. No gimmicks, no pandering to stars, only truthfulness to the intentions of the composer. It was at this stage that the slogan 'aiming for the sky' was born, which John loved to use in speeches, interviews and discussions to the end of his life. When the parameter of the task had been defined it was time for Carl to work out a detailed budget, so that the full damage of the exercise could be faced. After all, he had come to Britain in the belief that no private person could shoulder the burden of putting on opera seasons (he had no comprehension, at that time, of the financial resources of patrons like Lady Cunard, who had financed Sir Thomas Beecham's Covent Garden seasons for years – she never subsidised Glyndebourne). Carl put together an approximate budget for a two-week season of two Mozart operas. Since he had no knowledge of the exact cost in Britain of some items, it could not be 100 per cent accurate. Having worked till late into the night, he presented his paper to John after breakfast. My father was flabbergasted when John, having reached the sum total, calmly said 'All right.'

At this stage my father had to consult urgently with Fritz Busch on the totally unexpected outcome of his mission in Sussex. It must have taken hours to convey the unique feeling of the whole situation: walking across a legendary English lawn to a ha-ha beyond which sheep and cattle grazed, the park-like gardens, the opera house looking quite settled in its pastoral surroundings, the enormous, rambling manor house and, most impressive of all, John and Audrey Christie, who were determined to make this dream come true and who had shown that they had the flair and the vision to make it work. What was more, they seemed to have the means to realise their ambition.

Fritz Busch and Carl Ebert decided to 'knock on wood' and to dive into this extraordinary adventure. But one last and perhaps the most difficult condition for their participation had to be put to the Christies. Carl said to them that they probably could not meet it. John asked: 'Are you too expensive?' 'No,' was the reply, 'the fee is not our main concern. But we have to insist that Busch and I have the final decision in all artistic matters, if it comes to a disagreement.' This was a huge sacrifice to demand of those people who were investing so much in their brain-child. But John and Audrey had the greatness to agree.

The Christies wanted the inaugural season to be in May/June 1934. The works chosen were Mozart's *Le Nozze di Figaro* and *Cosi fan Tutte*. Intensive preparations had to be taken in hand at once. Luckily, singers were not booked years in advance at that time. The system of stars travelling about incessantly had not yet been invented. Not that Glyndebourne necessarily wanted stars anyway. The idea was to try to assemble a near-ideal cast for each opera – ideal in every respect, not only vocal. The fame of the individual singers was quite irrelevant in this context. Much more important was the blend of voices in ensemble, musicality and acting ability. In fact, Glyndebourne made conscious efforts to find unknown, young talents. Rudi Bing, who had worked for my father both in Darmstadt and Berlin, was given the task of working out the contractual details for continental artists once they had

99

been selected and/or auditioned, as well as looking out for new talent. Some of the artists Glyndebourne wanted were, of course, well known to either Carl or Busch. British artists had to be auditioned. An orchestra of the best available players had to be auditioned as well, and a small chorus had to be selected individually. There was an awful lot to do in two and a half months.

Carl would have liked to work on designs for the stage sets and costumes with a designer of his choice, because the process of getting to know each other is always an adventure of sorts, trying to find a common 'language'. But time was short, and the Christies had already promised a friend of theirs, Hamish Wilson, that he would design the operas if a festival ever got off the ground. Carl compromised for the sake of the whole and accepted Hamish, whom John called 'our little genius'. He was an extremely amiable person with a great deal of theatre experience. He had also worked for the Carl Rosa Company and was well versed in designing for small spaces. Furthermore, he was on the spot and had watched the theatre grow under John's guiding hand.

Hamish and Carl worked on conceptions for the two operas at Glyndebourne and in Cureglia in Switzerland, where Hamish presented his first sketches. My father's command of English was still rather primitive and had no idiom. After greeting Hamish with much hullabaloo on his arrival in Cureglia, Carl asked him: 'Hamish, do you want to disappear?' which is a straight translation of the German 'Do you want to go to the bathroom?', to which Hamish replied, rather nonplussed: 'But Charles, I have only just arrived.' The sketches Hamish brought were a problem. They were serviceable in technical terms, but aesthetically rather too sweet and pretty for Carl's ideas. They did not get anywhere near a new, critical look at the works of Mozart. In fact the designs appeared terribly dated after a few years, period pieces of the late 1920s/early 1930s. They represented the contemporary view of Mozart: pretty tunes and not very much psychology, ignoring his unparalleled ability to portray the minutest detail of human feeling in his music. Fritz Busch and Carl wanted to reveal Mozart's genius as he really was, with his deep insight into the human soul, and strip away all the chocolate-box wrappings and superficial coyness of the usual interpretation, which, it must be said, was rampant in Austria – and, I believe, in Britain at that time.

On the face of it, the fact the singer Audrey Mildmay was also Mrs Christie, the *chatelaine* of Glyndebourne, and indeed a member of the quadrumvirate, might have provoked one of the envisaged insurmountable disagreements, against which my father and Busch wanted to protect themselves with their demand for ultimate artistic control. Audrey wished to sing Susanna in *Figaro*. During the policy-working sessions of the Big Four, it had become abundantly clear that she was ideally suited to the role temperamentally and in looks. Fritz Busch and Carl were able to confirm at an audition that she would do more than justice to the part vocally.

Everything was finally set for the beginning of rehearsals. For Carl and Busch it had been an extraordinary experience even to have arrived at this point. The manner and atmosphere of the meetings of the top team were so different from what they had been used to. They were workmanlike, but informal, easy-going and completely open. I think these occasions introduced them to the 'British way of life'; it was a small beginning of Anglicisation for them. The mad scheme they had come to investigate was turning into an achievable dream. They still had nightmare worries, of course. Would they get only a snob audience? Would they get any audience at all? Who in their right mind would get into evening dress after lunch and travel by car or special train 50 miles to an opera house in the depths of the country, to see a high-priced performance, dine or picnic during a long interval and return home round about midnight? Had John taken on an inordinate risk? Busch and Carl needed all the concentration they could muster for their work. Within this incredibly unlikely set-up they had received the gift of ideal rehearsal conditions – the most precious gift for everyone working in the theatre.

It had been agreed with the Christies that all the singers' and staff contracts would stipulate continuous attendance at Glyndebourne from the first day of rehearsal (e.g. no leave of absence for guesting elsewhere). To begin with, there would be one week of purely musical preparation: final coaching and the all-important ensemble rehearsals which are essential for a homogenous musical style. At these rehearsals singers would be expected to put away their scores, to imbibe musical details given by the conductor. Busch either played the piano himself at these sessions or conducted the more intricate ensembles. However good the coach playing for these rehearsals, conductors invariably get irritated by the fact that the coach eventually fails to follow the conductor's beat, but accommodates the singers' – very slight – variations. At that point the conductor goes to the piano and bodily slides the coach off the piano stool while taking over playing the instrument himself, without losing a bar of the music. For a few seconds four hands play the same music. The singers have to be immune to these comical proceedings. Carl would often sit in at the ensemble rehearsals, to gauge the singers' vocal expressions and perhaps to discuss some nuances with Busch and the singers as they arose. His teamwork with Busch was remarkable in that the question *Prima la musica, poi le parole?* or the other way round simply did not enter into it. In the first place, Carl evolved his productions from the music, and secondly, they were both true servants of the opera ideal, which requires the various elements of this complex art form to be absolutely in tune with each other.

It has often been quoted that working at Glyndebourne was like a monastic discipline. It all depends. Certainly the rehearsal atmosphere was one of concentration, without distractions, traffic delays, non-availabilities, etc. This contained community tackled the Mozart scores in an adventurous mood, trying to jettison the baggage of decades of misconceptions about Mozart's work, but it was not a monastery. More like an invigorating oasis, in which periods of single-minded dedicated work were punctuated by relaxation on the boating lake, in the magnificent park or at Audrey's tea table. Over the years Glyndebourne was the catalyst for quite a few romantic adventures, often leading to the tying of knots. Roughly half the casts of the two operas came from abroad. For most of them, living the Glyndebourne mode must have been a culture shock. Apart from the unusual rehearsal conditions, there was the *Schloss*, as the German singers would call it.

Originally it had been envisaged that all the artists should be the Christies' guests at Glyndebourne, partly to save money, partly as an inducement. Very wisely, Audrey allowed herself to be persuaded that the idea was too dangerous. The work process was already programmed to be very intense. Everybody being cooped up together for 24 hours a day might bring about unforeseeable strain. The singers were told that it would be less strain on them and really for their own good, if they stayed in rented accommodation in the neighbourhood. Only the conductor, producer and heads of department stayed in the house.

As it was, Audrey had decided to fulfil her duties as hostess, beside having taken on one of the lead roles of the season. She was a wonderfully accomplished lady of the manor, always lively, interesting, full of spirit, given to mischievous banter, totally in control of any situation, including John's extravagances, and always reading her guests' needs. She was helped greatly by the butler, Mr Childs, who was a perfect – and soon to become famous – specimen of his unique profession. Childs had been with John Christie for 23 years, and when Audrey asked him after her wedding how he could have allowed John to marry, he is reputed to have said: 'I had to get my own back on the master, madam.' The tea break during the afternoon rehearsal sessions was taken in the magnificent, but comfortable, hall of the manor, with Audrey presiding over the urn of hot water and two silver pots of tea. There was a loose queue of people to get their cuppa, and Audrey automatically asked: 'China or Indian?' One day there was a faint clicking of heels and the answer: 'German.'

The rehearsal process which got under way at Glyndebourne in April 1934 was to transform the operatic scene in Britain totally. It began a renaissance which led to the establishment of many more opera companies, a spectacular increase in opera appreciation and a fundamental change in the style of productions. Carl's work in Germany in the 1920s and early 1930s was acknowledged to be revolutionary, ridding the operatic stage of the convention of stand, sing and wave your arms about to show emotion. But he never indulged in arbitrary, unmotivated change just to be different and to make headlines.

He concentrated in his minutely structured productions on transforming the conventional Carmens, Violettas and Don Giovannis into real people. He had elevated the chorus function to an equal partner in the scheme of things, making its new dramatic impact a revelation to audiences. He worked in great detail on

103

characterisation from the very beginning, not afraid to spend a long time on just a few bars of music if he felt the artist needed it to find an entry into the character of his role – within Carl's conception of the whole.

Because he was a very accomplished actor, he would often give a short demonstration of the expression, movement and stance he wanted the singer to use, simply as a guide, to inspire the artist. Sometimes he got carried away and would act out a whole scene – equally convincing whether he portrayed a coquettish girl, a romantic lover or a shady scoundrel. These 'samples' were so perfect that they might have made the poor artist at the receiving end feel inadequate. But Carl, through his infectious enthusiasm and pure strength of personality, managed to convince them that they could, in fact, do even better.

He always worked in a very positive way, not like some producers, musicians or singing teachers, who first need to destroy any confidence their poor victims have before they build them up again, making it easier to imprint their own will. The only things that would make him angry were moody or uncooperative artists or downright laziness. His anger was unmistakeable and loud. Busch was also a positive worker, who inspired rather than drilled his artists. One of the singers Glyndebourne discovered, the young Spaniard Pilar Lorengar, said in a radio interview about my father's work years later:

'At the audition in Paris this amazingly good-looking white-haired man came to me and asked would I please sing Cherubino's aria *Voi che sapete* (from *Le Nozze di Figaro*) with orchestra – it was the end of an orchestra rehearsal at the theatre. I was too frightened and said no, I couldn't, not without any rehearsal. But then I did it. He came back on stage and was enthusiastic. So I was engaged to work at Glyndebourne under his direction. It was one of the greatest experiences I have ever had. It was the most wonderful thing that could happen to a young singer. His humanity, his understanding of a singer's problems, his love of the music and voices. And his incredible patience in working with the singers. Most artists have times of insecurity, they need a lot

104

of help. A producer should, I think, perceive that. I believe Carl Ebert was one of the greatest "psychologists" in that sense. He rehearsed without let-up, for hours, tirelessly explaining what he wanted in expression, movement, etc. I sang *Pamina* at Glyndebourne in three seasons, and every time the rehearsal process was full of new nuances – it was exciting.'

In an interview at the opening of the new Glyndebourne theatre in 1994, Roy Henderson, who had sung the Count in the first *Figaro* 60 years earlier, put it very simply, talking about my father's work: 'He taught us to act.'

On 28 May 1934, Glyndebourne opened its doors to let the public stream in to the first performance. It was not a full house, actually, and quite a few of the seats were taken by singers' wives, off-duty staff members and their companions, etc. However, the most important critics had come. Some people had used the special train, some came by car, some picnicked in the interval, some used the restaurant. But the first performance of the first season, *Le Nozze di Figaro*, made a sensational impact on everybody present. The notices in the papers the following morning announced that nothing like this perfection in musical ensemble, production, etc. had ever been seen or heard in Britain before. *Figaro* is a realistic work, a kind of eighteenth-century *verismo*. Any use of gimmicks will destroy the piece. At one time it had become fashionable to overdo the elements of antagonism between the classes. The rationale was that the outbreak of the French revolution had been influenced by Beaumarchais' plays – and the 'Figaro' story is one of them. The 'revolutionary' streak is certainly present in Mozart's music (*Figaro*'s first act aria *Se vuol ballare* is an obvious example), but Mozart presents that mood as a subtle undercurrent, not a call to arms. Carl's production elicited from the singers exactly that simmering danger signal, where it is called for.

Morning Post, 29 May 1934:
'I have never seen so intelligent or imaginative a production of *Figaro*. Every movement told and helped to emphasise the various points of the music and action.'

Birmingham Post, 30 May 1934:
'The performances are as good as perfect.'
Sunday Times, 3 June 1934
'A better producer than Carl Ebert could hardly be imagined.'

The premiere of *Cosi fan Tutte* followed next night. It was possibly an even greater success than *Figaro*. It had for so long been regarded as a somewhat inferior Mozart – totally unbelievable storyline, overlong and, dare one say it, rather boring. That was the perceived judgement up to that night. What the audience saw and heard was a fascinating, true to life, psychologically revealing dissertation on human nature, expressed in Mozart's astonishing facility to enunciate feeling musically. For decades the work had been performed worldwide as a hollow meringue of cloying sweetness, with arbitrary lashings of comic business poured over it. *Cosi* is certainly difficult to get right, exactly because of the delicate balance between serious, even tragic moments and comic situations. But it is all there in the music: one (that is to say, conductors, singers, designers and producers) only has to listen properly. Mozart even manages to convey a double-track of mood at times. My father always made the soprano singing Fiordiligi listen to the French horn in the orchestra, mocking the schoolmistressy outburst in her big aria *Come scoglio*. It expresses to perfection that the outraged, puritan tone of Fiordiligi is not entirely genuine, for, secretly she is rather taken with this 'Albanian' suitor professing love. In other words, her singing of this dramatic aria must have an edge of insincerity, a certain self-righteous pompousness. The 'Albanian' in this case – it is Ferrando in disguise – also has a difficult balancing act to perform: on the one hand he has to sound ardent enough for Fiordiligi to believe he loves her, on the other hand he must make it clear (to the audience) that he is only play-acting – at this stage of the opera – for the sake of the wager he has entered into. All these subtleties are quite clearly contained in the music. Naturally an audience can not be expected to analyse consciously by which means the music expresses the fluctuations in mood, nor are they meant to, but a first-class performance will reveal them and will make the experience exhilarating.

There were signs of a needed reassessment of *Cosi fan Tutte* on the Continent in the early 1930s, but it was Glyndebourne which put the opera firmly on the map. It still remains one of the most difficult to achieve. Fritz Busch, the rather solid-looking Westfalian with a bullet head, was equally at home in Wagner and Mozart. He gave the *Figaro* and *Cosi* scores all the shades of expression which they contain, and made each work a rounded perfect whole. And that is what makes an opera memorable for the audience. He had a genial un-German manner with the orchestra and a thorough understanding of the singers' art – and their problems. But there was never any doubt that he demanded total dedication to the work at all times. Therein lay the foundation of the partnership of Carl Ebert and Fritz Busch.

The rave notices for *Cosi* and *Figaro* tended to emphasise the qualities of the production at greater length and in more exotic terms than the musical achievements. The reason was quite simply that in 1934 Britain had almost no opera production, as we understand the term today. Sadlers Wells was the only permanent opera company in the country, ploughing a lone furrow with its pioneering work. Established in 1931 in North London, under the leadership of excellent artists like Sumner Austin, it created a lot of interest among music lovers. The company offered an adventurous repertory and achieved some modern productions, but lacked, as yet, a real breakthrough as far as the establishment was concerned. Sadlers Wells was regarded as the 'people's opera' and attracted quite a different clientele from the Royal Opera House, Covent Garden, where production standards were unashamedly 'international conventional style'. This reflected the use of international star singers unwilling to spend too much time on rehearsals.

As far as I know, Busch did not really resent the greater attention being given to the production side when Glyndebourne burst upon the scene. Maybe he was a little sad that his contribution to the whole elicited fewer column inches in the notices, but no complaints are recorded. He probably understood that, in British eyes, the production was such a unique feature of Glyndebourne performances. Busch was criticised in the press on only two aspects of his music making: he played the recitatives (himself) in both operas on a piano instead of a harpsichord, and he would not allow the use of any *appoggiatura*. Both decisions were commensurate with current practice in many German opera houses post World War One. Where this somewhat barbaric tradition came from is not absolutely clear. Some sources put the blame on Gustav Mahler's 'puritan' attitude during his reign at the Vienna State Opera.

Spike Hughes' book *Glyndebourne* is the most comprehensive history of the opera house and is generally regarded as the definitive encyclopaedia of its birth and career. It is a pity that the book contains a lot of factual errors (such as a production being credited to the wrong person) and arbitrarily ignores important information (the existence of a choreographer, *et al*). Such inaccuracies lead to confusion. The Appendix, listing details of every production, even differs from textual information. What is really hard to understand is that Mr Hughes took it upon himself to misrepresent the nature of the partnership between Carl Ebert and Fritz Busch. Again and again he emphasises that Busch was the leader and spiritual head of the company, that he could make decisions without consultation or against the express wishes of Ebert, etc., etc. It simply was not so. Naturally there were lots of diverging views on all kinds of details between the two Artistic Directors, as they were later called, from choice of repertory to individual artists, but there was never a fundamental clash defying solution. On the contrary, in the thousands of letters they had to write each other over the years about all the issues concerning the next Glyndebourne season, there are countless mentions of 'if you will agree', 'I hope to persuade you yet', 'I am very keen to get so and so as Figaro but only if you can get to hear him and agree.' Any form of ultimatum never came into their relationship.

The over-the-moon press notices after the two premieres resulted in a healthy build-up of audience numbers over the rest of this short first season. Even so, John Christie had to bear a deficit of roughly £7,000 out of his own pocket, a proud sum in 1934. Ebert and Busch were convinced that no man could look such losses in the face and mentally said goodbye to their dream – for that was what it had become in the weeks of rehearsals and performances. However, John Christie would have none of it. He wanted

108

the 1935 season to be twice as long and to contain four operas. Apart from that, he was already working on plans to improve the theatre along the lines which Carl had suggested on his first visit. They could not all be achieved at once, but from here on Glyndebourne quite often became a building site in out-of-opera-season periods. Over the years the stage was much enlarged, the proscenium widened, a side-stage built to facilitate scene changes, a fly-tower for the same purpose, a rendered brick cyclorama (also useful for projections), vast storage capacity for scenery, more dressing rooms, finishing up with a whole quadrangle of dressing rooms which included the most magnificent 'green room' in the world for the artists, and finally, a rehearsal stage on the same level as the stage, so that the original scenery could be easily transported to and fro.

John Christie was clearly elated by the success of the first season, and must have been converted totally to his wife's maxim, 'Let's do it properly'. He had, however, no flair for diplomatic niceties. For some reason, he was always rather dismissive about Covent Garden. No wonder that Sir Thomas Beecham never replied to John's offer to be involved in the realisation of his festival plans. The outstanding artistic success of the first season fuelled John's ruthless onslaught on the British musical establishment. He vented his disdain constantly in letters to the press, lectures and private talks. In an openly patronising public statement he announced his willingness to mount a work by a British composer at Glyndebourne, if any of the operas submitted were found to be good enough for such an honour. He set up Glyndebourne as the final arbiter of operatic standards in Britain.

By implication, Fritz Busch and Carl Ebert were part of this campaign or, at least, were perceived to be behind it in order to safeguard their own nest. The establishment took these chastisements badly. By way of backlash Christie was attacked for having created a kind of German cabal at Glyndebourne, ignoring all achievements by British artists, relying entirely on foreigners, etc. These counter-accusations were patently untrue, but they stuck and made for difficult relations between Glyndebourne and 'the rest' for quite some time. They also set up an unjustified chauvinistic attitude towards the festival and its personnel, particularly the two Artistic Directors. Busch and Ebert were not fully aware of John's embarrassing, eccentric behaviour. Since they were working in various parts of the world during the rest of the year, they heard only occasionally, through messages from friends, about John's latest *faux pas*.

In hindsight, it looks like a missed opportunity in public relations on the part of Ebert and Busch. They failed to see the importance of wooing the British musical establishment a little. After all they had no need to be defensive: half the cast of the opening season was British. Perhaps their omission to do the right thing was partly due to their background. In the German theatre there was no problem about employing foreigners. In Britain the two artists' unions, Equity and the Musicians' Union, were very strong and also very strict about allowing contracts only for artists with an established career. The artistic directors probably did not realise how hard every management had to fight to get working permits for foreigners. In every single case managers had to prove that they had scoured the landscape for a suitable British artist, but that not one came up to the quality of the foreigner they wished to employ. Altogether a most invidious procedure. Even so Ebert and Busch, and especially the Christies, should have realised that the way forward was to hold well-publicised auditions to find up-and-coming young singers and generally to nurse contacts with composers, conductors, producers and managements – for the good of Glyndebourne.

But John was his own man. His idea of public relations was to tell everybody bluntly what he thought. If they did not like it or answered back, that did not bother him. Inevitably he hurt or irritated a lot of people with his uncompromising manner. If it had not been for Audrey's intervention, toning down letters and statements, relegating some of them to the 'pending' file, or just laughing him out of a particularly incendiary idea, the consequences would have been much worse. Unfortunately, her censorship activities were successfully circumvented by John many times. The accusation that John was a Germanophile was, of course, founded in fact. For some reason he did not like the French, neither their language, nor the people, nor their wine – of all things. He had been to German and Austrian opera houses many times, and was in fairly regular attendance at the Munich, Bayreuth and Salzburg Festivals. His favourite dress was German 'Lederhosen' (buckskin shorts) and heavy-knit white knee-length socks. Fairly startling in the Sussex countryside.

The 1935 season repeated the successes of the first season to even greater acclaim, because far more people saw them and the performances of the singers had grown in stature and assurance. Mozart's only two great operas to German texts were added to the growing repertory: *Die Zauberflöte* and *Die Entführung aus dem Serail* (known in Britain as *Il Seraglio*). Both works pose great problems, musically and for the producer. Ideally both operas need brilliant casts, vocally, in looks and acting ability, even more so than the two Italian-text Mozarts, *Figaro* and *Cosi*. In *The Magic Flute*, because there is a lot of ensemble singing, it is most desirable that even the timbre of the voices within each group should blend well, e.g. the 'Three Ladies' consist of a slightly heavier high soprano, a lower range soprano or mezzo, and a mezzo or alto. It is a tall order, but magic if the blend is right. For the Queen of the Night, as well as Konstanze in *Seraglio*, one needs a high coloratura soprano with an 'agile throat', as Mozart called it. (Luckily he had such an agile throat for his first Konstanze; he wrote an additional aria for her during rehearsals, the famous, very demanding *Martern aller Arten*.) Composers were pure pragmatists in those days and certainly did not have the holy, holy attitude to their work (or anybody else's), which we so often apply to our musical heritage.

On the production side *The Magic Flute* is a difficult nut to crack. For many years, until about the 1960s, it was presented in a very serious, not to say pompous vein, with the comic scenes running along on a parallel track. Producers have tried almost everything in getting to grips with the *Flute*. A Czech production had all the men in top hats and evening dress, Scottish Opera once played it as British Pantomime, a later Glyndebourne production left out all the dialogue (quite rightly Peter Hall resigned as artistic director over this decision, since he had not even been consulted). The producer, Peter Sellars, played the whole opera on and underneath a section of Hollywood Freeway and covered the missing dialogue links with bits of impoverished miming. I thought this

111

treatment reduced a sublime work into a Readers' Digest of the music with superimposed cartoon images – e.g. the Three Ladies were made to act like demented puppets, while the Three Boys (Spirits) arrived with skateboards, dressed in T-shirts, and the Queen of the Night sang her first aria to a TV screen showing a picture of Tamino. To my mind a futile, unacceptable, self-indulgent exercise, but some people found it 'entertaining'.

The Ebert 1935 production was perfectly straightforward, giving due weight to the serious and the comic elements, avoiding kinky interpretations, ignoring the inconsistencies in the libretto, which are insuperable anyway, and perpetuating the convention of certain cuts in the dialogue. He felt that the international cast assembled for the *Zauberflöte* simply would not be able to do justice to the German dialogue in its full-length version. The strength of his production was, once again, making real people, every person defined clearly in the different moods of his/her character. The result must have been literally 'magic', as it was judged by many people the greatest evening of opera they had ever seen.

In the first Vienna run of the work the librettist, Schikaneder, played the role of the bird-catcher, Papageno, himself. He was an experienced actor and loved to ad-lib asides to the audience. Carl thought it would be good to keep this vaudeville element, which the *Flute* undoubtedly contains, and to allow Papageno to make asides to the audience in English, while the rest of the work was, of course, played in the original German. Some members of the audience and the press corps considered this idea a strange 'lack of taste'. It is difficult to judge, after all these years, whether this strong reaction was simply a misunderstood feeling of awe for Mozart's genius. The *Amadeus* play by Peter Shaffer certainly demolished that kind of one-sided attitude once and for all, by emphasising the weird cohabitation in Mozart's psyche of his musical powers and his ordinary life – sometimes excessively 'ordinary'. Many people, particularly in Germany, found Shaffer's treatise shocking, but if they had cared to read Mozart's prolific jottings of anal humour, for instance, they would have arrived at a more balanced view. Perhaps in the case of the Papageno asides, the shock was due to the feeling that grand opera was being 'debased' by the device of using the vernacular for this special effect. Opera appreciation has become much less elitist since then.

In any case, the opening night of the season confirmed Glyndebourne's achievement of 'rediscovering opera for Britain', as one critic put it. The second new production of the 1935 season was *Il Seraglio*, again containing strongly contrasted serious and comic scenes and, again, very difficult to cast because of the vocal demands it makes. It became a worthy companion of the three productions which had already made such an enormous impact.

Carl decided to play two smallish, but important roles in the German operas himself. The *Zauberflöte* has a part called the 'Speaker', a kind of adjutant to Sarastro, whom Mozart has given only two short sections to sing, but a lot of fundamentally important dialogue in Act II. In those scenes the 'Speaker' completely commands the situation and atmosphere. Carl, tall and aristocratic, with a riveting stage presence and a beautiful authoritative voice, gave the scenes of Tamino's trials the full dramatic weight they should have, without being pompous for one moment – one of the dangerous pitfalls of the *Flute*. In the *Seraglio* he played the pivotal role of Bassa Selim. The Bassa is actually a Spanish expatriate, a renegade who lives and dresses like an Arab (a point which the audience usually does not appreciate and which is only revealed in the dialogue near the end of the opera). He is deeply in love with Konstanze, who rejects him because she still pines for Belmonte, from whom she was separated when their ship was taken by pirates. The Bassa is a middle-aged man with an aristocratic aura. He can, however, be extremely ill-tempered, even cruel in his outbursts of rage. Not before the denouement in the finale does he reveal that he was the rival-in-love of Belmonte's father. Only Konstanze's incorruptible devotion to her lover turns the Bassa's psychopathic hate against everything Spanish into benevolence – with a good measure of resignation. In short, it is a really difficult role, stretching over a wide range of emotions.

Glyndebourne was fortunate to have my father on hand to play it. His acting was so powerful, so sovereign, that it became the 'star' attraction of the evening for some people. In one of his programme notes John Christie wrote: 'Bassa Selim is usually played by an elderly singer who has lost his voice.' A little harsh, I would say, but perhaps not completely off the mark, given the resources of the normal opera company. I suppose Fritz Busch and Carl Ebert were so thoroughly tied up in their rehearsal schedule that they had no time to vet John's programme notes, which were sometimes rather weird, even outright embarrassing. They appeared unsigned, although the author was apparently known to all.

The deficit for the 1935 season worked out at £10,000 – a much improved result per performance compared to the first season. The dining hall had been used by the audience to a much greater extent, and indeed part of the relatively good financial result could be credited to the wine sales. John Christie had acquired a taste for and good knowledge of German wines over the years of his festival travels. He went on a central European wine-tasting tour from time to time, and had imported his choices for the Glyndebourne dining room as well as the opera patrons. Naturally all the wines were excellent and sold well. Since my school frowned on alcohol consumption at any time, I did not become acquainted with the Forster Johannisberg of John's until 1936, when it seemed nectar to me. Before then Mr Childs, the butler, had assured me that cider would be quite safe to drink, because it contained 'practically no alcohol'.

I had my first experience of Glyndebourne in 1934. When I came to Britain on my way to school in Morayshire, rehearsals for the inaugural season were under way in Sussex. I was allowed to stay two days and fell completely in love with Glyndebourne, the *ambiente*, the house, the Christies and the theatre – where I watched parts of rehearsals, but it never occurred to me then that I would work in theatre or opera one day (my sister Hidde had known from the age of five that she wanted to be an actress). The Glyndebourne dining room was, I thought, the most beautiful room I had ever seen. It was painted in that soft shade of beige which is meant to offset antique furniture most successfully. Looking at the long table set for a meal was a feast in itself. The polished wood was a gorgeous rich colour, and it was lit by two rows of black candlesticks with red candles and shades, black on the outside, off-white inside. This cunning effect does wonders for everybody's complexion. The only other source of lighting was hidden in brass shades mounted over the pictures along the walls.

But the moment leading up to entering this breathtaking room was a pure act of theatre. Audrey and John and their guests were standing about in the lovely hall, chatting, when the dining room door opened, Mr Childs came into the hall and announced: 'Dinner is served, madam.' He had an inimitable way of raising his eyebrows, and slowly closing his eyes while he said it, making us all feel humble and almost unworthy to be allowed into the feast. Mr Childs must have been interested in education. I was grateful for the whispered advice he gave me during dinner.

The 1936 season, only the third, one has to remember, was planned to include 32 performances of five Mozart operas – the great five, as they were called in the days before *Idomeneo* entered the general opera repertory. The newcomer that year was *Don Giovanni*. In the end there were one or two more performances to 'satisfy public demand'. Through the enthusiastic response to the first two seasons, Glyndebourne had arrived at the stage where 'Sold out' notices became the norm, at least until the outbreak of war. Its fame was spreading throughout the world, and an increasing number of overseas visitors were observed in Sussex. Glyndebourne was probably the only opera house anywhere which offered a repertory of all five of the most famous Mozart operas.

In retrospect, one must admit that the Glyndebourne casts in those early years were not uniformly brilliant. It was the musical and theatrical homogeneity which made the performances so unique and a revelation for British audiences. But there were quite a number of outstanding individual contributions. The most gratifying part of the work over the years was to realise the astonishing strides many artists made in their overall *Ausstrahlung*. It is a German word for which, surprisingly, no exact equivalent exists in English. It means the vibes or radiation emanating from a person and includes everything, from character via voice and demeanour, to the inner glow that people can bestow on their surroundings. Audrey Mildmay, Glyndebourne's *chatelaine*, is a good case in point. Busch and Ebert had been worried in case the promise she had shown would not come to fruition through the weight of responsibility she had chosen to carry. Audrey was a determined hard worker; in between seasons she went to Italy to study, for instance, and she was mentally tough. She simply blossomed under the guardianship of the Busch-Ebert treatment and became a highly accomplished artist (the word 'polished' always suggests to me a certain amount of superficiality, to which she never succumbed). Another artist who grabbed the chance to develop under Glyndebourne conditions was Roy Henderson, a marvellously genuine, humble and versatile singer. These two may be mentioned purely in lieu of the many, many artists who have tasted the Glyndebourne 'experience' and, as a result, have gone on enriched in their craft. Not least, of course, the chorus, who were fast becoming world leaders – even if their tasks so far were short in duration. What a relief, though, to see real people on stage and not just a crowd of robots all doing the same thing. It soon transpired that a number of young soloists, lured by stories of how differently Glyndebourne tackles opera production, came under assumed names, to profit from the novel methods.

John Christie was busy most of the year working on designs for improvements of the whole stage area. But these could not be ready until the 1937 season. *Don Giovanni* presents the same problems of pacing the dramatic flow as *Die Zauberflöte* and *Cosi fan Tutte*. In *Cosi* my father and Hamish Wilson solved the problem with what is called a front cloth curtain which allows an aria or another small scene to be played right downstage, while the set is changed, on tiptoe, for the next big scene. Thus action is continuous. It is a serviceable method, but not an inspired one, and died a gradual death. To be effective, one would need a different front curtain for each front scene – which is technically impossible. For the first *Zauberflöte* at Glyndebourne no solution was found for this problem, and there were scene changes of varying lengths. For *Don Giovanni* Hamish Wilson and Carl availed themselves of the 'front cloth method' once more and, therefore, the number of delays for scene changes was much reduced – but not eliminated.

One of the most striking effects of dramatic flow in Mozart's operas is the violent change of mood from the 'prayer' of the so-called 'Three Masks' (Anna, Elvira and Ottavio) to the revelry of the ballroom scene in *Don Giovanni*. The three masked aristocrats enter the park of Giovanni's house to infiltrate the party he is

116

giving for Zerlina and Masetto and their peasant friends. They believe he has immoral intentions, and also suspect him of having murdered Anna's father. Leporello invites the three formally into the house. As they go forward to follow him, Mozart interpolates a moment of reflection and gathering of spiritual strength which is pure magic. Another famous composer is reported to have said that he would gladly sacrifice his entire output, if he had had the inspiration of Mozart's three bars of transition from the park scene to the 'prayer' of the three 'Masks'. Their invocation to the gods to protect them during the dangers to come is a private prayer with three separate vocal lines, suggesting that each character is dealing with his/her problem in a personal way. The music has an astonishingly introspective, almost claustrophobic feeling about it. In that sense, pulling the trio out of the flow of the action is perfectly justified. But one can also argue that the three characters alone in a large, darkly menacing garden, trying to prepare themselves for their unknown fate, could be evocative, given the right staging and lighting.

In the 1936 Glyndebourne production the continuity of music and action must have been the deciding factor, for the impact of going straight from the trio into the violently different music of the ballroom is prodigious. In most productions there is – there certainly was at that time – a gap after the trio while the scene was set for the ballroom. But it seems that Mozart wanted the straight juxtaposition of the two contrasting moods, a very daring, modern device on his part. (For us today it is almost impossible to perceive how modern he was in his time.)

Some of the critics of the day considered this part of my father's production – the front-cloth scene for the trio of 'Masks' – a terrible *faux pas*, a barbaric, quite unmotivated idea. 20 years on, the use of the front-cloth solution had more or less died out in serious opera. Producers began using permanent sets with variable or additional elements, as well as sets which moved mechanically, changing shape and elevations using electric motors. Revolving stages were also used more frequently. At one point this emphasis on over-elaborate mechanical stage design almost got out of hand. Complicated stage design acquired a life of its own, overshadowing the human element in a performance. But then fashions in stage design change almost as quickly as fashion in clothes; the hemlines go up and down.

Another detail meeting with disapproval was Carl's introduction of three courtesans into the last scene of the opera, the so-called supper scene. In fact, it caused something like outrage. The *Daily Telegraph* used the school report phrase: 'We had expected better of Ebert', and the *Birmingham Post* called it a 'wrong-headed German tradition'. I am not sure whether it had ever been done in Germany, but it is not such a far-fetched idea, considering the behaviour of the Don as characterised by Mozart and da Ponte (maybe they thought such embellishments would be as naturally a part of productions as *appoggiatura* was of music – no need to write it down in detail). Anyway, it seems odd that the Don should sup alone, when he had spent the whole opera trying to get hold of girls of all shades and classes. This tut-tutting about 'lack of taste' was, one must suppose, an expression of the times. In a much later production of *Giovanni* at Glyndebourne, the producer made the Don bring on a three-quarter life-size wooden statue of the Virgin Mary – presumably he had levered it off its pedestal somewhere in passing, just for a lark. In the course of the supper scene he raped the statue. At the end of the performance there were some boos, but by the time the production was revived the following year, there were no more protests. Between the 1930s and the end of this century the perception of what is permissible on stage or in good taste has obviously changed dramatically.

In the 1936 season it was, once again, the overall perfection of the ensemble and of the production, plus the homogeneity of the two which thrilled the audience more than individual performances – and there were quite a few outstanding ones among these. The *Don Giovanni* production had the exact feel of what Mozart had written for a work that is compelling in its dramatic architecture. Perhaps it is the most important part of a producer's and conductor's art to achieve the right pacing and mould the change of emotions within that overall edifice. To interpret the composer's intentions in terms of a modern audience without vain self-indulgence or pandering to gratuitous fashion is the most difficult and also the most responsible task.

Both Fritz Busch and Carl had gained a great deal in stature and character during the first few years of emigration. It could hardly have been otherwise. The impact of so many new impressions and being lucky enough to be able to work in a variety of new, diverse cultures was bound to be strong. They had never known anything except the *ambiente* of the German theatre and arts scene. Admittedly, it too was very diverse and forging ahead in revolutionary experiments. But it was of their own kind, so to speak. Now they were confronted every few weeks or months with the need to adjust to different reactions of the people they were working with, in order to get the best artistic results. Having been surrounded completely by the rather stiff and formal German style of communicating with other artists, they were now breathing the much more open, informal British way.

Although the social structure of Britain was, and still is, far more rigidly divided into classes than in Germany, say, there is a greater sense of human respect, overriding the social scale. It is quite fascinating to observe these differences in human behaviour and, of course, more profitable to allow them to influence one's own actions and reactions, than to stick to the inbred rules. I think neither Carl nor Busch fell in love with the Latin American way of life, brash, not to say vulgar in the upper echelons, but abysmal poverty at the other end of the scale. Whatever the ideological pros and cons, however, Carl always found it fascinating to get to know a country, to smell the atmosphere. He was always intrigued to discover new shapes of life, hitherto unknown to him. Busch was a workaholic; he had no interests outside his music, I believe. But he definitely had a sense of humour. It was about this time, fresh from extended travels, that he started to tell the story of the conductor rehearsing an orchestra in Sweden, then in Germany and then in Britain. If he heard a bad mistake in one of the sections of the orchestra and looked across with a stern rebuke, in Stockholm all the players would be even more intent in looking at their music, in Germany one of the players would point unmistakably at his neighbour, and in Britain one of the players would half-rise from his chair and signal that it was his fault. Perhaps a little harsh on the Germans, but it is true that they are not good at owning up or taking the blame.

In this context, my father experienced an incident which

corroborated Busch's story. At one of the last rehearsals before a premiere at Glyndebourne, some lighting effect went drastically wrong. The one thing Carl always found inexcusable was lack of commitment. At the end of the act he went on stage and lost his temper, shouting: 'Who is the idiot who forgot to position that lamp?' My father's rages were quite frightening; as he used the full range of his beautiful actor's voice, they were actually very impressive. Not for the people in the immediate vicinity, though. When one of these storms was unleashed, the technique was to try and melt into the scenery. On this occasion Carl went on shouting his question as the stage slowly emptied, and after a while he became aware of a voice at his side repeating quietly: 'I am very sorry, sir.' Then he realised it was the tiny electrician from the first lighting bridge, who had climbed down to the stage to apologise face to face. It was all settled with a handshake. My father said this incident embarrassed him deeply and taught him to try to control his (Irish?) temper.

There were intense discussions at Glyndebourne among the quadrumvirate about the special effort needed in 1937 to mark the Coronation year. Strangely enough, nobody seems to have thought of mounting one of the operas by Henry Purcell. The new awareness of Baroque music in general and opera in particular probably only began after the war. That Busch and Carl had practically no knowledge of the British opera repertory is understandable, but it seems that even the Christies were not exactly conversant with the full choice available. The discussions got nowhere and had to be continued through the between-seasons-months by letter – a laborious process, which was kept going, though, by Rudi Bing, who had become Manager at the start of the 1936 season. The first Manager had been a competent theatre man, but lacked knowledge of the international opera scene, through no fault of his. In 1934 Bing had been entrusted with negotiating foreign singers' contracts at the behest of the Artistic Directors, and in 1935 he was given the same task again. To bring him into closer contact with the Christies, Carl arranged for Bing to spend some time at Glyndebourne as a kind of production assistant. It was his job to manipulate the flexible papier-mâché snake in *Zauberflöte*. I shared a room with him for three nights at the Green

Man pub in Ringmer during that period. He was terrified of spiders, so I had to eliminate the poor things every time before 'lights out'. Another hazard was walking through fields of grazing cattle, across the hill to the opera house. Neither of us was specially brave about that kind of obstacle.

When there was no breakthrough in the search for a British opera, various alternatives were discussed, from Gluck to Verdi. In the end there was no agreement – communications were too time-consuming, with Carl and Fritz Busch working flat out in Buenos Aires and then going their separate ways – so it was decided to repeat, for the 1937 season, the five main Mozart operas of the year before, rather a shaming climbdown on this special occasion. On the other hand, it was good for the budget. As John Christie had prophesied, the end of the season showed a small surplus of about £2,500.

1938 became the delayed turning point in Glyndebourne's history. Everybody had felt that it would be debilitating for the festival in the long run to restrict itself to a pure Mozart repertory. The Christies, quite legitimately, were keen on adding Donizetti's *Don Pasquale* as a vehicle for Audrey. The Artistic Directors were happy with that idea, on condition that a second new production would be added to the repertory, which should be of a heavier calibre. They were afraid that Glyndebourne might be trapped into an endless round of eighteenth century works (*Pasquale* was, of course, written in the 1840s, but was set in the eighteenth century). After many options had been considered Carl suggested Verdi's *Macbeth* which he had done with enormous success in Berlin. Everybody was worried whether there would be an audience for a completely unknown Verdi, but Carl thought that, in the four years of the festival's existence, a new understanding of modern production had been created among the opera public. One has to remember that there was so little opera in Britain in the 1930s that impresarios thought they had to rely largely on well-known works, so-called potboilers. Again Sadlers Wells was a lone voice in the wilderness, but that company's excellent efforts did not have the same resonance or effect with the public as the Sussex festival – which some remote newspapers still called the 'village opera'. Busch did not know *Macbeth* at all well, but agreed to the

121

suggestion. He had been scheduled to conduct a new production in Dresden years before, but fell ill and had to delegate it to another conductor.

The 1938 season benefited enormously from the many improvements which John had so strenuously worked on for two years. The auditorium had been considerably enlarged (under the same roof) by the addition of a fairly deep balcony as well as boxes at the back of the stalls. There were also four rows of seats with restricted view, which were intended to be sold (relatively) cheaply to students, a move which must have pleased Carl and Fritz Busch, who were still fretting about getting too many 'snobs' into the performances. These alterations resulted in the creation of the 'Covered Way', a kind of semi-open foyer with bar that became a landmark of the Glyndebourne way of life. More important for the continuing development of the festival were the improvements John was able to make on the other side of the curtain. The longed-for fly-tower was built, as well as a large side stage and a great deal of storage space behind the brick-built panorama. The quadrangle of dressing rooms containing some workshops, and the elegant 'Green Room' for the artists was now joined to the main body of the theatre.

The departure from a Mozart-only repertory gave Glyndebourne a boost, for the company itself, particularly the orchestra, as well as the audience. Finding as near ideal a cast as possible will always remain a headache. The *Don Pasquale* cast was settled quickly and brilliantly. Audrey Christie shaped a formidable Norina, on demand as demure or spitfire as you could possibly wish. Baccaloni, already a favourite for his Leporello, was the perfect love-hungry old fool Pasquale, endearing and touching in his disappointment. Mariano Stabile, intriguing in both senses as Dr Malatesta, had an uncanny way of using his eyelids and brow like Mr Childs – elegantly disdainful. Hamish Wilson devised sets which had charm and wit. The audience apparently rolled in the aisles – so much so that John Christie contemplated putting a ban on extended laughter. In the end there was no *diktat* – it was accepted that Donizetti's comedy is simply not as subtle as Mozart's. Much joy prevailed all round and, oddly, much surprise that *Pasquale* was such a good opera. Perhaps it had something to do with the superficial, slapstick way *Don Pasquale* is so often done. It is amazing, though, how deep prejudice can dig, even among critics.

For Verdi's *Macbeth*, the other 'novelty' in the 1938 programme, Carl secured the designer Caspar Neher, with whom he had worked on the Berlin production. Neher, a highly talented all-round artist, had quite a maverick personality. If theatre workshops asked him for further details on his designs, because they feared they might not interpret them properly, he just did not reply. As far as was known, he could only speak German. At Glyndebourne everything seemed to be going well, until one day he was discovered with 'Jock' Gough, the stage foreman, poring over designs spread on a little table in the middle of the stage. Neher was saying: '*Dieser Teil muss schwarz sein*', and Jock, in his magisterial way, countering: 'No, no, no, it's got to be black.' It became quite heated until bilingual help arrived on the scene. Neher's stylised, highly evocative sets and sharp, strong costumes made an enormous impression on audiences and critics alike, and the whole production had an intensity and expressiveness which completely demolished the attitude that early Verdi was just not worth it. Even so, some critics could not shake off their preconceived idea that it was 'inferior stuff', and said so in their notices. The actor Paul Scofield, a frequent visitor at Glyndebourne after the war, ventured the opinion that the opera was better than the play. Certainly music, in the right hands, can heighten the emotional range of a play. In some cases, the required condensation of the text for use as an opera libretto, also helps to tighten the drama.

Because the two main roles in *Macbeth* make exceptional demands on the singers, there were anxious times during the search for the right interpreters. After a few alarms, a marvellously well-matched couple were found: Vera Schwarz, a Yugoslav singer, had all the steely determination and ruthless seduction the role of Lady Macbeth requires, and the American Francesco Valentino conveyed the anti-hero side of the character perfectly: ambition mingled with fear, as well as total subservience to his wife (I think in most productions of the play the cowardly aspect of the character is underexposed).

Carl's production was possibly even more sharply focused than his first foray in Berlin. The characterisation was compelling; for the first time at Glyndebourne a really large chorus was needed, and its role was just as important as those of the soloists. Carl worked hard to make every chorister a separate self-contained character, and he found very willing collaborators in the young soloists making up the chorus. They enjoyed portraying several different facets of the drama: witches, murderers, courtiers, refugees, soldiers, etc. The finesse of their acting and singing was a revelation for the audience.

Within the marvellous spaces and levels which Neher had given him Carl produced a performance entirely built on 'personalisation'. There was only one stage 'effect' he used: after the announcement of King Duncan's murder and after the death of Macbeth, he utilised the new technology of the fly-tower. He made everybody on stage freeze in the middle of their action and brought down a painted cloth as a background to the static crowd, at the same time blotting out the scenery. This process removed the ensuing ensemble from the realism of action and switched over instantly into a communal thought process. This detail jarred with those people who liked their opera traditional and did not want to be made to sit up. During one of the final rehearsals of this scene there was a linguistic misunderstanding. Everybody on stage stood ramrod still, staring straight ahead – as my father had demanded on pain of death – when Busch suddenly pointed at one of the choristers and, continuing to conduct, shouted: 'You, woak' and again: 'You there, woak ... woak'. The terrified chorister looked about him, without moving his head and when Busch pointed again, but before he could open his mouth, started to walk slowly across the stage. Now Carl started yelling. Total collapse of rehearsal. It turned out that Busch had found the intensity of vocal input by this chorister somewhat wanting, and expected him to 'work' harder.

Toscanini, whom Carl had known quite well for some years, came to one of the performances and was very complimentary about Busch's and Carl's work, but the story goes that he growled when the cloth came down after Duncan's death and muttered: '*Tedesco* [German].' All the same, he invited my father to do

Macbeth with him at Verdi's birthplace. The eminent critic W.J. Turner wrote of the same performance in the *New Statesman & Nation*:

> '... the murder scene in Macbeth's castle is overwhelmingly thrilling ... Here we have a rare combination of acting and singing in equal degrees of virtuosity. In the culmination of this scene, when Mr Ebert masses the whole household of the castle with the murdered King's retainers before the curtain to sing Verdi's magnificent chorus, he achieves what is the most electrifying effect I have ever seen on any stage ... The production of *Macbeth* ... far surpasses from the acting point of view any production of Shakespeare's play that I have ever seen.'

Another famous critic, Ernest Newman, wrote about the same production in the *Sunday Times* in 1947:

> 'Carl Ebert's handling of the scene is dramatic ... Action of the ordinary type ... would be much less impressive here than an immobilisation of the crowd that has the effect of impersonalising and universalising it, making it a timeless and cosmic rather than a temporal and local element in the drama.'

Strangely enough, the famous German conductor, Furtwängler, came to the same performance as Toscanini. He was a fairly regular visitor, and always brought a message from the Nazi hierarchy suggesting my father and Busch should return to Germany. He always received the same reply: No way. Glyndebourne staff were carefully deployed by Bing to prevent Toscanini and Furtwängler meeting. Toscanini hated him for having stayed in Nazi Germany, allowing the Government to use his fame as a propaganda tool. Toscanini had turned his back on Fascist Italy and Germany.

It was roughly at this stage of his self-imposed exile that Carl used the expression 'Thank God for emigration' more and more frequently. He was thankful because emigration, with all its bitterness and anger and frustration, had brought him into contact with so many rich, new experiences. He enjoyed and was fascinated by observing the many national characteristics which he had been fortunate enough to encounter. Later in his career, he also confessed that: 'Glyndebourne is my favourite baby.' Everything came together to make it ideal, the atmosphere, the working conditions, the collaboration with John and Audrey and Fritz Busch, and the freedom of British life. Glyndebourne represented the same magic for almost everybody who ever worked there. The house and theatre protected by the high slopes of the Downs, the beautiful garden and lakes, the expanse of lawn which seemed to invite one to dance on it while music spilled out of every open window, the majestic trees – it all added up to a serene whole, an oasis of creativity.

1938 had been a vintage year. Glyndebourne was firmly established as an important player on the arts calendar of the world. The political rumblings, the invasion of Austria and the Munich crisis, had endangered some of Glyndebourne's personnel, but detailed plans were made for the 1939 season. It was decided to repeat the repertory of 1938 (the three Italian-text Mozarts plus *Macbeth* and *Pasquale*). On top of that there was talk of a close relationship with Covent Garden, the possibility of going to the Lucerne Festival in Switzerland, and a firm invitation to perform a season at the New York World Fair in August 1939. There were a few changes of cast for the operas, and the season was again a great success with the public. Within days of the last performance on 15 July, all the artists and personnel had dispersed. John Christie announced a programme for the following year's festival. Six weeks later war broke out, and Glyndebourne had become the home of a lively bunch of East London evacuee children.

9

Hitler's Stranglehold

By 1936 the world was in a fair amount of turmoil politically. Governments failed to find a way out of the world recession of the early 1930s and therefore fell frequently. The most stable countries seemed to be, paradoxically, the fascist dictatorships of Italy and Germany, and the USA under President Franklin D. Roosevelt. Italy finally conquered Abyssinia by capturing the capital Addis Ababa, whereupon the emasculated League of Nations lifted 'sanctions' against Italy. Germany re-occupied the demilitarised Rhineland without any protest. *Front Populaire* in France under M. Blum dissolved the new fascist party Croix de Feu. The Spanish Popular Front Coalition won the election against the Conservatives, but the right wing Falange led by General Franco revolted and started the Civil War, supported by Italy and Germany. It lasted until 1939. Germany abrogated the Locarno Treaty, under which Great Powers undertook to submit disputes to arbitration. Germany had already quit the League of Nations. King George V died in January and was succeeded by Edward VIII, who abdicated in December. The British Government began to consider re-armament, continually demanded by Winston Churchill. Germany signed Anti-Comintern Pact with Japan.

Hitler's programme of re-alignment and annexation functioned like clock-work. Re-introduction of general military service, phased re-armament, re-occupation of the Rhineland — hefty reminders of what *Mein Kampf* had laid down. But no single action was ostensibly big enough in itself to demand retribution

127

by the Western Allies – some of whom had plenty of internal problems of their own.

No wonder the annual Glyndebourne season, getting longer every year, was a haven of sanity and tranquillity for my father – admittedly only after strictly observing the adage 'Everything cometh to him who waiteth, as long as he worketh like hell while he waiteth'. His work schedule was hard, toing and froing between Switzerland, Austria and South America. There were many interesting and also gratifying assignments, but Glyndebourne was the only place where he felt he could really build up something new, something for the future, something permanent. That aspect of his work had been the most important to him throughout his career as an actor, teacher, producer and theatre director/administrator. Suddenly, out of the blue came an enquiry from Turkcy, asking whether he would be interested in creating something which did not exist so far, a National Academy of Music and Drama, with the final objective of establishing a Turkish National Theatre. The task seemed, on paper, tailor-made for him and appeared particularly enticing because of the exotic flavour of the Middle East, so far unknown to him. He decided to go out there to reconnoitre.

In the meantime he found his second-phase acting career more and more stimulating. Having started out with the comedy *Tovaritch* from sheer economic necessity, he soon felt the stage adrenalin flowing again. He was asked to play Peer Gynt and Egmont and other roles for which he had become famous, and which he now found he could approach in an even more mature way. Breaking away from the over-tight discipline of the producer-led State Theatre in Berlin 10 years earlier and gaining his first experience as a producer himself, gave an added dimension to his acting. He now had that overall perspective of a production which he had longed for in Berlin, but which was denied him, causing frustration in his work. The feeling of being in a strait-jacket had ultimately decided him to look for a post as *Intendant*, in which he would be free to test his ideas on modern productions and on the all-important actor-producer relationship. He felt instinctively that the era of the tyrannical dictator/producer was at last on the wane. It had become outdated, and its place was

128

slowly being taken by producers who sought to inspire rather than dictate. In Switzerland Carl also played several roles for the first time, which had not come his way before, such as King Lear.

Freelancing artists suffer the horrible fate of living out of suitcases permanently. Carl was fortunate in becoming acquainted with Herr and Frau Reiff, who lived in a large house in Zürich and ran the modern equivalent of a 'salon' for the arts intelligentsia. They invited him to stay with them while he was working in that area. It was a stimulating and luxuriously comfortable household, where Thomas Mann and other intellectuals were frequent visitors. The Reiffs had the knack and the connections to make their home into a centre for relevant discussions on the widest range of subjects, from the arts via politics to theology; so much more positive than the prevailing rumour mill of those days.

My father saw very little of his children in the years up to the outbreak of war. The three youngest ones stayed in Cureglia, the two girls went to the village school, learnt Italian very quickly and also learnt the pretty unfathomable Ticino dialect – very useful for conversations among themselves which they did not want the grown-ups to understand. The birth of my brother Michael on 15 January 1935 was greeted with great joy by the whole family. Very early on he developed a disconcerting habit of hardly sleeping at all. My stepmother, Gertie, became extremely worried and consulted the Swiss-Italian paediatrician, who tried to console her by saying: 'Children of old parents – often nervous.' Gertie, at 34, was not amused. My brother retained that quality of being a bit different all his life. He would go walking in remote parts of the Rocky Mountains in deep snow, accompanied only by his dog, or he would sit in a church in Italy plastered with Giotto frescoes, with his eyes closed (better to feel the atmosphere and forget the tourists). There was always an element of showmanship about everything he did. Yet he became a very good actor, without any help from Carl, sensitive and not at all showy.

My eldest sister, Hidde, also got her first theatre engagement without any help from my father. In fact he was negative, not to say destructive, about any of his children aiming for a stage career as performers. He was absolutely obsessed by the fear that they might not make it to the top, and therefore become part of what he called the 'artistic proletariat' – i.e. the lowest form of life imaginable. Strangely enough, he was very happy with my sister Renata's and my own choice of careers on the production side. Renata became his assistant when she had finished her schooling and had learnt to speak Turkish fluently. After the war in 1947 she also assisted him on one production, *Rigoletto* at the Cambridge Theatre, London, before going on to the USA to marry an American soldier she had met in Ankara. In the States she went into films and became very successful, first as a continuity girl and then as a producer.

Hidde had a rocket start at her first theatre in Bochum. She was chosen to play Desdemona when she was 19, and soon amassed a list of leading classical roles, including Iphigenia, Cleopatra and Gretchen in Goethe's *Faust*. I saw her act only once, when I was about 16, and felt rather embarrassed and sad that I had to be so critical. Maybe it was the producer's fault (and I cannot remember her role), but I thought she played it terribly ingenue-naive. She was a wonderfully warm, trusting, helpful, loving girl, determined to believe that everything and everybody in the world could be made to be good. Perhaps it was this extreme naivete which coloured her development as an actress – although she made a very good career, going on to Stuttgart and then to Berlin.

My father thought it would be something rather special if he and Hidde played opposite each other in Goethe's *Egmont* which he had been engaged to do in Basle. For both of them it was to be a special and exciting occasion, a kind of family festival. It was a disaster, because Carl told her after the performance that her acting was 'lowest provincialism'. Given his great kindness to colleagues and pupils, which is attested to hundreds of times in their letters, it must appear extraordinary that he could be so cruel to his daughter. I don't think he wanted to practise shock therapy; he simply would not accept anything other than the highest possible standards, certainly not from his own child. He offered to work with her at any time she could make herself free. Stuttgart to Basle was no distance. It may be that her performance was part of the professional crisis in which she found herself, triggered by a deep unhappiness in her private life.

It is touching to read the hundreds of letters the four parents wrote to each other, discussing how best to cope with the situation without hurting Hidde. They did not succeed. She had to fight her way through the agony in her own time. In parallel to that worry ran the question of the relentless approach of war and whether it would be possible to persuade Hidde to leave Germany. All four parents were very conscious of the need not to force discussions of these twin problems on Hidde when she visited them in Britain or Switzerland. When opportunities did arise to discuss the political situation, Hidde usually became evasive after a while. Somewhere in her heart she must have thought the parents – and the tens of thousands of others who had left Germany – were wrong in their assessment of the future under Nazi rule.

The situation was quite different for my step-grandmother, Hans Oppenheim's mother, who was Jewish by birth. She struck me as a strange apparition when I was a teenager. Tiny, dressed entirely in layers of black, she had beautiful dark grey hair piled high over a china-smooth face. She looked almost transparent to me, fragile, with a kind smile, at the same time aloof. She lived in Berlin in a small flat, which could have passed as a V&A Museum exhibit of Victoriana. Heavy, ornately carved furniture, dark patterned wallpaper and carpet, thick dark velvet curtains and pelmet, plus lace curtains, lampshades with fringes and any number of small pictures and ornaments. She looked an indefinable age – she might have been in her late sixties. Mama Oppenheim, as we called her, had decided that even Hitler would not drive her out of her home town. She lived, quasi in isolation, through the first five years of Nazi rule. When the persecution of the remaining Jews, the pogrom, reached a new pitch of intensity in the autumn of 1938, she decided to end her life. She took some drugs and left a note for her only son and her daughter-in-law, the Oppis:

'My dear, dear children,
'My last thoughts before going to sleep are for you. I am calm and happy, because I know I am doing the right thing at the right time – for you and for me. Do not grieve, do not begrudge me my peace. My dearest wishes always surround

you, with gratitude and love. Please forgive me, that I make you sad.

'Your mother'

Hans and my mother could not even dare to go to the interment.

The question of my own future had to be decided in 1936, when I passed the so-called Oxford and Cambridge School Certificate against all expectations. I was very interested in the diplomatic service and economics, which would have pointed to reading Modern Greats. But I also suddenly saw that it would be quite impossible for my father to finance a university course for me. A family conference was called for the earliest possible opportunity. It took place at Rules' Restaurant near Covent Garden, just the four parents and myself. The parents debated the issues before us assiduously while we ate, until one of them suddenly said: 'Peter, for God's sake say something.' I was well-known in the family for being rather quiet. Since the whole situation had arisen unexpectedly for me, I had not yet found an alternative professional interest. It was decided that banking experience would do no harm – and there was a certain amount of justice in that because my father had started the same way. I became a 'volunteer clerk', an apprentice in fact, at the well-known commercial bank of S. Japhet and Co. in London Wall. The experience was fascinating. I took out a student subscription for *The Times*, bought a hat and an umbrella, and travelled from my digs in Ennismore Gardens, South Kensington to Moorgate every day. The idea was that I should spend, say, two or three months in every department to learn the trade properly. After about 18 months I decided that banking was not for me.

The Oppis had in the meantime moved to Dartington Hall in Devonshire, which Dorothy and Leonard Elmhirst had chosen for an experiment in rural rejuvenation. It included several farms run according to different traditions, as well as a sawmill, cider mill, textile mill, glass manufactory and other commercial ventures. To make the scheme a round whole, the Elmhirsts also built a junior and a senior school and put a very modern educationist, Mr Curry, in charge. They also created an arts complex, which included Michael Checkov's Drama School and the Jooss Ballet as well as individual artists. Hans Oppenheim was charged with the task of building up a music department.

When I had finished with banking, the Oppis happened to hear that a teacher at the Senior School was about to start a small film unit to make classroom and documentary films. In a flash I saw that the combination of the artistic and the technical might be the right choice for me. Working in the theatre had simply never occurred to me as an option, although I was surrounded by it in the family. Perhaps there was a hidden psychological barrier in having a famous theatre man as father. He had never even hinted that it would make him happy if I chose a theatrical career. I lived with the Oppis and became a student cinematographer. Dartington was permanently alive with interesting activities. It was almost impossible to see and hear them all. The work of the Jooss Ballet and the Drama School represented world class.

Carl came to Dartington only once in those last years before the war. He was, after all, still looking for what he called 'a real task, something to develop and build with a sense of permanence about it, like Glyndebourne and Turkey.' After five years or so of 'guesting' – however satisfying and prestigious it was at the time – he just longed for something that would still be there in 10 years' time or more. I think he came to Dartington with an open mind. He found it not enough to his taste, not 'real' enough, not sufficiently brawny, too ethereal, in fact a little precious. It is a danger for places like Dartington that, in trying to build a rather special community spirit, they become too inward-looking, navel-gazing.

Soon after he had decided to leave Germany in March 1933 Carl was approached by certain people near the levers of power in Vienna. They were keen to have him on the throne of *Intendant* of the State Opera, one of the most famous houses in the world. Franz Werfel, the Austrian writer– and translator of opera libretti – was one of the people trying to use his influence in that direction. His wife Alma, the widow of Gustav Mahler, still had very influential connections as well. Nothing came of it at the time. The mill through which Vienna theatre appointments have to pass grinds more slowly and more deviously than any other. Again and again offers of productions came his way, but they always foundered. The saddest loss was the invitation from Bruno Walter to do

Masked Ball with him in Vienna. Carl felt he owed it to Fritz Busch to inform him of the plan and to receive his *placet*, because, together, they had had such an outstanding success with this opera in Berlin. He did not want to offend his friend Busch, but it needed delicate handling to make Bruno Walter see it in that perspective without offending him. He was, after all, the Music Director of the Vienna Opera. Busch was only one of the guest conductors. An endless correspondence ensued, quite a feat because all three of them were continually on the move. Busch was not particularly enthusiastic. He said he understood that it was an exciting opportunity for Carl, but it was a pity they could not repeat their Berlin cooperation on this work, etc., etc. He finally left it to my father to decide. To burden Carl with that dilemma was not generous, especially in view of the fact that hardly any other producer would have shown such loyalty – anyway, not under the prevailing conditions. So much time had elapsed with this correspondence that Vienna was unable to keep the offer open.

The Turkish proposition was some consolation, but, of course on a totally different plane. Seeing and getting the feel of Istanbul and then Ankara for the first time provided exactly that excitement which an explorer must feel and which Carl relished. Kemal Ataturk, Father of the Turks, was bent on modernising his country. He had demoted Istanbul to the status of a provincial capital because he was convinced that a totally new beginning for Turkey could only be accomplished with a brand new power centre. He wanted to run the state from a clean, purpose-built new town as an outward signal that the old power structure and its discredited mechanisms were buried for good.

Carl made his first trip to Turkey in late 1935. He spent 10 days assessing the situation. Ataturk's plan was simple, honest and uncompromising. He wanted to bring every aspect of technical, business, academic and cultural life up to the most modern Western standard. For that he needed experts from abroad to analyse the required reforms and, if their report was accepted, to see them through to the end. This always included the obligation to train Turkish personnel, so that they could take over when the foreign expert's task was done. The new Turkey was fiercely nationalistic and at the same time businesslike in its attitude and treatment of foreign advisers. But there was never any question of a foreigner being allowed to build a niche for himself.

Fortunately, the top civil servant in the Ministry for Cultural Affairs, Cevat Bey, was a highly intelligent man with whom Carl established immediate rapport, although Cevat had no direct knowledge of the performing arts. He had been to university in Berlin and had lived there for a number of years. He was fluent in German. He had apparently been given orders by Ataturk, after Carl's interview with the dictator, to treat the establishment of the academies as a priority. Ataturk discussed Carl's experiences in the field in detail and finally asked how long it would take for Turkish singers and actors to perform plays and operas. Carl replied: 'A minimum of three years for drama and five years for opera.' Ataturk said: 'Two and three.' Carl said: 'Out of the question. The performances could not achieve the standard which I myself demand for the first Turkish National Theatre.'

He was asked to prepare a written submission of all aspects of the proposed academies working up to the goal of a National Theatre. His comprehensive paper, delivered in April 1936, started with the history of the Turkish theatre, which had been provided so far mainly by Armenian actors. There was only one drama theatre in the whole country at the time, the remainder of theatrical entertainment consisted of the lowest kind of ad-lib comedies and light operetta/musicals. The standard of performances was unacceptable in every instance. The paper went on to stress that there could never be a national theatre without the emergence of an indigenous dramatic and musical culture – so far non-existent. Until such a time when Turkish dramatists and composers had emerged and gained some experience, the new theatre would have to rely on existing Western classical and modern masterpieces for its repertory. The translation of selected works had to be commissioned at once.

These first few paragraphs of Carl's report revealed in a nutshell the unique task set by Ataturk. As far as is known, there has never been an attempt to create a theatre culture out of nothing, in a desert. In due course Carl was to realise that the problems were even graver than he envisaged. But he found the task more exciting every day, the deeper he got into it. This work would be a far cry from establishing drama schools in Berlin and Frankfurt, which had automatically built on the extant wide theatre culture in Germany. At every step of his planning he had to remind himself that there was no background, nothing could be taken for granted. He found it weird but exhilarating.

Having established the primary need of encouraging the emergence of an indigenous dramatic art, his report went on to explain the difference between *stagione* theatre and repertory theatre. He argued that the repertory system would be the only possible route for the creation of a verdant theatre culture. The *stagione* system, he continued,

> 'had been allowed to flourish in some of the other so-called "young" nations, with dire results. In those cases the spiritual and musical needs of the people have been served by *stagione* ensembles, who carry home enormous star salaries, but leave behind no discernible cultural benefit. The great South American countries, for instance, present all the most famous names of drama and opera to an increasingly blasé public, stifling any home-grown art. It proves that art bought like consumer goods is devoid of any spiritual or cultural benefit to the nation.'

Carl went on to enumerate the advantages of the repertory system, saying the National Theatre could and must be:

> 'the cultural yardstick of the nation,
> its "moral foundation", in the sense of furthering people's attitude to ethic values,
> the intellectual platform for the discussion of contemporary problems,
> the "laundry" for cleansing and enhancement of the language,
> the motor for indigenous dramatic and musical creation,
> the place for the most effective visible national education in music.'

In this 'foreword' on the subject matter Carl was careful to praise the one or two (short-lived) success stories worth mentioning. The section was also sprinkled with a few highly complimentary references to the visible achievements of the new Turkish nation in other spheres.

The main part of the report dealt with the wide-ranging details of setting up the academies, not forgetting to pre-empt the argument: 'Why have all this effort in training? Genius will always win through anyway.' He pointed out that the purpose of academies was not to train a few outstanding talents, but to raise the overall level of achievement, which is much more important for a new theatre culture than a beautiful façade with only a genius or two. He cited the Turkish saying: 'Just a few flowers don't make a summer.' To safeguard the standard of the future Turkish National Theatre, he pleaded that completion of the academy course should be made obligatory for everybody wanting to enter the profession.

He then went on to say that:

'There is never a student problem, only a teacher problem. We must recognise the fact that an actor or singer most of all needs a thorough grounding in his/her craft. That and artistic discipline are the two main pillars of training. We have to find "experienced" teachers, but not in the shape of retired singers or actors who lack educational experience. They are simply looking for a sinecure. The educational nous and the passionate joy of working with the human material entrusted to the teacher – those are the qualities which the student senses most readily and which will speed the learning process. The second main ingredient for a successful academy is a carefully balanced and comprehensive curriculum.'

The planned timetable left nothing to chance. Apart from the obvious subjects which every opera school has to offer, such as vocal training, music theory, role study, staging rehearsals and their subdivisions, the students had speech training, dialogue, languages, body training, e.g. Martha Graham, Dalcroze, ballroom dancing and fencing.

A few months later, in the autumn of 1936, my father's report was accepted in its entirety, and he was given unusual powers to see the scheme through. The first task was to find the best possible teachers and to attract the right students. To collect the right body of teachers was just a question of endless letter-writing to friends and others in the profession, asking for recommendations, followed by more correspondence and interviews. The time was propitious for attracting good people to such a way-out venture because of the political uncertainty in Europe. Carl also had to find a deputy for himself, as it was intended that he would be in Turkey for only four to five months. All this was accomplished fairly easily, with most of the teachers coming from German-speaking countries, but other nations were represented too.

Finding the right student material posed quite a different problem. Since there was no theatre culture, how could one reach potential performers, how could young people know what a 'Drama Academy' meant? The Government paid for a publicity campaign, with posters and leaflets throughout the country. It also paid for the swarms of youngsters who wanted to come to Ankara to audition. One typical example may stand for the unusual circumstances under which the panel of judges had to decide whether a candidate was suitable material for the academy. A young shepherd girl from the Anatolian plain came to the audition with her grandfather as chaperone. She was asked the usual question: 'What would you like to sing?' She gave the name of a song from a musical. After she had finished, the routine question came from the panel: 'What else have you brought?' Nothing, was the answer, she had not learnt any other Western music. 'How did you learn this song, then?' 'It was in a film I saw.' 'But you can't have learnt that song, by just hearing it in the cinema once.' 'I liked the film so much, I saw it through twice.' The panel thought she was obviously musical, quite apart from her promising vocal material. She was asked to sing a few scales which the accompanist would play on the piano, to test the range of her voice. The pianist played, but nothing happened. It turned out that she could not hear or associate the chords played with singing scales because the Turkish musical scale is quite different from the Western scale. She was accepted, and became a star pupil. It was exciting, adventurous work for Carl and the other teachers.

138

Although Carl was such a talented linguist, he found it impossible to learn Turkish. Apparently, it has nothing in common with any other language except Hungarian and Finnish. This was a minor disaster for him, because he depended so much on using the inflexions and colours of his voice to put across his meaning. But worse was in store. One of Ataturk's reforms had been to cleanse the Turkish language of all the foreign accretions it had collected over the years, mostly from the Arabic. New words were being 'invented' all the time. Some were abandoned again after a while as impractical. For the time being, all Carl's work with the students had to be done through interpreters. One day he became aware that different people pronounced the same words in different ways. This led to the discovery that the problem lay not in regional accents, but in the fact that there was no such thing as 'High Turkish'. Carl set up a commission of four experts, plus himself as chairman, to lay down phonetically how the language should sound. It seemed absurd, but it did pay dividends.

My father had great respect for Ataturk. He was a ruthless dictator, but only interested in the cause. He hated pomp and pompousness, never wore uniform or medals, never put on a 'show' about his own position, nor did he want to be idolised as a saint. He was a proud Asian, and stubborn. And he was wise as well as clever. Ataturk worked immensely hard, but had a tiring habit of asking ministers and other leaders of departments to appear at his house in the middle of the night to report on their work.

On one such occasion, Carl watched from a first-floor window where he was waiting, how a car drove up to the entrance. Ataturk stumbled out and had to be helped up the steps. Five minutes later the door swung open and he strode in, fresh and alert, and commenced a searching interview with Carl about progress at the academies. He was always clear and decisive, fair and respectful.

Carl also had wonderful support from Ataturk's friend, Ismet Inoenue, a former general, comrade-in-arms of Ataturk during the revolution, and now Prime Minister. He was a highly educated and sensitive man, and believed in the importance of the arts for the nation's well-being. When Ataturk died, Inoenue became President. Other eminent emigrants, such as the architects

Clemens Holzmeister and Hans Poelzig, the politician Ernst Reuter – who became Mayor of Berlin after the war – and the composer Paul Hindemith, had also been asked to submit proposals for the rejuvenation of Turkish life, each in their own spheres. Their presence in Ankara counted for my father as a guarantee of the seriousness of the Turkish Government in their quest to rebuild the country. He made many new friends over the following 10 years.

It took a little while for Carl and Gertie to adjust to living conditions in a totally strange environment. Up to the outbreak of war, though, their stays in Ankara were confined to only two to three months at a time. The family, at home in Switzerland, was, of course, keen to have a picture of what their new life was like. Gertie wrote:

'Ankara is not really a city yet, more of an ambition ... The little old Kurdish town of Angora sits on two small hills, and around it they started to build the new town Ankara about 14 years ago. They began with masses of little stone houses in a kind of colonial style, with corner shops and uneven pavements and the occasional enormous, ugly building in between: the first bank and a ministry. That was the beginning, the so-called centre. From there the town is spreading out further and further with great complexes of colleges, institutes, hospitals, ministries and stadia, great estates of villas and apartment buildings and the diplomatic quarter. High above the town on a hill, the house of Ataturk. A few grand boulevards criss-cross the city, but many ordinary streets are still not made up. Everybody has to have rubber over-shoes, galoshes. After a heavy shower the city's music director, Mr Praetorius, has to pull up his trouser legs to walk, like a flamingo, the two minutes from his house to the music school, to conduct the weekly "people's concert". The city is spreading enormously far and looks like a vast exhibition site at the moment. All the bits in between have not been filled in yet and the parks and trees lining the wider streets are still missing.

'For our entertainment there are two cinemas and the

140

"people's palace", where you can see amateur performances (unbelievably dreadful) and go to political meetings. That's all. There is one excellent hotel and two good ones, one very expensive Western restaurant and two Turkish ones (we visit the Turkish ones in turn) – and there is a cafe, decorated in ice-grotto-blue.

'This strange, developing landscape is peopled by several thousand civil servants, perhaps a similar number of foreign experts, a large diplomatic corps and finally the original inhabitants, Kurds and peasants.

'We had to go to a charity ball one evening. Ataturk was there. He had one or two ministers and generals at his table and his adopted daughter of whom he is very proud. She is an army pilot. He wore an ordinary suit, because he hates evening dress. The impression he made on us was completely different from what we had expected, or rather what one would expect of people in his position. He has an arresting head, grey-blond, lines around the eyes and mouth, a man nearing 60, who has had a hard life. One feels the presence of an exceptional personality and authority, but an outsider would not think of the man sitting at that table as the Turkish Dictator. His behaviour is easygoing and natural. Even among this very elegant crowd he has the aura of a stern, but much loved teacher among his pupils. He dances very well and talks with great animation – sometimes so loud, that people at the other tables listen, those on the dance floor stand still and the music stops. He accompanies his words with strong, hard gestures. An elderly general counters his argument softly but with emphasis. Ataturk finally stops the argument with: "I give the order for flags to be hoisted, I decide when to declare a holiday, I alone". The band strikes up again, the dance continues, people talk and laugh.

'It is really hard for us to get to know the Turks. They seldom say precisely what they mean, so one has to filter what one hears and guess and combine what they hide behind their unmatched politeness. Carl is very lucky to have Cevat Bey. He can be completely open with him – and that saves a lot of time.'

141

The first winter of the Turkish adventure was largely devoted to the immense task of creating the whole organisation, engaging the right staff and selecting the fortunate 40 students, 20 each for the opera and the drama schools. From the beginning Carl relished the, somehow, unreal experience of working with students absolutely clean and untarnished and without any preconceived ideas. What began as a far-fetched, romantic notion for him slowly developed into a hard-to-believe dream.

In 1938, at last the way was clear for Carl to do two productions in Vienna, *Carmen* at the Opera, with Bruno Walter conducting and Caspar Neher responsible for the designs and, at the Burgtheater, the State Drama Theatre, Shakespeare's *Julius Caesar*. The *Carmen* was hailed as epoch-making, Vienna having experienced only the traditional blouse-slipping-off-the-shoulder presentation of the opera so far. There were the usual alarms of timescale, such as getting together with the designer early and often enough to deliver agreed concepts to the workshops on time. This was followed by the usual complaint that the workshops could not read Neher's brilliant designs. But it all happened and the audiences were amazed, partly because the trawl for a new, untraditional cast had also been very successful. At the reception after the premiere, the Austrian Chancellor (Prime Minister) and the Minister for Education pulled my father aside and offered him the combined directorship of the Opera and the Drama Theatre. Carl later recalled: 'I was taken unawares, and said I would have to have a little time to think about it. Three minutes later I realised it was the most stupid thing to say.' Three months later the offer was to become irrelevant.

Working at the Burgtheater was a more difficult task. Carl had to cope with remnants of the Court Theatre tradition, which he thought he had helped to sink without trace 15 years earlier. The roster of principal actors was flexible and willing enough to help Carl in eliminating empty rhetoric. The smallest roles gave him the biggest problems. There was one actor with years of service to his name, who only had to say something like: 'There is a messenger waiting outside with letters.' He made such a lugubrious, pompous meal of this factual line, that Carl was still rehearsing him half an hour later, by which time the actor was so flustered the line became: 'There are letters waiting outside with a messenger.' Work on *Julius Caesar* proceeded against the background of a continually vacillating political situation in Austria. Kurt Schuschnigg had taken over as Prime Minister in 1934 after the assassination of his predecessor Dollfuss by Nazi supporters. In 1938 it seemed that Schuschnigg would have the majority of Austrians behind him in his defiance of German threats. But nobody was quite certain. Carl had got as far as the pre-Dress Rehearsal of *Julius Caesar* when the German army crossed the Austrian border on 15 March. He described the last days of an independent Austria in a letter to me after his escape:

'Cureglia, Tuesday, 23 March 1938

'My boy,
'there are experiences that, in spite of being awake intellectually, we can not quite bring ourselves to analyse: was it real or a dream? That's how I feel at this moment. I just can not get it into my head that situations of such extreme opposites can exist so near in time and space. So, I shut my eyes and hang on as long as possible to the dream that I am lying in the Ticino sun and, while Gertie tends my injured knee, I just listen to the birds singing. Without opening my eyes I can savour the white, yellow and blood-red blossom of the trees in the garden, I can caress the soft rhythm of the outline of "our" mountains, which I love so much and thought, a little while ago, I would not see again for a long time. For my ear is still blocked by another rhythm – of marching columns and the chanting and shouting "Sieg Heil" of an unruly mob looking for victims.

'How it all happened? Nobody who didn't experience it could possibly imagine the incredible speed of these events. And those who did experience them can hardly trust themselves to reconstruct the order of events and, somehow, can not account for their inner logic. The individual was powerless – as in the face of a natural catastrophe. I have only experienced this once, at the outbreak of war in 1914.

'Rudi Bing will have told you what a *gemütlich* evening we had at his sister's on 10 March. Frau Ilka put on a Joan of

Arc act prophesying an election triumph for Schuschnigg, spreading calm throughout the country. He could be sure of 70–80%, she said. For myself, I was just uneasy about the sudden, spooky silence across the border. (Now I can't understand, why I did not continue my line of thought logically...)

'When we drove home that night the town was quiet, almost too quiet. On Friday morning, at rehearsal, I didn't notice anything either. The few Nazis in the ensemble, who had been pointed out to me and whom I had been watching with curiosity, seemed to me a little distracted and overtired. Who could have guessed that they'd had meetings and made preparations all night, as they told me proudly later! This pre-Dress Rehearsal for *Caesar* was ghastly – nervous, lacking cohesion. At four thirty I arrived back at the hotel, exhausted – Gertie and Peter Paneth were waiting for me. It was quite noisy in the streets, I heard groups singing "Down with the swastika".

'There was a lot of nervous toing and froing, but most people were drifting towards the city centre. I was thinking "if only it could hold until Sunday" – but where were the Nazis? (They were gathering, quietly organising, they were on alert, small advance parties were already appearing on some main roads.)

'Half an hour later, the waiter bent lower as he served me: "The election has been postponed!" I could feel myself turning pale – the explosion was imminent! This was Schuschnigg's self-immolation: his people were ready for a confrontation, yesterday it still seemed to be 80% – if he now gave the order to retreat, there was no stopping them, I knew my Nazis too well!

'Bing rang, already very frightened, he had witnessed bloody confrontations in the Kärntnerstrasse, couldn't come to our hotel any more, wanted to leave the city that night. Now cries of "Heil Hitler" began to well up from the street, cars sped past, the town was in turmoil – like a disturbed antheap. We sat on the edge of our bed and weighed up the situation. Should we flee?

'On 20 February I had already considered leaving, as soon

as the first wave of Nazi unrest had surfaced. But at that time the rehearsals had not even begun, now we had almost reached the first night (such ridiculous considerations sometimes have a curious influence on our decisions). It seemed to me like desertion. But it wasn't only this "romantic" notion: wouldn't quitting look as if I had a bad conscience? And could we be certain to get across the border still? What if the Nazis were even quicker and I were to run straight into their hands in Innsbruck (that province was said to be more Nazi than Vienna)?

'We decided to stay, quietly packing our things. Gertie would buy the rail tickets in the morning (who could know what the following day, Sunday, would bring?). We drove to the opera house where I had a meeting about *Masked Ball*. Gertie did not want to be parted from me, so I got a seat for her in a box. They were playing *Onegin* that night. I sat with Neher in the technical director's office, looking at the models for *Masked Ball*. We did our utmost to control our nervousness. Somebody burst in: "Schuschnigg has resigned. He has just said goodbye to the Austrian people, on the radio." Then the marvellous stage foreman Klepp flung open the door: "The Germans have started to invade, across all the borders. Now we've had it, now we shall be sucked dry like lemons. Austria's finished, now we are only a colony, just blacks." He slammed the door behind him. We had all turned pale. The two Austrians laughed in embarrassment, I was taken aback by this outburst. When Klepp returned after a while, I pulled him aside and begged him to control his tongue. It didn't help much. 24 hours later he was arrested.

'The performance comes to an end, I go to look for Gertie, but I can't find her in any of the usual places, none of the ushers know where she is. Neher brings news that the Nazis are gathering at the exits, intending to beat up all Jews coming out of the theatre. Through the window I can see an incredible turmoil, the Ring[strasse] and Kärntnerstrasse are black with people, torchlight processions are forming. I must get out of here – look for an exit at the back of the stage. But where on earth is Gertie? I limp about like an idiot – if Gertie

145

gets into this maelstrom looking for me ... where is she? Then suddenly she's standing in front of me, by pure chance she happened to come along that corridor. Now that the performance has ended it would be impossible to find her in the crowd making for the exits. Outside the dark masses are waiting to scrutinise everyone's face. As we leave the opera house with Neher we are met by wild cheering – screaming, singing people thrust their outstretched arms into each others' faces with the bellowed greeting [Heil Hitler], which seems to intoxicate them, they ride on the running boards of cars, driving around wildly for no apparent reason, waving little paper flags with that brutal cabalistic symbol – where do these thousands of paper flags suddenly come from? On the Ring heaving black masses of people, torches are lit. From our hotel we ring Rudi Bing again. He's ready to leave for Prague on the night train. He suggests I should go with him. We speak very calmly on the phone, it might be bugged, and say goodbye formally. How and when will we see each other again? It is 5 years to the day, since they occupied the *Städtische Oper*. Sent us into exile. Gertie and I talk about it for a long time, and what we should do now. The town seems to have gone completely mad. Now the people have formed great processions, have brought out their hidden flags, have mobilised their sympathisers – and the flotsam of the big city follows in their wake. Many many thousands are marching down there now, who, only six hours ago, were "decided" to vote for a free Austria. Had they not been deserted [by their political leaders]? Weren't the German motorised divisions already rumbling towards Vienna along the main roads? Wasn't it futile to ask further questions? Only the future counted, tomorrow. And tomorrow you had to be a Nazi, or you would get crushed by the wheels. We lay awake half the night. The "Heil" and "Hitler" shouts and the chanting never ceased.'

Rudi Bing was in Vienna on Glyndebourne business at that time. He had a heart-stopping experience on the Prague train that night. Every passenger's papers were scrutinised carefully. Bing

146

The pre-war Städtische Oper, Berlin (now Deutsche Oper, Berlin)

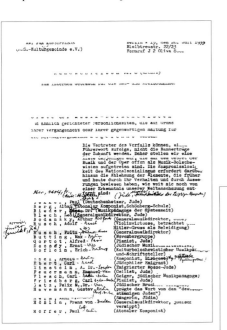

Nazi blacklist of banned artists
('Music Bolsheviks') including
Busch, Fritz and Ebert, Carl, 1935

'Towaritsch' poster.
Back to acting in emigration 1935

Hitler outside Vienna Opera House after 'Anschluss' 1938

C.E. working with Turkish students at new Ankara Academy 1938

'Men of Glyndebourne' John Christie and C.E.

Photo: *Sussex Review* 1949

Original Glyndebourne auditorium with Act IV set of first *Figaro* production 1934

Photo: Reeves, Lewes.

Alberto Erede and Salvatore Baccaloni: rehearsing 1936.
Photo: *Weekly Illustrated*

Rudolf Bing, Fritz Busch and C.E. 1936   Photo: Debenham

Glyndebourne Organ Room and Stage Tower of Opera House 1938

happened to be carrying with him a special invitation and visa he had procured for a British MP. He took a gamble: instead of showing his passport, he held out these documents. No further questions were asked, the officer saluted and Bing was free to continue.

Carl and Gertie came to the conclusion next day that it would look like flight and even an admission of guilt if they tried to leave, only a few days before the *Caesar* premiere. A further consideration was the effect of an early departure on Hidde's career and on the renewal of Carl's own passport, without which he could not travel. So he went to the Burgtheater for the scheduled technical rehearsal. The doorman greeted him with an, as yet, unpolished 'Heil Hitler' to which Carl replied with a jolly '*Grüss Gott*'. People walked about slightly disorientated, whispering the latest information, strain showing in their faces. Carl made himself play the unconcerned, calm boss-doing-a-job to good effect. One of the worst actors of his cast, the Cassius, who had already been pointed out to him as one of the chief Nazis, came to him during the lighting session. He took my father by the arm and jovially assured him that there was 'Nothing to worry about, he had a firm grip on the situation, all the necessary changes had already been decided during the night and he would make sure the problem of the "poor Jews" would be solved humanely.' Carl saw his work through to the end and decided that he and Gertie had a better chance of passing the increasingly vigilant border controls if they travelled via Italy, the 'Axis' brother of the Nazis. The planned production of *Masked Ball* with Bruno Walter and Neher was, of course, cancelled.

On 27 April 1995, the fiftieth anniversary of the setting-up of the second [post-war] Austrian Republic, the Vienna State Opera gave a concert consisting entirely of *Entartete Musik*, i.e. music suppressed by the Nazis. [This silly term, meaning 'music, robbed of its true genes' included all atonal music as well as works by Jewish composers.] This memorial concert was a magnificent gesture. The above excerpt from my father's letter to me was printed in the programme. This also contained articles about the most prominent musicians affected by the Nazi ban and a kind of 'hit list' of living theatre people whom the Nazis regarded as enemies of the regime. It included Carl Ebert and Fritz Busch.

Hitler's programme of bloodless conquests continued on schedule. In the autumn of 1938, six months after swallowing Austria, Hitler demanded the cessation of the so-called Sudetenland, the strip of Czechoslovakia along the German frontier which contained a large proportion of ethnic Germans. Six months later, in the spring of 1939 Hitler grabbed the whole of Czechoslovakia. Protests were just a matter of form by then. But, punctually on 1 June 1939, a new Glyndebourne season began, the sixth.

It appears quite surreal, considering what was happening on the world stage in 1939, that Fritz Busch and Carl planned the 1940 Glyndebourne season in every detail, that they both went out to Buenos Aires again as just another episode in an on-going series, that Carl and Hans Oppenheim met in New York, as it happened, on separate career-building missions. Carl went on behalf of Glyndebourne to investigate an invitation from the forthcoming World Fair, which wanted a season of four different operas, all details including costs agreed. The only outstanding problem was the venue(s) for the performances. Glyndebourne was not prepared to compromise in a make-or-break situation regarding entry into the American music scene. The air was full of other schemes to bring Glyndebourne to the States, possibly on a recurring basis. All this had to be vetted. New York made an overwhelming impression on my father and step-father. Oppi wrote home: 'It is wonderful being with Carl on this trip. He makes me enjoy the experience of New York as only he can.'

Unfortunately, Carl was not satisfied with the theatres offered to Glyndebourne. His report on available venues for a season at the World Fair was negative. Within a few months, all plans for the near future had become redundant through the outbreak of war.

Carl prepared for his return to Ankara to fulfil his annual winter commitment to the academies. The travel route through the Balkans was still open. Turkey remained neutral.

With Hidde in Germany, the Oppis and myself in England and Gertie's parents in Switzerland, my father had ample opportunity for worrying. The main agony was the uncertainty, and sometimes extreme slowness, of postal communication. However, through the neutrality of Switzerland and Turkey there was always a way of keeping in touch, even when letters had to go all the way round the Cape of Good Hope and took up to three months. The greater problem was whether one could take at face value what had been written with censorship in mind. The well-being and activities of the various members of the family were the main topic. Everybody was continually asking for more news. Even then, certain information of location or activity had to be in coded language.

The great puzzle for all of us lay in Hidde's letters. Did they represent her true feelings? On the outbreak of war my father had written to her to suggest 'a visit to Cureglia to see the "old" grandparents; who could know whether and when they would see each other again', etc. It was a simple feint to give her a chance to apply for leave from her theatre and get a permit to cross into Switzerland – and safety. She replied, enumerating her workload of rehearsals and performances, and continued:

'9 Sept.1939
'You will understand that it is impossible for me at the moment even to visit my dear grandparents. And should we not be able to perform any more, then the fatherland will immediately call on me for some other service . . .'

Was the 'fatherland' a sop to the censor or what? 13 months later, after the German forces had carried all before them on land, she wrote:

'31 October 1940
'. . . Above all write to me, dear Daddy, whether you would not like to visit me soon – or have you so much to do and no wish to see your child and your friends again? They are all longing to see you. But if that is not enough to tempt you, perhaps you could combine pleasure with a business trip. Then you could at last have the interview, long overdue, with Prof Hermann [code for Reichsminister Hermann Goering]. Should you have no contact with him any more, a friend of mine here could re-establish it easily, she is quite intimate with the Prof. Hermann household [a reference to the actress Kaethe Dorsch, who had written and wired my father a few times during the early years of emigration]. . . .'

149

This strange pleading could only be explained by her desperate fear for my father's safety, under the influence of Herr Goebbels' triumphalist propaganda. Hidde would not have dreamt of listening secretly to foreign radio stations, and it was a fact that the war front was far beyond the German borders. The answer to Hidde that made my father's attitude clear, for the umpteenth time, without jeopardising her political safety was a tightrope act.

On 23 April 1941 she wrote an even more puzzling letter:

'23 April 1941

'Darling father,

'I am so sad, because I feel I must tell you: do not let yourself be influenced in this whole family quarrel by Hans and Cissi. You see, I was always closer to you and must be even closer to you at this moment ... after all the sad things and the unsavoury enmities within the family you have to decide where you stand, even if that is difficult. I have to tell you, it is impossible that you agree with Hans and Cissi wholeheartedly and also be as one with me! There is no chance of a reconciliation between them and myself, it will surely come to an open breach ... If they try to blacken my character, you will support me, won't you? For you are my father and when we meet again, then everything will be quite wonderful ...'

There was no explanation for this extraordinary outburst, other than that it was once again a code. But nobody in the family managed to decipher this one. It seemed far-fetched but possible that she had come under surveillance when the censor noticed that she wrote frequently to a Mrs Oppenheim [our mother] c/o a Swiss address, and she may have thought she had to wipe her slate clean, so to speak. The mindboggling strain told on all four parents.

In contrast to these on-going nagging worries, Carl's work in Turkey had become a realisable dream, his task had a fascination for him such as he had never found before. Previously he had sometimes, vaguely, thought how useful it could be as a teacher to be able to obliterate all tradition, an ideal opportunity to start a completely new approach to the art of performing. Here in Ankara

150

it had suddenly become reality. He did not even have to search for a new approach, it came quite simply through the opportunity of working with his selected group of young people – fresh, enthusiastic, uncluttered minds, untroubled by cultural ballast:

> 'It was a tremendous experience for me, one of the most profound in my whole theatrical career. It meant very hard work, but it was wondrously exciting. We literally threw tradition into the incinerator and started from the beginning, the very beginning – it is hard to imagine what that means. The only factor which sometimes seemed to block progress was the difficulty of vocal communication.'

After a while he found two or three promising young assistants, who were sent to Germany and Austria to perfect their German. They were then better qualified than the normal hired translators, to convey the exact meaning of Carl's words in theatrical terms.

Working with such malleable material as these unspoilt students is, unfortunately, full of danger – for the students. In the performing arts there are too many people, talented and not so talented, who ply their trade as teachers in a mystic guru fashion. In many cases, this is quite unnecessary because they clearly have the talent. I suppose it gives the guru-addicted teacher a sense of greater power – and a longer career(?). I went to a session of the famous Actors' Studio in New York after the war and thought it rather annoying, personally, to find the atmosphere quasi-incense-laden, rather than workman-like. The place had the aura of a shrine, rather than the smell of a craftsman's workshop. The teacher had not appeared yet, but everybody was talking in hushed tones and there was a build-up of expectancy, whether imagined or engineered I don't know. Eventually the teacher came in, the hush became almost oppressive. The teacher asked in a kind of whisper whose turn it was to show the exercise they had worked on. Three people put up their hand. Pause. 'All right, let's start with the Hamlet monologue.' Nothing happened for a long while. Nobody moved. Then a young man went on to the stage area and sat down. Another long stillness for concentration – perfectly justified – and then: 'To be, or not to be . . .' he interrupted himself:

'Here I have a problem.' I left quite soon soon after that. No doubt the Actors' Studio have done excellent work for a whole string of actors, some of whom became famous.

'Motivation' was the great slogan then – as if it were something new. Carl had approached his whole acting career on the principle of motivation, the intellectual grasp of the inner life contained in the dramatist's words. He had built up that power of revealing the hidden meaning of a play's lines ever since his first years with Max Reinhardt. Carl had a strong, almost magnetic personality – and he was conscious of it, but he never abused this strength. All his working sessions were intense and required everybody's concentration, but he would ease into a more relaxed mode when he thought a 'breather' could help. He never set up a 'guru worship' atmosphere or anything approaching it; in fact, he loathed it, and considered it cheap. One of his most pronounced qualities was his humanity – to which generations of colleagues and pupils have referred. The Turkish students quickly became devoted to him – in an overzealous way, to our thinking. They looked on him as their 'father', father of the theatre. Sometimes I received messages from completely unknown individuals, students, calling me 'Dear brother Peter'. Their close relationship to their teacher obviously included all his family. Carl was a big man, slightly heavy at this time, with a beautiful head, very expressive blue eyes and greying hair. He had always been confident of his good looks, and made use of that knowledge in an unobtrusive way where needed. For many people who worked with him the most surprising feature about him was his ability to, not just portray, but to become a totally different person through body language, movement and facial expression – a desperate young girl, an exuberant man, a caressing old woman, whatever the role demanded. These demonstrations, however, always had a soul, they were never merely a facility, a brilliant technical device. You could feel his whole person living the role he played.

The Turkish students were 'raw' material in the sense that they had nothing to which they could compare their own efforts. To them theatrical 'reality' was a particular problem. Carl did not have to worry about the students sliding into empty rhetoric, or posturing or declaiming their lines – they would never have seen or heard it anywhere before. To teach them natural expression without going to full realism was an important aspect of their equipment as performers. On one occasion a young student, rehearsing a passionate scene in which the character he played threatens to throw himself out of the window, actually jumped out of the first-floor window of the rehearsal room. He came back running up the stairs, breathlessly happy and beaming. The poor man received a terrible ticking-off, but it was an ideal moment for a lecture to the class on the difference between acting a situation and doing it realistically.

After about a year's 'bedding down' into their new routine and new surroundings, the students made fast progress. They also proved to be well chosen. The students were not burdened by the knowledge that they were partaking in the creation of a new profession, a new culture in their country. But my father was all the more conscious of the 'overwhelming responsibility', as he called it, which he had shouldered. But he was practically inebriated with the joy of his work. The first year was the hardest because of the endless stream of meetings and interim reports with which he had to deal, beside guiding the students through their first steps in acting.

Getting the whole organisation set up and functioning was just as much pioneering work as teaching the art of acting. He had to 'invent' every detail of the whole institute, the organisation, procurement of facilities, budgeting and, of course, the schedule of rules governing the academies. Carl was able to call up his experience in setting up the academies in Frankfurt and Berlin, years earlier. However, those occasions could not compare with his present task. For one thing, in Germany there were a lot of experienced civil servants to help with the paperwork, and there were many role models from which to cull the best ideas. All these recall experiences would not always suit the conditions in which he found himself in Turkey. Responsible budgeting in such a one-off situation was the most hazardous task. But once the whole apparatus was running smoothly, the administrative burden lessened and Carl could concentrate more on launching the first batch of students into their new element.

The two academies occasionally presented evenings of selected scenes from plays and operas to the public. They helped the students to test their stage presence and provided much publicity for the eventual launch of the first full production. There was a considerable build-up of excitement in Ankara at the prospect of regular theatre in the near future, particularly among the European exiles. Carl was able to keep his promise that the first production of a Western classic play, translated into Turkish, would be presented after three years. The first opera production – *Madame Butterfly* – saw the light of day five years after the academies had started work. Within a short time Ankara had its properly equipped theatre, suitable for plays and music theatre. Some years later a palatial, very modern theatre building was erected in Istanbul. It was the expression of the national will to have its own theatre culture.

Carl attributed

'the success of this wholly unusual venture to the enormous talent of the modern Turks for adaptation and assimilation of foreign experience and influence.'

Certainly, without this quality Ataturk's command could not have been fulfilled. But there was more to it than that. It is quite impossible to imagine the amount of basic groundwork which Carl had to put down on paper, unless one was directly involved. Down to the minutest detail, such as the book which the stage manager had to keep to record the beginning of every rehearsal, who was present, who was late, what was rehearsed, when the rehearsal ended, whether all the props were accounted for etc., etc., plus 15 rules laying down to whom the book had to be shown and who had to countersign it, etc. In fact, it was not only the rules and disciplines of the academies which Carl had to set out in minute bureaucratic detail, he had to call on his long experience as an actor, producer, theatre director and union member to draw up the even more complicated regulations which govern everything concerning the running of a theatre.

Work at the academies and the theatre had reached a steady rhythm when war broke out in September 1939. Carl had planned to return to Ankara for his annual winter presence about mid-

October. The war necessitated a difficult decision: whether to go at all, or whether to go alone to try to assess the likely position of Turkey in the longer term. In that case Gertie would stay with the younger children and the grandparents in neutral Switzerland. It was very hard to guess whether Switzerland would be the safer place for the family. Hitler might think it advantageous at some point to swallow the country for its Alpine passes and its bank vaults. My father sensed a certain amount of panic feeling in the country, and work prospects were very thin. But shifting the family out to Ankara could mean a politically even more uncertain future. He decided to go alone and reconnoitre. Just before Italy entered the war in the Spring of 1940, the parents decided to unite the family in Ankara. The nervous tension over which side Turkey might join in the war had given way to the realisation that the Government was going to await further developments and in the meantime profit from being a neutral broker and trader. Turkey, just like Portugal at the other end of Southern Europe, automatically became a hotbed for political intrigue and spying.

Hitler must have considered Ankara a valuable staging post for gathering information and disseminating propaganda, covering the whole of South-East Europe and the Middle East. He sent Herr von Papen to be the German Ambassador. Von Papen was a right-wing conservative from the Junker class, one of the short-lived predecessors of Hitler as German Chancellor (Prime Minister) during the death throes of the Weimar Republic. He was a wily, urbane diplomat who had thrown in his lot with the Nazis in order to survive. His nickname was 'The devil in the top hat'. The German-speaking community in Ankara consisted mainly of experts who had gone there on time contracts to help build up Turkish institutions and train personnel. Some were political or Jewish refugees, others had simply been attracted by an interesting job and good pay. The latter were now required to decide whether to return home to join the war effort on Hitler's side, or whether to jump ship. There was no problem, presumably, for German and Austrian party members – most of them would want to go back to the 'Reich'.

The outbreak of war had rather awkwardly disturbed the

155

perfectly harmonious and normal relations between the 'opposing' groups of temporary immigrants. The composer Paul Hindemith was head of the Ankara Music School, whose task it was to train potential music teachers. He had been a close friend of my father's since his Frankfurt days (1915–22). Hindemith was a leading member of the musical avant-garde at that time, while Carl was helping to forge a new understanding of the role of the theatre in society as a member of the modern Frankfurt ensemble. When Carl met Hindemith shortly after the Nazi take-over he asked him whether he would be emigrating too. He replied: 'Why should I? The Nazis should be left to get on with it. We'll be better off with them. You'll see, they'll do many things much better than we did.' Carl was aghast at his attitude, but they continued to see each other and remained good friends.

Hindemith had a chequered career. Before the Nazi take-over his music was attacked for being un-German, but after 1933 a slow rehabilitation began, led by the conductor Wilhelm Furtwängler. This was sabotaged by Goebbels personally. Finally Hindemith moved his home to Switzerland, where his opera *Mathis der Mahler* had its world premiere. Hindemith was not very happy in Ankara, in fact he was not particularly interested in other nations and their ways. He once said to Carl he could only compose in Germany; he needed the forests and rivers and old towns. Politically he turned out to be blandly pragmatic. The crisis in their relationship, while they were working in Ankara, seemed to be based on Hindemith's envy that Carl managed to get his requests granted by the authorities much more quickly than Hindemith did. Probably the creation of a theatre culture counted for more than the training of music teachers.

Ambassador von Papen had to try to ensure that all able-bodied Germans returned home, while keeping a wary eye on the political nonconformists. My father ignored all invitations to functions at the German Embassy. Over the years he had become acquainted with many foreign diplomats stationed in Ankara, and was often invited to the British Embassy. It was the time when the famous spy 'Cicero' was the valet of the British Ambassador. When he was caught, it was said that 'Cicero' had furnished his German masters with detailed information about the Allies' strategic plans

– which they thought was a little too perfect, and they paid him in forged dollar notes.

Sometime during the war my father's passport ran out, which meant he could not travel any more, not even in a wartime-limited way. Since he had left Germany he had never lived anywhere long enough to fulfil the residential qualifications for naturalisation. And he certainly did not want another German passport. He was perfectly happy with that situation, because his work was still fascinating and satisfying to him. The academies were attracting more and more students, and the theatre was able to give more performances as the whole complex grew through the annual intake. Yet again, the intimate confrontation with a new culture and the need to convey his own teaching and his experience in a different way were a boon for his character and personality. They increased his versatility. The freshness, uninhibited talent and ambition of his Turkish students fuelled my father's own imagination.

In 1941 Rudi Bing, the by now unemployed caretaker manager of Glyndebourne, wrote to Carl about a puzzling development in New York. Fritz Busch had requested the loan of the scenery and orchestral parts of *Macbeth* for a short season of *Macbeth* and *Cosi fan Tutte* in a New York theatre – not one of the opera houses. At the same time Glyndebourne was made aware of the fact that a theatre management were advertising this season as a 'Glyndebourne Opera' event. Fritz Busch had been invited to conduct, and his son Hans, Carl's assistant since the first Sussex season, was to produce. Hans had the production scores of the two operas with him. Such scores contain every detail of a production, every move, every expression, every lighting change, etc., etc. It is quite inexplicable that neither Busch nor his son made any attempt to inform Carl or the designers about the projected season.

Glyndebourne turned down the request to ship scenery and orchestral music, which was probably impracticable in wartime, anyway, and John Christie wrote to the Buschs: 'What about Charles?' [my father] Still no attempt to inform him or get his agreement to the scheme. Christie insisted that the description 'Glyndebourne Opera' must be taken off the advertising material. My father wrote letters to the Buschs and finally wired: 'Urgently

157

request you refrain copying Glyndebourne productions otherwise forced to protest publicly.' He did not go public, but the first response he had was after the event. And that letter was, he felt, an attempt to blame the victim instead of the murderer. Carl was devastated by this wanton betrayal of trust, as he saw it, particularly after the long, harmonious period of close collaboration with Busch and after he had jeopardised his own *Masked Ball* production in Vienna in order not to hurt Busch. One can only assume that the Buschs were so concerned about their survival during the war in a difficult, if not hostile climate, that they lost touch with the ethics of the situation temporarily. It caused my father immense pain, and he took a very long time to get over his disappointment.

At the same time he was still worrying a lot about Hidde, especially when the bombing raids on Germany began to build up, and he always wanted to know where I was in Britain and what I was doing. I could not always give him detailed information. When France fell – and not until then – the British Government decided, quite naturally, that all Germans, whether refugees or suspected Nazi sympathisers, should be interned. I was released after 13 months and then worked in factories in London and later on the land.

Only his demanding work enabled my father to ride the personal and political anxieties of 1941 – when Germany invaded Russia and was advancing on all fronts. Turkey was forced into a non-aggression or 'friendship' pact, a bad omen remembering a similar pact which Germany concluded with Russia just before the war. For most of the German emigrants in Turkey it became a major preoccupation to guess what would happen if the German armies were to reach the Turkish frontier, which looked increasingly likely. For those emigrants whose passports had run out or who had abandoned them, the Ankara Government arranged with the Czechoslovak Embassy that it would issue them with temporary Czech passports, so that they could at least try to get out of the country. This generous, reassuring facility was, of course, withdrawn again as soon as the war ended.

In 1944 Hitler made the futile gesture of declaring 'total war'. All theatres were closed, the men were called up, women had to go into arms factories. My father tried to get leave for Hidde and her husband, Walter Richter, to go to Turkey as 'urgently required' staff for the burgeoning requirements of the Drama Academy. It was of no avail, of course. On the contrary, it might have proved dangerous for the two, because an official in the Ministry of Cultural Affairs became suspicious and ordered Richter back to Berlin from Vienna, a relatively safe haven where he was fulfilling a guest engagement. Soon all communication between Turkey and Germany was cut. Occasionally a second- or third-hand trickle of news filtered through, with the help of friends in neutral embassies in Ankara. But basically the news blackout lasted until the capitulation of Germany. Even then the mail was sporadic and unpredictable, in consequence of the widespread devastation the war had caused.

Now Hidde appeared in a completely different light through her letters. She spoke of the Nazis as 'these inhuman criminals' and similar terms. In 1946 she began to write about the unbelievable resurgence of theatrical activity and how many colleagues had spoken to her about their plans, always ending with the question: 'Would your father come back and be part of this?' She wrote:

'14 July 1946
'... That I could not promise – I could only say that you had always told me you would return once the Nazis had gone. But so much has happened since we last spoke to each other ... even last summer one could not have imagined what Berlin would look like now ... or that a single German would want to return ... that you, for whom the whole world is open, should want to come back to this heap of rubble? And I thought of Gertie and the children. On the other hand it is incredible how busily this antheap is working again and how the city is beginning to function ... And then we heard that some people outside still have a longing for Germany, this ghastly country, which stank like a bubolic boil, this of all countries. That one fact, that there are people who want to come back, was the most moving thing for me ...'

Carl was under the impression he knew Walter Richter, Hidde's husband, only from their correspondence, which started earlier in the war. Richter was then on the way to becoming one of Germany's star actors. The style of their early letters was charmingly old-fashioned. They were feeling their way, trying to get to know each other by correspondence – at a time when one could not write completely openly anyway. Richter first addressed my father as 'Hochverehrter Herr Profesor Ebert', a term of politeness reminiscent of olden days. Richter reminded Carl that they had indeed met once before, in his box in the Darmstadt theatre, because Carl had heard about him and wanted to meet him and, perhaps, offer him a contract. But Richter had to tell him at the time that he was no longer free. On saying goodbye after a lengthy talk, my father admonished him with: 'Well, Richter, before you finalise your next contract, promise to let me know first.'

Now, during the war, Richter wanted to steer round to another contract. He wanted to ask the Professor formally for the hand of his daughter. There was no reply. He wrote a second time, mentioning that he and Hidde had postponed their wedding, hoping that they would still receive her father's blessing. It was a nice, sensitive gesture, recognising that Carl must have felt sad at being cut off from his first-born at that moment. Hidde was 28 by then. This time the mail functioned, the wedding took place and Richter started to write to 'Dear father-in-law' and finally arrived at 'Dearest Carl'.

The relationship blossomed into discussions about the state of the theatre, the 'Turkish experience' and the defence of artistic values. Carl was happy to discover in Walter Richter an actor after his own heart, uncompromising in his demand for the highest standards. My father wrote to my mother in Britain that he thought Hidde had, at last, found the right man, and that they were obviously very happy. As it turned out they were also unbelievably lucky in avoiding, by pure chance, some of the most devastating bombing raids which were beginning to rain down on major German cities. Carl, who was a living example of functioning telepathy, must have felt that fate held its hand over the two.

When Hidde and Walter had overcome the trauma of the last months of the war and postal services had become reliable again, Walter wrote a brief account of that final stretch and what had been happening since:

'Beloved Turks!

'... Today I can only give you a telegraphic style account of the last months of the war, when we were not allowed to write. After you had been trying for some time to get us contracts for the Ankara academies, I was suddenly ordered to return to Berlin from Vienna. The minister himself had made the order that my leave for Vienna must be cancelled (I heard later that they thought we might go "absent without leave"). At the end of August all theatres were closed and the actors, with few exemptions, put into uniform. The head of UFA immediately gave me a year's contract. But Herr Hinkel of the Ministry (you know him from your experiences in 1933), countermanded the signed contract and ordered that I should join the forces at once. Another film producer acted more quickly, he gave me a contract and started shooting the following day, so that the authorities were outmanoeuvred. We made two films in quick succession. But then, one morning at six, the doorbell rang and I was handed a note: "You are called up to take part in an exercise, you will bring two days' rations and meet at 11 am outside Wannsee station."

'Well, it had to come. Quite often the telephone had rung in the night, even during air raids with the bombers flying overhead: it was the army, calling up civilians, collecting them in lorries after the raid and sending them to the front just outside Berlin. Without any training. Anyway, Hidde came with me to Wannsee station. The men had to line up and a roll call began. Suddenly a good angel appeared in the shape of Titti Lennartz [an actress friend]. She went straight up to the commander and gave him a piece of paper demanding my immediate release to the radio station for recording a feature of the greatest importance to the Reich. The paper was a fake. I was released and we spent all day mobilising contacts. I had to return to barracks for three days ... I took part in one exercise. We were given rifles and 9mm live ammunition. Never having held a rifle before, it was not difficult to miss the target altogether. I was put into the second rank of call-up ... I went to see the senior consultant at Wannsee hospital. He

161

gave me a certificate that I was suffering from an enlarged thyroid and must not take part in training for three weeks. After three weeks he renewed it for another three. At that point even the handicapped and severely ill people were called to the "colours". The Russians were now within rifle range. Wannsee was beginning to look like a fort. Right outside our garden wall the army had built a defensive line ... I hid in the cellar with two actor friends. The house above our heads filled up with soldiers. When the artillery and air bombardment became even heavier, the soldiers came down into the cellar as well. We three men moved into the tiny air raid shelter in the cellar. Our wives stood guard outside the door and asked the soldiers not to use the shelter as well, because it harboured three babies ... Finally, on 27 April, we decided we had to flee towards the West to get out of the battle zone. Outside the house we saw a lot of soldiers, artillery, waggons, horses, any amount of ammunition, a radio mast etc. As our row of refugees passed through the ranks of soldiers there were astonished faces. One of the "babies", myself, had a beard. We trudged as far as we could through the dark, the sky to the left and right aglow with fires. We rested in the basement of a house. The bombardment became even more intense...

'On 30 April at midnight the first Russians entered the house. We left at first light, walked through the smoking ruins of Potsdam, past corpses and dead animals lying in the streets and carried on and on ... One day, moving through a little village I met the chief sleeping car attendant with whom I had done at least thirty trips between Berlin and Vienna. Just ran into him in the street. He had been appointed "Commissar" for this village. We stayed there for 6 quiet wonderful weeks – relatively so, I should say...'

When the war front had swept across Berlin and onwards, Walter Richter made a few trips into the city to discover what was happening to theatre and film production, if anything. Amidst all the destruction four theatres remained usable, although damaged, where there had been over 50 before. But enormous activity in planning, looking for funding, putting together companies, etc. was already under way. Within a few weeks over 30 ensembles had started rehearsals and prepared makeshift venues for performances. In all this chaos the population was hungry for live theatre, it seemed. It appeared even more important than something to eat. And from all accounts the name Carl Ebert was thrown into the discussion wherever three or four people met, to find the best way to start the renewal of the Berlin theatre scene. Many of his former colleagues were, of course, still 'in harness', but they lacked an obvious leader on the spot, to whom they could all look up, whose integrity they respected.

All this reached Carl's ears through different channels, but it was also noticed by the appropriate authorities of the occupying powers. With the unprecedented destruction all around, it was difficult for them to understand this extraordinary will of the people to have some kind of theatre. The reasons are twofold, I believe: people's sense of freedom after years of unrelenting Nazi propaganda in all the media, and the realisation that theatre could be played almost anywhere, under the most primitive conditions. Houses, hospitals, schools needed 'real' building operations and vast resources – which were simply not available. Not all the hastily set-up theatre companies survived, but in their place new ones sprang up, offering performances. The venues included pubs, church halls, studios, large cellars. Audiences paid for tickets with lumps of coal or bread, small bags of potatoes, a pot of jam. The Allied Occupying Powers were intrigued and asked my father whether he would be prepared to undertake an extended tour through all the regions of Germany and report to them on 'the theatre situation'.

Naturally, Carl accepted the invitation. He realised that he was better qualified than almost anyone else – through his wide experience in Germany and abroad – to judge the situation and make the most viable recommendations. More than anything he wanted to help in rebuilding the quality of performance which had previously had such an outstanding impact on world theatre and which the Nazi regime had almost totally squandered. He had by this time received several offers to take over theatres. He told people quite unashamedly that he was not interested in just being an

Intendant somewhere. If he were to return to Germany he would have to be given a wider responsibility, to include training young artists, for instance.

A tour of Germany was arranged for Autumn 1946. The Allies had agreed that the whole trip should be organised and accompanied by Ashley Dukes, the Chief Theatre Officer of the British Zone. Unfortunately the Russians pulled out of the agreement, so the trip was confined to the British, American and French zones of occupation, plus Berlin (it was under Four-Power Control). Ashley Dukes was a highly experienced theatre man and writer, and knew Germany well. He was married to Mme Rambert, the famous choreographer. My father asked that I should be allowed to accompany him as secretary, to facilitate the compilation of a report. We flew from London to Bünde, an army base in Westphalia, in a military aircraft (benches down the two sides of the fuselage, facing each other). In fact, we were now civilians within the military set-up. Ashley Dukes greeted us in uniform; we could only stay in hotels requisitioned by the forces and we had at our disposal a jeep, which the driver proudly told us had been through the El Alamein battle and on, right to the end of the war in Germany.

We were overwhelmed by contrasting impressions. Travelling almost exclusively on the network of motorways, the countryside seemed to us just as we remembered, well-cared-for fields, tidy farms, endless pine forests. At one point I said: 'Aren't the woods lovely?' Ashley replied: 'I hate them.' I suppose they were rather dark and forbidding if you had not grown up with them. Although I had never been homesick for the German landscape, it was touching to see it again after 12 years. Actually, we did not talk much while travelling. For my father it was far more emotional than for me, having gone into voluntary exile after Stormtroopers had occupied his theatre. The towns we passed through or where we stopped were an unexpected shock. In spite of all the newsreels and photos one had seen, the endless ridges of rubble framing the roads, the hundreds of people sorting it into different narrow-gauge trucks, the sallow skins of passers-by, the horrible scramble of people for a discarded cigarette butt, these impressions were worrying in their intensity. The main railway station of Frankfurt was more than a little frightening: Dostoievski's *Night Asylum* in *cinema verité* – obsessively fascinating for us, but we did not stay too long. Although we dressed down as much as possible for walking about the streets, we were obviously recognisable as coming from the 'opulent' West. We visited some of the biggest centres like Hamburg, Cologne, Frankfurt, Stuttgart, Munich, Berlin, and a few smaller ones.

Everywhere it was the same: we inspected the ruins of the local theatres and talked to the current leaders of the resident company. Carl was either treated with awe, like a visiting archangel, or practically squeezed to death by the people he had known personally and worked with in pre-Nazi days. There were quite a few tears of joy. We also looked up as many as possible of his former colleagues who were retired or ill or simply not part of the new companies. Naturally, we made courtesy calls to the local arts or theatre officers of the Allies. Travelling about like this was doubly tiring: to digest emotionally what we saw and heard and the very long hours involved, combined with the relative discomfort of crawling along the motorways. All German motorways were built as sections of reinforced cement. Through lack of maintenance over the years, the end of each section was a little higher than the beginning of the next, so that the brave jeep landed with a bone-shaking rattling bump every one and a half seconds. After about 93,000 of these it felt like the Chinese water-drip torture. I persuaded Ashley Dukes and our driver to let me take turns in driving the jeep. It made it less exhausting for me. Speed limits were strictly enforced. For emphasis, the Americans had put up a lot of large signs saying: 'Death is so permanent'.

Even for Carl, who had done productions of plays and operas under wildly different conditions, it was good to witness the resourcefulness with which some companies were tackling the obstacles. The situation differed from group to group. The theatre might still be usable, but the stores of scenery and costumes might have gone up in flames. Or the stores might be all right, but the theatre ruined. One could not buy materials of course, so these had to be gleaned from bomb sites – like wood, metal, bricks and so on. Or one had to think of quite novel ways of designing a performance. New materials were perforce finding their way into stage

165

design, a development which continued over the next few decades and procreated a separate stream of modern theatre design. The necessity to be inventive instead of just ordering what one wanted, also made for a refreshing paring-down of the visual aspect of a work, which in turn tended to bring the whole interpretation nearer the essential truth of a piece.

We saw an excellent example of this 'minimalism' at the Hamburg Opera: a performance of *Traviata* produced by the *Intendant*, Günther Rennert, who later made a name for himself on the international opera scene. The auditorium of the Hamburg State Opera had been completely burnt out, but on the other side of the Iron Curtain the theatre was still serviceable. The designer Neher had created a festive auditorium out of the enormous stage area with the simplest means, a few beautifully painted hangings. The cramped backstage, very wide but shallow, and normally only used for storing some scenery, was made to serve as the stage. The decor for *Traviata* suggested the lush Parisian *ambiente* required for two scenes of the opera, with only a few telling elements, rather than enormous built scenes.

It is a strange phenomenon that the perception of what constitutes the optimum visual aspect of theatre always works in cycles. Scenery and costumes tend to get more and more elaborate (and expensive), even superficial over the years, until they become so much an end in themselves that a violent reaction sets in. The revolutions shaped by Adolphe Appia and Gordon Craig in the late nineteenth and early twentieth century are symptomatic for the sudden rejection of overweening visual effects which swamp the actor/singer and therefore rob the performance of its most expressive constituent, and its true meaning. Caspar Neher and Wilhelm Reinking were two designers in the Appia/Craig mould. They were among Carl's preferred designers because they were exponents of the 'economy of means'. As Reinking put it:

'To show wealth, richness, wanton waste the theatre does not have to cover the stage with silks, velvets, Brussels lace and gold thread. By sparing use of strong elements in decor and costumes as "signals", the theatre can best convey the production's intention to the audience. Even the monumental,

166

over-dimensional can be projected through a simple signal. Such a scenic signal will relate the wanted atmosphere much more precisely than stage "reality" – which must inevitably remain "pretend" reality.'

In other words, copying Old Master paintings in detail and materials for the costumes of any work with a historic context is simply not theatre. Carl had already pioneered the economy-of-means style in his productions, when he had become *Intendant* in Darmstadt in the late 1920s. The post-war German stage did not have these questions of principle to worry about, since there were no materials to create reality. During the Nazi time the emphasis had veered more and more to outward show (just as in Nazi architecture), rather than content. So the shortage of resources actually saved the German theatre, forcing it to go back to the roots of each play or opera, discovering their essential truth instead of playing on the obvious outer trappings. This cleansing effect did wonders for artists and audiences alike. German theatre once more became innovative. That part of the up-and-down cycle lasted between 25 and 30 years. From the middle 1960s onwards, the emphasis on outward show began to come to the fore again. Newspapers started to talk about the Erté *Rosenkavalier* or the Hockney *Magic Flute*. Some people continued to think these operas had been written by Richard Strauss and Mozart respectively, and not by the famous fashion designer or painter responsible for the current productions.

Although not all new companies in the post-war German theatre were as successful as the Hamburg Opera, the will was visible everywhere and the general atmosphere was confidently hopeful. Artists and administrators did not even complain about the shortage of everything. They accepted the reality of the situation and celebrated the fact that they could work unfettered by ideology. They also had access, for the first time in over 12 years, to what had happened in the 'decadent' rest of the world, as the Nazis would call it, in art, literature, drama and music. There was great intellectual hunger – as well as the physical type. All this needed to be absorbed and assimilated into their new life expectancy. Naturally, there were personnel problems.

167

The Allies had set up a 'De-Nazification' process. Tribunals were created to check on everybody's moral/criminal conduct during the Nazi period. I don't think it was intended to punish the orchestra musician, sitting at the third desk of the first violins, for having been a member of the Nazi party – unless he had, say, harmed people by denouncing them. It would have been impossible in any case to comb through the records of some 50 million people. Quite rightly it was thought, on the other hand, that the big fish, whether in the civil service or judiciary or the arts, should be investigated. At the time of our trip through Germany not all of these personnel problems had been sorted out, and some of the decisions of the tribunals naturally met with scepticism.

When the war ended my father was in Turkey. There were a number of prominent German refugees working in Ankara in diverse fields. One was the politician/philosopher Ernst Reuter, teaching politics at the University. He told Carl that he would be on his way back to Germany on the first available train, would Carl be coming too? He replied that he could not decide so quickly, he felt that he could not bring himself to shake hands with people who had actively supported the Nazi regime. By the time of our trip my father had changed his mind. He felt that each individual had to wrestle with their own conscience in this matter, there was no point in harbouring resentment for ever, and once a tribunal had given its verdict relations should return to normal.

From Hamburg we continued our trip to Hannover, where the theatre had been completely burned out. The company played in the orangery of the Summer Palace in a lovely park just outside the city. Our next stop was Berlin and the prospect of reunion with Hidde and meeting her husband Walter Richter for the first time. The Russians were getting more uncooperative by the day, in fact working up to the full-scale Cold War. The area of Berlin formed an enclave completely surrounded by Russian-controlled East Germany. We had to travel from Hannover in the nightly military sleeping-car train, which was inspected by the Russians at the border of their zone, after which the doors were sealed. It was strictly forbidden even to raise the window blinds while travelling through the zone. To use this train we had to be military personnel,

168

so we were given the very temporary rank of Colonel Carl and Lt Peter Ebert.

To be with Hidde again was wonderful, as if nothing had happened. There was so much to talk about, previous misunderstandings were not mentioned at all. What did it matter? Hidde and Walter were living reasonably comfortably in a small apartment, they had help from the theatre for food and other necessities, and my mother sent parcels with coffee, chocolate, soap, etc. which were simply unobtainable. Within an over-full schedule my father had insisted we should have the first evening entirely free for family business. Hidde had provided supper, consisting of herrings and boiled potatoes – and we heard from her next day that it had cost a week's salary on the black market. Restaurants were non-existent for people like us. Walter had borrowed, bought or confiscated some wine, and in the course of a very long night several theatre friends of theirs and my father's dropped in for joyous, intense discussions on the future of the theatre and the arts in general. It sounded as if the whole theatre community was straining at the leash to build and explore and experiment. One felt tremendous optimism all round, and difficulties were just waiting to be annihilated.

The impact of the city on Carl was devastating. The endless mounds of rubble in the streets, with jagged outlines of destroyed buildings looking over the top, were enervating. Somebody told us that it had been calculated it would take 30 years, at the current rate of progress, to clear all the rubble. It seemed an astronomical figure, like the distance of stars. At the final count, it was not far out. Berlin had never been a beautiful city; its strength lay in the atmosphere generated by its people. And exactly that was the strongest bond for my father, who was not German, with the city, it had been and remained 'home'. After the first few 'Look, the French Embassy has disappeared – just look at the *Staatsoper*', we stayed silent as we drove past the landmarks from one appointment to the next.

The theatre situation in Berlin was still at a more chaotic stage than elsewhere. This was partly due to the division of the city into four administrative sectors and the emerging non-cooperation of the Russians. It became evident too that the jockeying for position

169

among potential leaders prevented the evolution of a properly structured theatre policy. Too much politicking and not enough art. It is not surprising that many of the more serious artists among the theatre community urged or begged Carl to 'come back to Berlin'. He was politically completely untainted by the Nazi era, his reputation as an artist and person was well remembered from pre-Nazi times, and even word of his achievements during the period of emigration had reached the German public.

Given a functioning political entity for the city, I think he could not have refused such a 'call to duty'. He did receive an official invitation to take over the *Städtische Oper* again, which he had left more than 13 years earlier. The old opera house in Charlottenburg had been completely burned out, and the company were playing in the so-called Theater des Westens, a smaller, less well-equipped house near the Bahnhof Zoo. But it was not the venue which decided Carl against accepting the Berlin post, rather the political instability, which he felt would take a long time to resolve.

The tour of Germany continued, including Cologne, Frankfurt – where Carl had spent seven decisive years as actor and teacher – Darmstadt, his first post as *Intendant*, Stuttgart and Munich. It was a very moving journey.

Everywhere the question recurred: 'When are you coming back?' Even the people who might have felt threatened in their own positions by Carl's return urged him to come back 'for the sake of rehabilitating the German theatre'. The most eerie part of the trip was our entry into Darmstadt in the jeep. We had lived in the town for several years and knew every street, every prominent landmark. Driving towards the centre along the main artery, we both suddenly realised that we had no idea where we were, how far we had gone along that main road which we had used every day. It was uncanny, disturbing.

From Munich we took Carl the relatively short journey to the Swiss border on Lake Constance, from where he went home to Cureglia before returning to Ankara. I drove back to Bünde with Ashley Dukes and flew home to London. It took me several weeks to digest the welter of impressions and emotions the trip had imprinted on my mind. It felt like an assault from which one could not escape. The happiest incident was, of course, being with

170

Hidde, even if it only added up to a few hours all told. She wrote an ecstatically happy letter to my father on 12 October 1946, in her typically over-romantic, word-caressing style, thanking him for our visit, ending with:

'On the 14th I shall thank God from the bottom of my heart, that I have the most wonderful parents in the world.'

Two days later I received news from Berlin that Hidde had taken her own life, on her thirty-third birthday. It fell to me to inform all the rest of the family. She had left no note, there was no indication of what might have provoked her decision. My father did not come to terms with Hidde's death for the rest of his time. Having seen her so thoroughly happy so recently made it all the more baffling. His recurring thought was to blame himself, that he had caused a deep scar through the break-up of his marriage to my mother, when Hidde was only 11 years old.

10

Glyndebourne Post-war and Los Angeles

As soon as the war in Europe ended it became imperative for Carl to travel to Britain, to discuss the future of Glyndebourne with John Christie and Rudi Bing. Clearly the opera festival had to assess its role afresh. Financial conditions were quite different compared to 1939, and wide-ranging restrictions, like food and petrol rationing, would affect artists and public alike. The question had to be addressed, whether Glyndebourne should go in a new direction, continuing its pioneering 'mission', or keep to its proven recipe. It had built up a phenomenal reputation for quality in the six seasons of its existence. Perhaps it was time to specialise in some way, such as concentrating on rarely performed works of the great composers and operas by living artists? And there was the wide field of operas of the Baroque period to be explored. The character of potential audiences was changing as well: a growing appreciation of opera was noticeable, and countless servicemen had been exposed to opera abroad and had found it to their liking.

Only one problem stood in the way of a quick trip to Sussex to discuss all these implications. Carl had had to return the Czech travel documents issued in case of a wartime emergency. He had no passport and counted as stateless. In the confused postwar situation it would probably have taken months to get a so-called Nansen passport, an international travel document for the stateless. Carl decided to bluff his way through. Gertie made up a good-looking document herself, with high-faluting phrases, titles, dates, a number – and, of course, several faked rubber stamps. The only way to fly was via Cairo, changing planes there. The

Egyptian officials at the passport control were a little nonplussed about the travel document and finally fetched the officer in charge to adjudicate. He scrutinised the paper carefully until his eyes met the name Ebert. 'Are you the son of the German President Ebert?' he asked, with a look of disdain for his uneducated staff. My father responded only with a shy smile, looking at the floor while he made a noncommittal movement with his hands, like somebody who wanted to avoid having to throw his weight about. The officer immediately took a stamp off the desk, slammed it down on the document and handed it back with a 'Bon voyage, sir.'

In Britain my father was confronted with a long list of schemes, on which John Christie and Rudi Bing had worked for some time. They were options of what Glyndebourne's future might look like, but these seemed to have been thrown together like a jumble sale lot, without prior discussion in depth. John Christie had been trying to buy the freehold of Covent Garden Opera House, Rudi Bing had been working on a scheme for a drama festival in Oxford. There were plans of weekends of music at Glyndebourne itself, attempts to raise outside finance for a Glyndebourne season, which John Christie could no longer pay for out of his own pocket. It all seemed a bit disjointed and lacking a direction.

Carl found that it was indeed very difficult to come to a clear decision on the future of Glyndebourne because there were, as yet, too many imponderables. In view of the financial restraints, it was decided to pursue the idea of linking with the 'new' Covent Garden, which was being set up with Government money. For the first time in history, it was proposed to fund a permanent opera company through a state subsidy, somewhat like the system used on the Continent. Since there were not all that many people in Britain who had experience of establishing and running a permanent opera company, it appeared sensible to harness the expertise which existed ready-made at Glyndebourne. One of the options was to establish a merger to provide summer festival seasons at Glyndebourne and to play at Covent Garden for the rest of the year, the whole organisation to be under one management, with Carl as Artistic Director (possibly in collaboration with a conductor of international fame) and Rudi Bing as General Manager. The music publishers Boosey and Hawkes had bought the lease of

Covent Garden, and a Board had been assembled to appoint a management team. Many semi-official contacts had already taken place to sound out the general attitude to a merger scheme.

One day Carl was asked to meet the Board at Covent Garden for a formal discussion. John Christie had been very active in promoting the merger idea, but unfortunately in his incorrigible, rough, not to say rude manner. Almost every sentence in his letters or conversations implied that nobody outside Glyndebourne knew anything about opera. These cannon shots undid all the patient diplomatic work of other people in an instant. Christie was so keen, however, that he suggested at one stage that he himself would abstain from any involvement in the scheme, as long as 'my men' were to run the whole operation.

The atmosphere at Carl's meeting with the board, which I had been invited to attend, was icy, even hostile, from the start. The Board members were asking questions as if they were Inquisitors. Quite obviously they had been hurt and annoyed by the criticism that they were just amateurs and had to be taught how to manage an opera company. Carl and Rudi Bing had, of course, studiously avoided any critical comments, implied or otherwise. But it was no good. The Board had already made up their minds. From being naturally curious but a shade suspicious of the idea of cooperation or merger with Glyndebourne, they had become convinced that the whole scheme had been hatched for the sole purpose of swallowing Covent Garden for its facilities and its subsidy. I also felt during the course of the meeting that there was an element of xenophobia as well as envy – perhaps not so surprising when the war had barely finished, and remembering the earlier resentment of the 'German cabal' in residence at Glyndebourne and its singular success in turning it into one of the world's major festivals within a few years.

John Christie, who had started out with a much simpler vision of opera at Glyndebourne but had been convinced by Audrey's insistence on 'doing it properly', had turned into an intrepid fearless fighter for the highest standards in the arts. Many people thought he sounded arrogant. That is unfair to a man who was single-minded in the pursuit of what he believed in, but was not prepared to waste time on diplomatic niceties. In August 1946 he sent a paper on 'Music and Drama' to Mr [later Lord] Wilmot, a staunch supporter of the arts and at that time Minister of Supply, which is almost frightening in its staccato thought process, but contains a perfectly valid argument:

'I believe the approach to these Arts is through respect rather than through familiarity. It is easy to scatter round bad and uncostly performances. The uncritical accept them, but that overlooks two important sections of the audience: those who are critical and those who are prejudiced against anything that is not common. Those prejudiced are a larger portion of the community and they have to be won over. I submit that all three sections can be won over by respect and not by familiarity. At any rate it is unthinkable that the critical should not be catered for.

'I. Supreme performances

'I believe therefore that England must have in London, her capital, the World's supreme performances. Londoners will attend them and in lesser numbers provincials. They will then become critical and this leads to the next stage – "the aim at the supreme" ... There are hardly any operatic artists in this country, because opera offers them much less financially than concerts, whilst orchestral players are paid many times their orchestral salaries for film work ... Competition is therefore not based on artistic purpose. At any rate Art is not yet a competitor with commerce and commerce is apt to be contemptuous of art; yet they are expected to go to bed together.

'II. Combined opera

'I submit therefore that all four Opera Units be joined into one: Covent Garden, The Carl Rosa or Touring Company, Sadler's Wells and Glyndebourne. All artists should be engaged by headquarters, who would direct artists where they are to perform. As it is, Covent Garden have several times approached the Glyndebourne artists at Glyndebourne with a view to next year. [David] Webster (Covent Garden) has told [Benjamin] Britten that anyhow the artists would be

175

bought out with State money. Such things are bound to happen if all four are separate.

'The central management should teach the local management. At present there is no standard in England. Standards have fallen terribly. The achievement of supreme standard depends on the co-operation between British artists and great foreigners ... The young British singer must work side by side with the world's great artists ... What is important is the contact in rehearsal rather than in performance ...

'III. Expert Executive

'Central headquarters must be the expert executive, who must accept the whole responsibility for what is actually done. The Expert Executive must be the servant of the group of non-professional Trustees or Directors, who are the contact between the State and the Public on the one side, and the Executive on the other side.

'Money must be the servant and not the master, but art wants the best possible business control and no muddle, and as little waste as possible.'

John Christie continues with sections on orchestra provision, the buildings in which the scheme is to operate, the vexed problem of acoustics, an advanced opera school, drama companies, and concludes:

'My scheme may be criticised on the basis of Dictatorship. But we – the expert executive – should be the servant of non-professional Trustees and that, it seems to me, is the necessary protection.

'Artists directed by headquarters have to be directed as artists and they want handling. Headquarters have the authority and experience for this. Local managements have not.'

It is safe to assume that Mr Wilmot did not show this memorandum to anybody, but it is equally safe to believe that all the people to whom John Christie refers so ruthlessly knew his thinking, because the paper echoes all his speeches on the subject in style and content. Naturally, other people's attempts to forge a closer understanding with fellow organisations, let alone cooperation or mergers, were at a disadvantage. When he went to the Covent Garden Board meeting, Carl could not possibly have guessed that this was the picture of Glyndebourne's ambitions which people feared.

On his first return to Britain in 1945, my father was still considering the possibility of accepting a post in Germany – which he had not revisited yet after the end of the war. A remit to rebuild the German theatre after 12 years of Nazi vandalism in the arts would have interested him very much, particularly with his experience of creating a new theatre culture in Turkey successfully completed. 30 years earlier, when he had founded the Frankfurt Drama Academy, he had already condemned the inadequate and misconceived training for young actors. He had spoken out and written articles against the outworn traditions of teaching which had been carried forward from another age. Now he felt an even more radical programme should be devised, with the added incentive of having to eliminate the effects of Nazi ideology, which had used the theatre as a vehicle for propaganda and, worse still, as a means of indoctrinating the people. Naturally, he realised that the basic conditions existing in Germany, even after the collapse of the Thousand Year Reich, were quite different from what he had found in Turkey. But his work with the uninhibited, enthusiastic students, free of the ballast of tradition, had given him a new vision of the shape and ethics of future academies. It was only the spectre of having to deal with many people tainted by their willingness to work under the Nazis and allowing the regime to use their names as propaganda tools, which made him doubt the wisdom of returning to Germany.

Carl would have been happy to settle in Britain, which he had come to love and where he felt the seeds sown by Glyndebourne before the war were beginning to bear fruit. The decision to establish a quasi 'National Opera' at Covent Garden, with a permanent company funded by the Government, was a major departure from the previous system of privately funded *ad hoc* seasons. The wartime organisations ENSA and CEMA had paved the way for this radical rethink on arts provision. The example and unparalleled success of Glyndebourne had undoubtedly created a much wider appreciation of and interest in opera. Carl felt that Britain was suddenly on the brink of an opera renaissance, and he wanted to be part of the 'building' process. But a great deal had still to be done to create a resilient British opera culture.

After five years' continuous work in Turkey, in a benign Asiatic dictatorship determined to force-feed its people the achievements of the Western world, it was strange for Carl to return to the most democratic and conservative of European nations, emerging from the enormous strains and sacrifices of a devastating war. He was disappointed at his failure to win over the Covent Garden Board. The quest to find a new role for Glyndebourne was halted through the uncertainties of funding. He had offers from film-makers, from American entrepreneurs and other projects, but they all had a nebulous feel about them.

Carl returned to Ankara to complete his remit before turning over the academies and the National Theatre to his former pupils to run without his help. In the meantime he had acquired a recognised travel document. It was a heavily disguised blessing, because for every country he wanted to visit or through which he needed to pass on the way, he had to get a visa, which meant filling in long forms in triplicate at many Consulates.

It soon became clear that Glyndebourne would not mount its own season in 1946. Instead, a group of artists round the composer Benjamin Britten made a contract with John Christie to put on a season of Britten's new work *The Rape of Lucretia* in Sussex. He had premiered his large-scale opera *Peter Grimes* at Sadlers Wells in London the previous year, with tremendous success. *Lucretia* was a new departure, the first of a series of chamber operas scored for a small orchestra of instrumental soloists. The Britten Group were not billed as Glyndebourne Festival Opera, they were 'guests' at Glyndebourne. But John Christie paid the losses of the Sussex season as well as the subsequent tour of England. He found these losses unexpectedly high, and it remains a mystery why, under these circumstances, a 'real' Glyndebourne season was abandoned.

Back in Ankara, Carl found himself cut off again from the outside world occasionally. It seemed grotesque, so many months

The 'big four' of Glyndebourne

Photo: Roger Wood, *The Sketch*, London 1951

C.E. directing

Life 1951

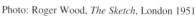

Fritz Busch conducting

Life 1951

C.E. rehearsing Darya Bajan as Gilda
Picture Post 1947

C.E. rehearsing Marko Rothmüller as Rigoletto
1947

Design for *Macbeth* by Caspar Neher

Design for *Barbiere di Siviglia* by Oliver Messel 1954   Photo: Armstrong Jones

Design for temple scene in *Alceste* by Hugh Casson 1953

Carl Ebert   Photo: Eschen, Berlin.

after the end of the war, that postal communications were often interrupted, that letters were censored and sometimes lost altogether. It was difficult to negotiate new contracts and evaluate different projects under such conditions. One of the most interesting approaches was made by an entrepreneur, Mr Jay Pomeroy, who had founded the New London Opera Company at the Cambridge Theatre and had spent a considerable fortune mounting opera and ballet productions presenting a mixture of star performers and young artists. The nature of Mr Pomeroy's resources did not become clear until a few years later, when the British Government made a retrospective alteration to financial regulations. He had found a loophole in the law which allowed him to make enormous profits, perfectly legally, in whisky deals. He was required to pay hundreds of thousands of pounds in tax, and Britain lost a promising cultural asset.

In 1946 Mr Pomeroy proposed that Glyndebourne and his organisation should enter into a deal of cooperation or even merger. At the same time, he asked Carl to do a production of *Rigoletto* at the Cambridge Theatre as early as possible. Carl wanted to obtain the Christies' approval, because his first loyalty was to Glyndebourne. John and Audrey thought his first post-war work in Britain must be at Glyndebourne – on the other hand, at this stage they were still not able to guarantee a Glyndebourne season for 1947. Negotiations between Mr Pomeroy and Glyndebourne ensued, but stumbled once more over the question of managerial control.

During a visit to Edinburgh in 1940, Audrey Christie is reported to have said to Rudi Bing: 'This is the place for a festival.' By 1946 Bing had persuaded the City Council that a large-scale International Festival would be of immense financial and prestigious benefit. The first festival was announced to run for a three-week period in August/September 1947. Glyndebourne would participate with two opera productions, and provide the organisation for booking all the other 'events', ranging from exhibitions via drama and ballet and chamber music to orchestral concerts. At one stroke it was to be the largest International Festival in the world, incidentally cashing in on the fact that all the famous European pre-war festivals were still struggling to rise from the ashes of the war.

179

In July 1946 my father came back to England to discuss all these developments with the Christies and Bing, at the same time meeting the Britten Group and seeing the *Lucretia* production. Travel was still so haphazard that it took 20 hours to fly from Ankara via Cairo, Malta and Marseille to London. Many decisions were waiting to be made urgently. The Britten Group were polite but distinctly distant. They emanated a strong feeling of an intellectually elitist group unwilling to be contaminated by outsiders. The question arose of whether and how another 'guest' appearance of the company in 1947 would integrate or overlap with Glyndebourne's own proposed season. The length and content of that first post-war Glyndebourne season was the central problem which influenced every other decision. Various innovative combinations of operas had already been discussed at length by letter. They ranged from Stravinsky's *Histoire du Soldat* (Carl had produced and narrated the German premiere in 1923) in a double bill with a short Mozart, via Martin's *Le Vin Herbe*, a stage-oratorio of great beauty, to Richard Strauss' *Ariadne* or *Intermezzo*. It was even discussed whether Glyndebourne should do its own production of *Lucretia* (it owned scenery and costumes, having funded the Britten season), coupled with a new production of another opera. In the end it was decided that Glyndebourne could only do one work, and it would be its first production of a Baroque opera: *Orfeo ed Euridice*, the pathfinder, so to speak, for Gluck's drive to reform opera in the middle 1700s. His crusade had been directed against the sterile, formal use of music into which opera had degenerated. Gluck wanted the musical language to express dramatic situations more explicitly.

The next most pressing problem was the choice of two operas for the first Edinburgh Festival in 1947. Glyndebourne had approached Toscanini and Bruno Walter for the two operas, but neither could fit such a commitment into their timetables. Walter had already been booked to meet up with his beloved Vienna Philharmonic Orchestra for the first time since the war, at Edinburgh. It was decided to revive two of the most successful pre-war Glyndebourne productions for the festival: *Le Nozze di Figaro* and *Macbeth*. Rudi Bing had been given two assistants to manage the avalanche of work which now descended on the office: Moran

180

Caplat for Glyndebourne, and Ian Hunter for Edinburgh.

Carl returned to Ankara to do another production with the theatre he had created and to arrange the transfer of the whole family to Switzerland and Britain respectively. The Pomeroy contacts continued, and Glyndebourne was ready to set aside its misgivings about doing a production at the Cambridge Theatre before the 1947 festival season. *Rigoletto* was pencilled in for the Spring. In October 1946 Carl was informed that the Britten Group had submitted a plan for the joint operation of an opera school. Such a plan had been discussed at Glyndebourne in detail before the war, and Carl thought it was essential to carry it out to safeguard the future of the festival. In his opinion, the training of young singers and actors was inadequate to dismal all over the world at that time – with very few exceptions – and was responsible for the equally disappointing quality of average performances. Being in the process of winding up his 10 years' work in Turkey, he was, of course, very keen to apply his latest experiences to any future activity in teaching. He considered the plan of the Group totally unacceptable, primitive and old-fashioned. Only musical studies, 'Movement' and 'Dramatic Action' appeared in the proposed curriculum. Movement to be taught by a dancer and Dramatic Action by a singer, not a producer. The paucity of the proposals seemed quite ludicrous to my father. He warned Glyndebourne not to have anything to do with it.

During his summer visit, the Britten Group had invited him to produce the new chamber opera which Ben Britten was writing for the 1947 festival at Glyndebourne. Carl was very interested in the project and looking forward to receiving the first pages of the score. Ben Britten had the unusual ability to compose to precise deadline dates with unfailing certainty. It soon became apparent that Carl's idea of deadline was rather different from Benjamin Britten's. He always took a lot of trouble in preparing a new production, and therefore needed the music very early. In the end he had to turn down the offer of producing *Albert Herring* because, as he wrote, he 'could not start on preparing a production when I do not know how the piece ends'.

After she had finished school, my sister Renata became a valuable assistant to my father in Ankara because she spoke Turkish

181

fluently. She also proved to be ruthlessly efficient and have a flair for accurate, easy-going communication. As a reward, she was invited to be my father's assistant for his production of *Rigoletto* at Mr Pomeroy's Cambridge Theatre. The whole family said goodbye to Ankara early in 1947, to the biggest send-off ever recorded.

It meant a further adjustment for my father to work in Western conditions again. However happy he had been to teach young artists free from the encumbrance of tradition, to work with experienced performers needed a slightly different technique. Communication was quicker and easier. Perhaps he now had a tendency, even more than in pre-war days, to demonstrate what he wanted by acting it himself. This can be frustrating for professionals, but the working atmosphere at the Cambridge Theatre was excellent through the intensity and humanity of his personality and the quality of his 'performances'. The frequently performed 'potboilers', as they are so aptly described, of Verdi's and Puccini's output suffer terribly from performances which are simply vehicles for big voices, elaborate decor and extravagant costumes. These performances, whether repertory or 'gala', seem to set out to prevent the audience from understanding what the pieces are all about. The whole thing easily degenerates into a celebration of glorious sound and a feast for the eyes. Nothing is more inappropriate – and more galling for the producer – than to hear audiences saying: 'Oh, I loved *Rigoletto*, the costumes were so pretty'. Verdi, after all, intended it to be the most shocking and harrowing piece.

Carl used the traditional period for his production, but brought out its brutal drama through the psychological characterisation of the protagonists.

With the help of the conductor Alberto Erede, a pre-war colleague at Glyndebourne, Carl managed to eliminate all the false, pompously heroic singing in which these operas so often drown. Every minute of the evening was alive and real, particularly strong were such scenes as Rigoletto's monologue in the second scene '*Pari siamo*', often degraded to a vocal showpiece. In this production it showed the agony of the man who hated his job of entertaining the Duke's court, the self-indulgent, uncaring Duke himself, and it clearly showed how fearful the widowed father was for the safety of his daughter, at a loss how to shield her from evil. In this way Rigoletto's own cruelty against others is based believably on psychological circumstances. The whole opera was analysed and treated in the same way. The humanity of the vocal expression conveyed the endless suffering contained in the opera. 30 years later, to get away from the 'pretty picture' syndrome of the work, other producers successfully attempted to heighten the incisiveness of the drama through, for instance, an almost surrealist stylisation (Scottish Opera), or by updating to the Mafia *ambiente* of New York (ENO).

The Cambridge Theatre production was highly successful, but it did not show tangible results for closer cooperation between Jay Pomeroy and Glyndebourne. The premiere of *Rigoletto* happened to be on Renata's twenty-first birthday. At the reception after the performance, Mr Pomeroy made a speech revealing that the real genius behind the production was Renata and her father was only the front man. He also presented her with a first-class ticket on the *Mauretania* to New York, to sail in style to her wedding and her new life in the States. He was a generous man.

The wedding arrangements had had to be postponed because of Renata's involvement in *Rigoletto*. Carl was quite a modern father in many ways. He loved to be argued with, and what made him laugh more than anything else was to be teased by the family. In other ways he could be most patriarchal. Like most fathers, he hated to lose his daughters and had no sympathy for the poor fiancé who had the hassle of reorganising everything. Hassle? What hassle? My father rarely used the flights he had booked originally – he did not understand about hassle. Lou Stoia, the young American of Albanian origin whom Renata had met in Ankara, bore my father a slight grudge all his life about the patriarchal aspect of our clan. In the family it had been a joke for many years that all the daughters were expected to marry oil sheiks or similar. Some time later my father 'joked' that his younger daughters had married the only two poor Americans. He was proved to be thoroughly wrong. Both sons-in-law became highly respected university professors.

While the whole family were still in Turkey packing up their household, Rudi Bing rang me in London to ask whether I would be interested in coming to Glyndebourne and Edinburgh as Assistant to my father. I had nothing much to do at the time, and agreed. I am not even sure whether Carl had been asked about this idea, but there were not many people about in Britain who had the faintest notion of what an opera Production Assistant's function was. The beginning of rehearsals for *Orfeo ed Euridice* came as a revelation to me and, as far as I was concerned, settled my future.

Orfeo is the most frequently performed opera of Gluck, and any attempt to bring it nearer to a contemporary audience meets an astonishing amount of prejudice. Baroque opera seems to conjure up for many people stately, measured behaviour – which is exactly the opposite of what Gluck wanted. He wanted the drama to be intensely human and not courtly. The three singers Glyndebourne found for the soloists were a perfect team in looks and voice. Kathleen Ferrier had been recommended by Roy Henderson some two years earlier for future use. Glyndebourne had drawn the Britten Group's attention to her for the part of Lucretia the year before. So in 1947 she was already an old Glyndebourne hand. Radiant or tragic, she had a wonderfully real personality coupled with an exceptional voice, strong and expressive. Ann Ayars, a beautiful young American girl with a sensuous limpid soprano, sang Euridice, and Zoë Vlachopoulos, a well-rounded joyous creature from Greece, played Amor. There was no problem in assembling an excellent chorus; Glyndebourne's reputation accounted for that. From there on, the exceptional quality of the Glyndebourne chorus became a permanent feature.

Orfeo ed Euridice also needs a group of dancers. The vital choice of the right choreographer presented a problem. Carl had been away for too long to know the 'market'. He wanted to accentuate the personal interplay in the story within an only slightly stylised frame. There was no question, therefore, of using a conventional 'ballet' group, but he also shrank from using the excellent Jooss Ballet because he feared that they were too fixed on their own expressionist style of performance. With the help of outside advice, another modern choreographer was found and entrusted with the task. Before any stage rehearsals had got under way Carl met the choreographer in London for two days to explain his whole concept and show him the stage plan and then to go through the whole opera, bar by bar, setting out his conception of the production and explaining in detail what he wanted from the dancers. There were clear indications of style, expression and of the integration with the cast and chorus. The plan was for the choreographer and dancers to work by themselves for a while in London while Carl rehearsed soloists and chorus at Glyndebourne. At a certain point the whole would be put together to adjust and fine-tune before going into stage-orchestra rehearsals. The great day came, and the dancers showed what they had been working on to my father on the Glyndebourne stage.

Their two big numbers were the 'Dance of the Furies' and 'The Elysian Fields'. It was a total disaster. For the 'Furies' the choreographer had worked a kind of 'robot ballet', like a Paul Klee painting entitled 'The Revolt of the Engine Room', all jerky, violent movements and contortions. In the 'Elysian Fields' the dancers portrayed an Indian ritual of navel-gazing, beautifully calm, but one-sided. It was as if the two men had never talked to each other. This was an entirely intellectual, abstract concept, while Carl had made it abundantly clear that he wanted only a degree of stylisation. There was only one solution: to rework the dancers' tasks from the beginning, which Carl set out to do with the choreographer's help. The result was certainly not a world-class exhibition of modern dance, but it was integrated with the rest of Carl's production – and that is always an extraordinarily difficult result to achieve, because on the whole the two 'languages', opera and dance, are so different. For myself, this meeting of cultures had the happiest result imaginable: I set eyes on my future wife, who was one of the dancers.

The 1947 *Orfeo ed Euridice* was probably not the definitive answer to the challenges of the work, but it had the outstanding portrayal of Orfeo by Kathleen Ferrier. Her serenity, her suffering and her passion were so moving because they were utterly real. And she was just that as a person. Her career blossomed from that moment.

It is very typical of Audrey Christie's thoughtful kindness that she sent little presents to my father and Gertie at the first-night with this note:

'A little devil for Charles to remind him (whenever it knocks) of how my heart knocked with wild delight at his devilish Hades scene! The rose may remind Gertie that she is "Elysium" not only for Charles but also to some of her friends – including
Audrey'

The remainder of the season included the Britten Group's new work, *Albert Herring* and a few performances of *Rape of Lucretia*. After that, contact with the Group ceased.

The excitement of preparing for the first Edinburgh Festival took hold of us as soon as the last car had left the car park at the end of the Glyndebourne season. Two operas designed for the Sussex stage had to be transferred to the King's Theatre, Edinburgh. Alterations to the scenery had been taken in hand some time earlier. A delegation, headed by Carl, went North to thrash out all the remaining problem details that we could think of, including lighting bridges hung over the stage (unheard of in Britain at that time) and exact size of the orchestra pit. The 'pit', only about two feet deep, could not be extended sufficiently to take the *Macbeth* orchestra, so an additional row of seats (some of which had already been sold) had to be taken out. The players would be sitting at stalls level and on a slight slope. It was all a bit primitive compared to a 'real' opera house; on the other hand, there was such a sense of pioneering about the whole enterprise that one just had to be optimistic. We were told that there was a chance of improving some details for the second festival – if it ever came to a second one. One luxury Glyndebourne insisted on: that the theatre would be dark, i.e. totally at our disposal for two whole weeks before the start of the festival.

Rehearsals for the two operas, *Figaro* and *Macbeth* took place at Glyndebourne. George Szell was engaged to conduct both operas. He was a very experienced opera and concert conductor who had recently moved to the United States. Apart from the unprecedented hiccough of the pretty American soprano, scheduled to sing Susanna, having arrived without any knowledge of the long and complicated recitatives, everything was going well. The Susanna must have thought she could pick up the recitatives

186

during rehearsals. She had to be replaced after three days. Szell attended all production rehearsals. He never said very much, but after a short while he started to tap his music desk with his baton to emphasise his beat. Soon it became irritating for everybody. He never made it clear whether he felt the singers were not looking at him enough. Among themselves they called him 'the woodpecker'. One morning a note was found that he regretted not being able to work under such conditions. He had left Glyndebourne at dawn, but nobody was any the wiser as to what had been so unacceptable for him. During the rehearsals he had concentrated on time keeping, never trying to breathe with the singers or encourage them. Carl had thought it very important to have a well-known conductor for the first Edinburgh Festival, which was also the first time Glyndebourne would play outside its own theatre. But it was too late to find another famous maestro.

Berthold Goldschmidt, who had first recommended *Macbeth* to Carl for his 1931 opening in Berlin, was entrusted with conducting the work for the Festival, and Walter Süsskind, the head of the Scottish Orchestra, took on *Le Nozze di Figaro*. The Scottish Orchestra had never played for opera before, but they acquitted themselves well. At one orchestra-alone rehearsal, I was intrigued to hear Goldschmidt trying to teach the players to attack the cackling rhythms of the witches' music in a brutish way. They were meeting new experiences.

We had plenty of excitements and alarms on the way to getting our contribution to the Festival ready, but the most wonderful feature was the scheme whereby all the 'workers' at the Festival were given passes to attend each others' rehearsals. It was a brilliant idea, particularly because so many of the world-famous artists were meeting again for the first time since the war. The most touching moment came when Bruno Walter started to rehearse with his beloved Vienna Philharmonic Orchestra after nine years of enforced exile. Quite naturally, that inaugural Festival engendered more excitement than any other since then. From the opening fanfares of the trumpeters at the St Giles' Cathedral service to the closing concert in the Castle gardens, the Festival signalled a positive new beginning after the war.

New plans were made for 'real' Glyndebourne seasons in 1948

and 1949. They involved lengthy discussions, endless correspondence and travelling. In retrospect, it is difficult to understand that there was no attempt to work out an artistic policy or a theme for Glyndebourne's future development. Suggestions for repertory, conductors, designers and artists were flying about, were investigated and then changed again. It all came down in the end to the central problem of finance. As John Christie had warned in 1945, without help from other sources, whether state or business, Glyndebourne would have to close its doors. The enormous success of the Edinburgh Festival had postponed the unthinkable for the moment, because the Festival bore the full cost of Glyndebourne's productions shown there. As welcome and as generous as this was, it could not last for ever – other European theatres could probably be 'bought in' for much less, because their visit to Scotland would be subsidised by their own Government. Although Glyndebourne's involvement at Edinburgh was perhaps secure for a few years, there would be no Sussex season until a fundamental financial reorganisation had taken place.

The once eagerly pursued link-up with Jay Pomeroy withered slowly, without resentment on either side. Pomeroy was, however, still very keen for Carl to do as many productions at his Cambridge Theatre, London, as he could find time for. He was engaged to produce Verdi's *Falstaff* in March 1948, his first acquaintance with this unique work, the supreme example of Verdi's genius. The designer, Hein Heckroth, was in that period involved in two epoch-making films, *Red Shoes* and *Tales of Hoffmann*. He devised a clever set consisting of levels and ramps for *Falstaff*, which allowed for quick changes and gave Carl varying acting areas to work with for the different scenes. The actor in my father relished the Shakespearean text, brilliantly turned into Verdi's libretto by Arrigo Boito, and he had a lively cast to work with, led by the veteran Mariano Stabile.

Glyndebourne refurbished the pre-war *Giovanni* for the 1948 Edinburgh Festival, and embarked on a new *Cosi fan Tutte* with sets and costumes by Rolf Gerard – whose work for Peter Brook's innovative *Romeo and Juliet* in London had attracted much attention. The 'new look' could hardly have been more startling for people who had seen the pre-war *Cosi*. The sets were light, elegant

188

and skeletal. To emphasise the unreal frame to a very turbulently real human tragi-comedy, Carl had asked for a set without real walls or real doors. Gerard devised a set of elements which were in themselves only outlines of, say, panelled walls, etc.; like line drawings stood up on stage, a see-through effect. An incidental advantage was that the audience could see people approaching a door from outside, either in character or 'spying', as required. At last my father had been able to throw off the over-sweet designs of 1934. With only one member of a pre-war cast in both operas, it was like a new beginning.

Cosi fan Tutte was conducted by Vittorio Gui, with whom Carl renewed a partnership that had been so successful in the early years of the Florence *Maggio Musicale*. He became addicted to the Glyndebourne spirit very quickly, and remained an influential member of the team for years. His true Italian *brio* was good for Glyndebourne, and so was his Anglicised Italian sense of humour, except, that is, when he played the dictatorial Roman Emperor – a ploy he used from time to time. *Don Giovanni* was entrusted to a young Czech conductor, Rafael Kubelik, who had just decided to leave his native country with his family – an echo of my father's decision in 1933 – because he did not want to work under the new (Communist) regime. Kubelik was also a wonderful musician, very sensitive, but with infectious enthusiasm and great warmth.

The response to the performances was overwhelming, at least as far as the audiences were concerned. The critics were already beginning to get a little blasé about the amazing range of world-class events which Edinburgh had to offer. The 'modern' decor for *Cosi fan Tutte* was too difficult to understand for some. Carl had found a new impetus after the long years in Turkey, where he missed the stimulating contact with other theatrical events. His productions were even more intense and detailed and had greater energy than before. But there was not a shadow of a permanent assignment that would have made full use of his powers and given him the artistic satisfaction which he needed. Not that he was short of work. He had offers for guest productions in Vienna, Zurich, Florence, Milan and some German cities. But it all seemed so pointless to him. However good the productions might turn out to be – and the quality depended on so many ingredients coming right – their effect would be gone after they had finished their run. He enjoyed producing *Orfeo ed Euridice* at La Scala, Milan with Furtwängler conducting. It was their first cooperation, and they understood each other perfectly, save for the conception of Orfeo's great aria *Che faro* over the dead Euridice. He was blissfully happy to have found her, but he had killed her by ignoring the Gods' decree not to look at her until they were safely outside Hades. Furtwängler kept saying: 'The key in which this aria is written is always joyful, in all music ever written.' Carl insisted that there was more subtlety in the shades of expression within the aria to express Orfeo's emotions. They had long inconclusive arguments and were again arguing about it two years later when they met in London.

The 1949 season at the Edinburgh Festival repeated the success of the new *Cosi fan Tutte* and presented a new production of Verdi's *Masked Ball*. The success Carl had had with this work in Berlin in his collaboration with the designer Caspar Neher lay 17 years back, and he was keen to find a new solution to the visual aspect. He was afraid that the designs might have dated – which they had not – and that the reduction in size to the much smaller measurements of the King's Theatre stage would look feeble compared to the wonderful effect they achieved in the Berlin house. Neher could not free himself so easily from the old conception – anyway, not in the time available. His adaptation of the old idea was just as powerful in the smaller frame, but more difficult for my father to work in. A brilliant cast was assembled, and the opera again made a tremendous impact through its dramatic force. Ljuba Welitsch as the tragic 'Amelia', a tempestuous lover to the highly-strung and moving 'Riccardo' of Mirto Picchi; Alda Noni played a brilliant and cheeky page 'Oscar', while Paolo Silveri made 'Renato's' transition from a devoted Chief Minister to the unforgiving hatred of a betrayed husband frighteningly real.

With Glyndebourne still unable to mount its own festival, surviving solely through the productions for Edinburgh, my father decided to accept an invitation to create an Opera Department at a private university in Los Angeles, the University of Southern California.

As always, my father approached this new life in a most

positive mood. He found Los Angeles incomprehensible, but fascinating, the Americans (Californians!) polite, generous, friendly and willing to take any amount of trouble to help. He and Gertie and the two youngest children, Christiana and Michael — henceforth known as Christa and Mike — also found a small colony of immigrants, good friends, whom they had known previously in Ankara. So their entrée into yet another completely new culture was made much easier. They soon secured a nice apartment in West Los Angeles: 11009 1/2 Strathmore Drive, which amused us Europeans. I asked how long their street was. Only 400 metres or so. The 11000 gave an instant indication of the location of the street (to Los Angelinos) in the grid system of this vast conurbation. The 1/2 was the result of their block of apartments having been built against a steep hill, with each apartment set back about 20 feet from the one below, so everyone enjoyed a wide, secluded terrace.

Carl started to organise his virgin department with the whole-hearted help of the staff. He was fortunate in having an excellent, erudite Dean of Arts, Ray Kendall, to support his ideas. They soon became close friends. Within a short time everything was set up and Carl started his teaching, production classes and two lectures per week. Since he had not yet enough money to buy a car, he had to travel to the university by bus, 90 minutes each way. His lectures soon achieved stardom; he could not understand why there were regularly far more students present than were accredited to the Opera Department. In the American system, students can get extra 'points' or 'credits' by attending lectures outside their own departments. Carl never relished giving lectures, he preferred hands-on practical work. He was a little astonished when many students came up to him at the end of lectures and said: 'Hey, that was a lot of fun.' He had not allowed for the culture shock to be quite as marked. In Germany personal relations had been warm, but a certain formality was regarded as normal. He would have been called 'Herr Professor'. In Turkey he was the father figure, the revered teacher — and he managed to quash the dreaded rise of a guru culture. Here in California it was just 'Hey'. And 'fun'?? He wrote to me:

'I thought I had conveyed to them something of the incredible beauty and theatrical significance of the development of Baroque opera. So it was "great fun" to the young people. I am having to learn a lot myself. Fun is not only joking and laughing, it means giving pleasure – and what could be better than teaching the deep pleasure which a well-understood performance of opera can give? I'm learning fast.'

After nine months in Los Angeles, he was already preparing the first public performance at the university, Richard Strauss' *Ariadne auf Naxos*, no less. The cast of this extremely demanding work consisted exclusively of full-time students, and some of them possessed outstandingly beautiful voices. But Carl was far from convinced that he had made the right decision. He loved the easy-going, uncomplicated ways of Californians, their friendliness, generous welcome and their way of pushing worries to the back of the queue: 'Take it easy'. The shallowness of that opt-out did not become apparent to him till later. He enjoyed the climate too, and was keen to explore the city and the country. But he thought he had come to 'the West' at the wrong time:

'I am 20 years too old or, to put it differently, I have come here 20 years too soon, because it is impossible to accelerate a development which is still in its infancy. There is a chance that it will bring forth a rich harvest in the end. I have lived and worked here for nine months now, and I still can not tell whether our move will be for good nor whether it was sensible at all. There are masses of projects under discussion, but everything is vague, amateurish, impermanent and irresolute. I think I would grab the chance if La Scala came back to me with the same offer as last year, or if Covent Garden would repeat their offer of '46 – since no one can tell at this moment whether Glyndebourne will ever rise again.'

Although Los Angeles was home to an incredible number of talented people – not counting the fakes – including many European intellectuals and artists, it gave the impression of being a cultural desert. Through a Freudian slip, he often referred to it as 'Los Ankara'.

192

The performances of *Ariadne* were a sensational success, which is perhaps not all that surprising, since the provision of opera in LA was basic, both in quality and quantity. The San Francisco Opera mounted a short season at the Shriner Auditorium, a Masonic Temple holding somewhere around 6,000 seats, with a stage that was wide and deep enough for regular basketball matches. It was said that the San Francisco company could not survive financially if it were not for the income from the Los Angeles visit. The Boston Opera and one of the New York companies also came out to Los Angeles occasionally. Apart from these short seasons, necessitating concentrated bouts of overindulgence on the part of the patrons, there were a number of semi-professional organisations who put on *ad hoc* productions of – normally – well-known operas. These were under-funded, under-rehearsed, with scratch orchestras and chorus provided by 'fixers' – all really rather unworthy of a metropolis like Los Angeles. The one redeeming feature was the immense enthusiasm and seriousness with which the artists pursued their task. The community obviously contained much performing talent, but it lacked support and direction. On the other hand, if one talked to outsiders of the state subsidies enjoyed by 53 opera houses in West Germany, there was much disbelief and remarks like: 'But that is communism.'

Carl's new opera department at the University of Southern California flourished, attracting many students who later made international careers, like Marilyn Horne, Lucine Amara, *et al*. He had the facilities at his disposal to mount a wide range of productions, including world premieres of modern works. The freshness and eagerness of the budding artists gratified him – the country had not experienced the ravages of war and consequent shortages. Once they had left the university ('school' as they called it), young performers accepted the fact that there was no such profession as 'singer'; they were cinema usherettes or delivery boys for liquor stores. However, even at the school stage there was the recognisable spectre of the influence of Hollywood superficiality. Carl's teaching eliminated this fungus for the time being, but he worried about the long-term effect of the American preoccupation with 'stardom'.

Soon after his auspicious start at the university, a group which called itself Opera Guild approached him. It was one of those groups that tried to put some culture on to the stages of the city. Their brainwave was to put on annual seasons of opera at the Shriner for schoolchildren between 9 and 11 years old – in conjunction with the City's Education Department. Its Music Supervisor, William Hartshorn, was a member of the Board of Opera Guild.

Detailed feasibility studies had to be made and counterchecked. It was clear from the beginning that it would take military precision and extensive safety precautions to get 5,000 children – it was decided not to sell the worst 1,000 seats of the Shriner Auditorium to the children – to and from the theatre and into their seats in the time allotted for performance and transport. No child would be eligible for an opera visit for more than three school years, so it was decided to mount three different operas and perform them in a tri-annual cycle. These were *Hansel and Gretel*, *Bartered Bride* and *Cenerentola*, Rossini's version of Cinderella.

In the autumn of 1950, Opera Guild created their performing subsidiary, Guild Opera. The first performance of this experiment was scheduled for early Spring 1951. The Executive Committee realised that 5,000 young children could not be controlled by only a few teachers, unless they were meticulously prepared for the experience they were about to have. The education department ran a thorough and probably unique scheme for inoculating the children. All classes of every school which had booked for the opera received a set of records and material for the teachers, so that every child knew not only the exact story, but also the music, learned about the composer and even knew about his life and times, before they came to the theatre. In 1957 I took over these Guild Opera productions from my father, and added the *Magic Flute* to the cycle. To watch the children coming to these performances and to experience their reactions belonged to the most moving moments of my theatre life. There is, for instance, nothing to compare to a pantomime-related open scene change in *Cinderella* and 5,000 children breathing 'Aahaahaahaahaah'.

My father had felt for some time that there should be a reconciliation with Fritz Busch: 'Such sad disappointments should not be carried over into the life beyond.' The chance to make it up presented itself when Busch came out to Los Angeles with the Metropolitan Opera Tour. Adolf Busch and the pianist Rudolf Serkin, both good friends of his, asked Carl to forgive and forget Fritz' unethical behaviour at the beginning of the war. They met and had a relaxed review of times past, but:

> 'We would easily be able to renew the old heart-felt friendship; however, it is unavoidable that the passage of time makes one more critical, one discovers blemishes and wrinkles on the face of ones former flame – which one had actually already suspected in the Spring of the affair. In honesty, temperament, work ethos etc. we are as one, but it has become clear to me that there is actually a generation gap between Fritz and myself in our attitude to the art of opera. We were jolly, honest and wise enough to demonstrate this fact with an example. Fritz beamed when he told me that my view of the *Macbeth* ballroom scene, where I had made the action stiff, jerky and nervous, was totally wrong, because it was written in a jaunty 3/4 Polka rhythm. Naturally we did not quarrel about this; he laughingly accepted my riposte that his, the "old" generation, had obviously never heard of a visual counterpoint.'

All of a sudden, the hard work that had gone into finding new finance for the Glyndebourne Festival had borne fruit. In 1950 sponsorship arrived in the shape of cash gifts and materials. Spedan Lewis, the founder of the Lewis Partnership, gave the lead. It was a cautious beginning, but it came as a great relief to Glyndebourne's well-wishers and former patrons, that its productions were not to be confined to Edinburgh in future. The new *Cosi*, first seen at Edinburgh, shared the bill with a new *Entführung aus dem Serail*, also with designs by Rolf Gerard. Both operas were conducted by Fritz Busch. The old partnership was resumed with a flourish. Edinburgh financed two new productions that year: *Le Nozze di Figaro* and Richard Strauss'*Ariadne auf Naxos*. The seldom-performed first version was chosen, in which the opera follows Moliere's play *Le Bourgeois Gentilhomme*,

Ariadne being the entertainment which M Jourdain provides for his guests. Strauss must have thought of this delicious hybrid as eminently suitable for the normal German repertory theatre, which has singers, actors and dancers permanently at its disposal. But the work did not catch on, partly because the three groups of artists normally do three different things on any given night, and to put them all together into one performance is a planning nightmare.

At last Sir Thomas Beecham agreed to conduct a Glyndebourne company, after countless unfulfilled invitations. (The Christies had approached him even before Busch and my father arrived on the scene. Some of these overtures had ended in acrimony.) Miles Malleson played M Jourdain, and Mme Rambert brought her company and choreographed the dances. Another new designer, Oliver Messel, came to work with Carl for the first time. (Fritz Busch could not conduct the operas at Edinburgh that year, because he had a previous engagement to appear there in concerts with his Danish Radio Symphony Orchestra.) Operagoers often feel slightly uncomfortable with the first version of *Ariadne*. It is as if the world was divided into opera and drama fans, and the two shall never meet. The performances of this true festival piece were excellent, even if they did not set the city alight.

In Los Angeles Carl had produced the second version, which Strauss was prevailed upon to write after the mediocre success of the first. In place of the play with incidental dances Strauss had written a 40-minute prologue, which is one of the most brilliant things he had ever composed. Therefore the second version is the one normally performed. Oliver Messel was an important acquisition for Glyndebourne. He was really an eighteenth-century specialist. His sets and costumes were highly decorated and very beautiful, meticulously researched and therefore authentic in every detail. Whether that is the true meaning of theatre is debatable. At that stage, so soon after the war, his style, elegance and sense of colour combinations were certainly most agreeable, and he designed a succession of delightful productions. Some of them had, however, dated after 10 years or so.

1951, the Festival of Britain year, was the only season for which Glyndebourne received a Government grant. It was put to good

196

use with the provision of two new productions: *Don Giovanni* with designs by John Piper, and the practically unknown early Mozart's *Idomeneo*. Piper created wonderfully sombre, evocative sets, consisting of flat painted surfaces, using perspective and providing markedly different shapes of acting areas for the large number of scenes in the opera.

To offer up *Idomeneo* for approval, or at least for discussion, was an act of faith. The opera had never entered the normal repertory since it was written in 1781, one year before *Entführung*. It is possibly the perfect *'opera seria'*, the first one of Mozart's 'great' operas – he was 24 years old when he wrote it, and by that time he had definite ideas about dramaturgical structure. But – it is too long. Several respected composers have tried to 'save' the work for posterity by creating their own versions, but they have all superimposed their own style on Mozart's. Glyndebourne asked an Edinburgh musicologist, Hans Gal, to cut *Idomeneo* into a better dramatic shape and thus to an acceptable length. Fritz Busch was heavily engaged in this, and Carl to a certain extent. The designer Oliver Messel could, in this instance, not be true to period and style, since the opera is set at the end of the Trojan war. It was probably a good thing, because he could allow his imagination full rein. Messel loved to tell the story of how he sat on the floor in his house at Carl's feet and, while my father described the plot and the musical expression and developed the characters of the various roles, he, Oliver, started to draw. After three days of concentrated sessions, the groundwork of the visual conception had emerged. It was a Baroque version of Antiquity. He devised a permanent set of different levels and wide steps and the means, through the use of decorative curtains, of changing elements of the set while the action continued in front.

Idomeneo is one of the richest scores of Mozart's genius. He uses musical language which he never took up again. The biographer Hildesheimer thinks it was due to his having a good and friendly orchestra – some of the players he knew from his Mannheim days – and he was writing the score while he rehearsed. In this way he could make adjustments and also transcribe new inspiration instantly, in a happy working atmosphere. The score is full of the strongest and most persuasive characterisation. An astonishing aspect is the choral writing, which looks forward to Beethoven and Verdi, both in its dramatic ferocity and its lyrically reflective moments. It is unique within Mozart's total output.

His happiness in writing the opera was transported into the Glyndebourne rehearsals. They were intense and exciting, as if a new work was being tried out for the first time. I think everybody was under the spell of this 'unknown' music. Busch had one of his therapeutic, impish 'let's all relax' ideas when we were sitting in the organ room after a strenuous rehearsal. He said: 'Must get away from all this sugar music,' sat on the organ bench and played the *Lohengrin* wedding march, thumping it out with a hairbrush.

Idomeneo was a triumph for Glyndebourne, and it achieved six series of performances in 13 years. There was also a new production for the Edinburgh Festival in 1951: Verdi's *Forza del Destino*, in honour of the fiftieth anniversary of the composer's death. Sadly, it also marked the end of Fritz Busch's busy life. He had already been unwell at Glyndebourne, and his doctor had asked my father to help him to persuade Busch to cancel his Edinburgh commitments. But Busch was stubborn, and insisted on going through with it. He died in London, a few days after the end of the Festival. Carl had lost a comrade in arms, and once more had to carry the responsibility of the artistic directorship by himself. In a radio talk my father said of Busch:

'... Men and women from the most diverse professions, races and languages have honoured him on many occasions. In his shyness, he would try to dampen the over-excitement, tell a joke and an anecdote, and then turn to somebody standing in a corner, whom he recognised, perhaps a copyist from Dresden, or an oboist from Buenos Aires ... He never looked out for prominent people who could help his career, he wanted to meet human beings, because he was an unassuming person himself, not the "General Music Director" – the human factor in art was the valid measure of all his work as a reproductive artist. He was not the person to indulge in that kind of exhibitionism on the conductor's rostrum which has become almost obligatory today. He had the power to give the listener a satisfaction, a calm and certainty which says: this is right, this is exactly what the creator of the work intended...'

The 1952 season opened with *Idomeneo*, which Fritz Busch had done so much to bring to Glyndebourne. The first performance was a special memorial one in his honour.

The season also contained performances of *Macbeth* and *Cosi fan Tutte* and the first Rossini to be done at Glyndebourne: *La Cenerentola*. Vittorio Gui conducted, and Oliver Messel designed. Carl seemed to have found a new lighter touch in his wanderings through so many cultures. The performance achieved an aura of all-round perfection. *Cenerentola* joined the line-up of Glyndebourne audiences' favourites. One can never understand why some operas become so popular and then lose their appeal, to be happily resurrected in the course of imaginative programming. Rossini's music is witty and full of colourful characterisation. It toys with some bizarre situations, but is also brilliant or lyrical. It demands quartz-clock accuracy in several ensembles for six voices, often singing the same text, but with different expressions. These became what the world of musicals calls show-stoppers. Carl had done his usual careful study of the score by the time he met Vittorio Gui to talk about his conception. Gui played sections of the score as they discussed it. When he came to the so-called wine cellar scene, Gui said: 'That scene is no good, we'll cut it.' Carl was surprised, and said he thought there was good material in it and it was funny. After some discussion, Gui said he would play it for Carl. A couple of minutes later, he stopped and agreed that it was excellent: 'I have never heard it or looked at it before. It is an old tradition to cut it.' One of those dangerous traditions.

Since its rebirth after the war, Glyndebourne had found, nurtured and brought to fame a generation of young singers, many of whom worked with the company for years. Among them were Richard Lewis (who sang every single performance of *Idomeneo*), Ian Wallace, Juan Oncina, Sesto Bruscantini, Geraint Evans, Sena Jurinac, Alda Noni, Sari Barabas, Elisabeth Söderström, Pilar Lorenger, Grazielle Sciutti, who all became specialists in the Glyndebourne work ethos. Before the war, all the people working there fell under the influence of that unique family spirit which the quadrumvirate of the Christies, Busch and Ebert had achieved from the beginning. Such a feeling can so easily become a precious cult, introspective, self-satisfied or arrogant. Glyndebourne did not fall into those traps; there was quite simply that ideal feeling of serious professional work and selfless humanity. Once Glyndebourne had started to mount its own regular seasons again after the war, that same feeling of a family unit appeared once more. My father worked with all the artists right through the months of rehearsals. He had probably the most decisive influence on the working atmosphere. When he arrived at Glyndebourne for the beginning of his stage rehearsals, word spread round the company in a flash: 'The Prof is here.' There was an immediate rise in voltage.

In place of Glyndebourne, the Edinburgh Festival had invited the Hamburg State Opera for 1952, but there was such an unfavourable reaction in the press and among the public, that Glyndebourne was called back in 1953. It presented *Cenerentola* and *Idomeneo* in the Scottish Athens for the first time, and added the first modern opera to its repertory: Stravinsky's *Rake's Progress*. Carl had produced the world premiere of the work in Venice, with Stravinsky himself conducting. That occasion was a little fraught; some of the singers were still holding their vocal scores during stage/orchestra rehearsals – enough to drive a producer to murder – and Stravinsky had an odd habit when he conducted his own music of looking as if he had never seen the score before.

The Glyndebourne preparation also had a hiccough when the singer chosen to portray the name part was suddenly 'hospitalised', as the telegram said, and was forced to withdraw. Richard Lewis had already proved his superb musicianship and versatility as Idomeneo, Ferrando in *Cosi* etc. He was offered the role of the Rake, and since it was only a few weeks to the start of rehearsals, Glyndebourne offered to lay on a repetiteur to help him learn the incredibly difficult score. He said he could not sacrifice his holiday after a very strenuous season, but would learn his part on the beach. Glyndebourne swallowed hard, but decided to trust him – and he came back to the first rehearsal music- and word-perfect.

The Rake's Progress had caused a great stir among the world's critics at its premiere. It certainly had nothing whatever to do with what everybody expected from the composer of *Le Sacré du Printemps*. Some critics thought they had been taken for a ride, others dismissed it as a 'Mozart pastiche'. Neither is correct, of course. The opera is highly individual, has some tentative-romantic stretches, some raucous, aggressive patches, a wonderfully amusing, scatter-brain auction, a sparing, powerfully ominous graveyard, and the most moving finale, the madhouse scene. The work also has one of the best libretti in all opera, written by Auden and Kallman. Carl made the most of the wide range of emotions, which is this condensed biography of Tom Rakewell, from the double standard of the opening love duet, the sincere and insincere involvement of Anne and Tom, to the beautifully simple lullaby with which Anne says goodbye to the crazed brain of Tom. He drew brilliant individual performances from the chorus, who shone particularly in the brothel and the auction scenes, as well as the frightening madhouse.

Two new designers came into the Glyndebourne fold in the 1953 season, Osbert Lancaster for the *Rake's Progress* and Sir Hugh Casson. Lancaster worked with flat, painted surfaces, looking like book illustrations. He developed tongue-in-cheek and dramatic situations as equally strong statements. Sir Hugh Casson, the architect, was engaged to design Gluck's *Alceste*, the only new production in the Glyndebourne season proper. In both cases Carl enjoyed the conceptual discussions on these two very divergent works with two strong individual artists. Sir Hugh created a monumental-looking set for a relatively small stage (*pace* John Christie, who loved to tell everybody that the Glyndebourne stage was bigger than Covent Garden's – it all depends how you interpret statistics). Sir Hugh established dramatic spaces for Carl, which were eminently effective for the way he used crowds and for individual scenes. Again, there was a perfect synthesis of sets – incisive angles of architecture this time – with Gluck's dramatic music.

Alceste also has important work for a group of dancers. Carl engaged Pauline Grant as choreographer. He had first worked with her on *Falstaff* at the Cambridge Theatre, and found a good rapport. She was one of the few choreographers capable of distinguishing between dancing as a separate entity within an opera, and dances which have to develop out of the crowd. There was nothing Carl hated more than a dancer standing among the chorus on stage and looking unmistakably like a dancer. Pauline Grant created beautiful, sensitive dances for *Alceste*. By this time it had almost become a ritual for the music critics to pan all dancing in Glyndebourne operas. The moral is: do not allow music critics anywhere near writing notices about dancing.

Audrey Christie had an enormous influence on the development of the special atmosphere of Glyndebourne, but her most decisive act was certainly that she pointed her husband John in the right direction when she said: 'For God's sake, let's do it properly'. When she returned to Britain after her wartime exile in America, she had hoped, naturally, to continue her singing career for a few more years. But an illness had already begun to sap her strength, and she never returned to the Glyndebourne stage. A few days before the opening of the 1953 season Audrey Christie died, at the age of only 53. She had requested specifically that the start of the season should not be disturbed. My father wrote of her:

'Audrey Christie, Audrey Mildmay – the same person, yet two different personalities, each perfect in its sphere. That nature could combine and harmonise them within one mortal being in such uniqueness, is a miracle that will forever be remembered by all connected with Glyndebourne, members and audience alike.

'I first met Audrey and John Christie in February 1934, when I was invited to discuss their project of an Opera Festival at Glyndebourne. I was fascinated by Mrs Christie's grace as hostess of a big house, by her versatility in leading the conversation, and by her repartee, challenging everybody who liked to join in a tournament with congenial weapons of wit and spirit. Her natural domination, rendered so charmingly, was cheerfully achnowledged by every guest in the Christies' house and at their table.

'Few of these guests, however, were fortunate enough to see the same Mrs Christie slipping daily into the other part of her existence, the one that was her own, perhaps, even more.

Here she discarded the elegant foil-fencing game with words for the perennial fight to achieve an ideal which seems to elude one's grasp, as soon as one believes to have achieved it. In my long experience I never saw a more modest artist; not only in her attitude towards her fellow singers – the moment she joined the ensemble the Mistress of the House vanished and she became part of the artist family, this unique tie which unites all those who work in the atmosphere of Glyndebourne – but also in her very personal feeling of humility toward the creative genius and his work. These were the hours when Audrey Christie, the hostess, turned into Audrey Mildmay, the artist.

'We all admired the "Grande Dame" of last night's reception working for hours and hours on the stage next morning, demanding the utmost from her fragile physique with untiring willpower, and asking for censure and advice with the eagerness of a young student. Audrey Mildmay was not only endowed with a beautiful voice, genuine stage presence and disarming charm, but she was also an outstandingly ingenious and receptive artist concerning stage-production in general. Her unfailing instinct for the truly artistic, her imagination and her sure judgement of style and character together with an unconditional devotion to her task, made her the conductor's and producer's "dream".

'There may have been greater singers in the world, but Audrey Mildmay's was a personal quality which made her personifications unforgettable. Was it the warmth and sweetness of her voice, the sparkle in her great dark eyes, or the sensibility that was expressed in her every movement? It was most likely the combination of all these gifts which caused Fritz Busch and myself to feel: we never shall have (and never had) a more moving and convincing Susanna and Zerlina.

'Giving up singing, after the vacuum of the war years, must have been a heartbreaking decision for Audrey Christie. I cannot forget when once in those days of discussing her future activity on the stage, I found Audrey alone in the Organ Room, playing and singing Dido's last aria, "Remember me" . I was so struck by the expression in her voice that I could not withdraw. Upon finishing the aria she closed the piano, discovered me, and rose; I saw tears in her eyes, but she smiled. It was the resigning smile of the *"Feldmarschallin"*.

'Yet what the stage lost in Audrey Mildmay, Glyndebourne fully regained in Audrey Christie. Her enthusiasm and willpower was now free to focus on one primary target: Glyndebourne's perfection. The amount of inspiration and energy she radiated in the ensuing years, her absolute devotion to Glyndebourne's artistic ideals and her initiative in every phase of its ventures cannot be expressed in words. To those entrusted with the responsibility for the artistic achievements of the Glyndebourne Festival her unshakeable belief will serve as a guide thoughout Glyndebourne's future existence.

'To follow her "Remember me" shall constitute the best, indeed the only genuine form of gratitude and love that could be dedicated to Audrey Christie.'

Although not a single person lacked in respect and admiration for Audrey, it worried my father until the end of his time at Glyndebourne that there was no memorial for her until the Mildmay Garden was created, a romantic, secluded dell close to the stage. There was no headstone on her grave at Glynde, until after the transfer of her ashes to Devonshire. Clearly my father felt more formal about such things than John Christie.

1954 became another important landmark in Carl's career. He had finally decided that there would be no dramatic developments in the field of opera in Los [Ankara] Angeles in the foreseeable future. Almost all artistic enterprise lay in the hands of committees of the wealthy upper crust of society. He felt very awkward having to go round the circuit of meetings to explain wonderful schemes of future activity and to solicit funding (something which, unfortunately, has become an unavoidable feature of the British arts scene in recent years). He made up his mind to accept a renewed invitation from Berlin to take over his former opera company – the original theatre had been completely destroyed, but the

Städtische Oper performed in the somewhat smaller Theater des Westens. His new contract allowed him to continue working at Glyndebourne.

At this stage, Carl was probably at the height of his powers as an artist. He had retained all his old dedication and energy and had become even more versatile, but he would not contemplate any compromise in the working conditions for his productions. His workload had become so heavy, on the other hand, that he was forced to make life difficult for the Glyndebourne Managers. From the early post-war days, when artists were freely available at relatively short notice, a marked change had come over the opera scene. Singers, conductors and designers all had to be contracted much earlier, and were not always ready to tie themselves to one place for a longish period. The Managers, first Rudi Bing, until he went to take over the Metropolitan Opera in New York, and then Moran Caplat, tended to forget or take no notice of the fact that Carl could not always make, say, a vital artistic decision by return of post. The Managers tried occasionally to usurp the power of decision-making, which Carl had to resist forcefully.

The 1954 Glyndebourne season marked another step in the creation of a Rossini repertory. *The Barber of Seville* opened the festival. Vittorio Gui conducted a 'cleaned-up' score – it is quite incredible how many mistakes and inaccuracies the scores of popular operas accrue over the decades. Oliver Messel devised another delicious period set, with the bonus of an unexpected open scene change in the first act – from the street scene to the interior of the house – which invariably invoked a round of applause. The new generation of young singers added to their laurels with a perfectly timed example of spontaneous comedy.

The second version of *Ariadne* is a rather awkward piece for Glyndebourne, because the first half lasts only some 40 minutes, which is hardly long enough to work up an appetite for a one-and-a-half-hour dinner interval. It was decided to add Busoni's one-hour-long opera *Arlecchino* to the bill as a curtain-raiser. Moran Caplat suggested to Carl and John Christie that I should produce this piece. I was very reluctant at first to accept, fearing accusations of nepotism. In the end, of course, I could not refuse the honour. It was the first production in the history of the festival not to be produced by my father. *Arlecchino* is a Commedia del Arte-inspired piece of much fun and some social comment. The music, although extremely expressive, tends to strike audiences as slightly cerebral. John Pritchard, who had taken over some of Fritz Busch's Glyndebourne heritage, conducted, and we ran a competition to find a young designer to join us in this production. The winner was Peter Rice, who evolved perfect decor and costumes. Pauline Grant choreographed the group of masks who expressed the changes of mood between the scenes. The silent role of Annunciata was taken by Silvia Ashmole, my wife. Perhaps there was some nepotism, but I don't think so.

The Edinburgh season of 1954 included yet another opera by Rossini, this time an unknown work: *Le Comte Ory*. Like so much of Rossini's output, it was created during his long stay in Paris, and it has an unmistakeable French air in the cheekiness of much of its music. But it also contains an incredibly sensuous love trio (!). Had Richard Strauss heard the work, one wonders, before he wrote the last act of *Rosenkavalier*? *Comte Ory* is perhaps performed so rarely, because it is difficult to cast. It needs a supremely agile, high-coloratura soprano with a voice big enough to ride the large ensembles. It also calls for a high tenor, singing the highest register *pp*. The soprano also needs to look like a medieval chatelaine from the *Tres Riches Heures*. All this was achieved and more. The 'Rossini team' of Gui, Ebert and Messel were in charge again. Sari Barabas played the Countess Adele, Juan Oncina was Comte Ory, Sesto Bruscantini his buddy Raimbaud, Fernanda Cadoni the page Isolier, and Ian Wallace the stern Gouverneur. The opera plays at the time of the Crusades: Adele's husband is away fighting, Comte Ory and his supporters are draft-dodgers trying to get close to Adele and her entourage. So does the page. The Gouverneur's mission is to put spanners into the machinations.

The music is saucy, the story outrageous and the performances were a riot – even in Edinburgh, where it had been feared that the Presbyterian background might find the piece objectionable. Carl was in particularly good form, and was occasionally carried away by the irresistible situations. In one scene, after the obligatory Rossini storm, voices are heard from outside Adele's castle: poor pilgrims asking for shelter. They are admitted, and we recognise Comte Ory and his men, behaving meticulously well, disguised as nuns. Left alone, they start a reconnaissance and discover the wine cellar. The ensuing drinking bout is tempting for a producer – it is beautifully scored with many dynamic changes. Carl enjoyed himself very much, but it was essential that the scene should not go 'over the top' and should always appear spontaneous. After a spell of promising rehearsal, he could not constrain himself any more and acted the whole scene himself. It was very, very funny. Cutting short the laughter, he said: 'Do it like that – but very discreet.'

11

Berlin 1954–60 and Retirement

Carl started his second period as *Intendant* of the *Städtische Oper*, Berlin, in the autumn of 1954. By coincidence, the first Ebert production the Berlin audiences were able to see since the Nazi Stormtroopers had occupied the opera house, came from abroad. The Berlin Festival had, quite independently, booked the Glyndebourne production of *La Cenerentola* for its 1954 programme. And since all the Festival operas were presented at the *Städtische Oper*, Carl became a guest producer in his own theatre. Naturally, he was both nervous and excited about the outcome of the occasion.

Glyndebourne had never performed on foreign soil before. The whole production, scenery, costumes, props and special effects, as well as artists and staff, had to be flown to Berlin, because the city had effectively become an island. It was surrounded on all sides by the communist-controlled East German State, the so-called 'German Democratic Republic'. The attempted blockade of West Berlin had been foiled by the Allied airlift, which the Berliners called the 'raisin run'. But the authorities in the East continually thought up new regulations to make life in and access to Berlin more difficult.

The whole company felt a sense of adventure. Berlin had never been a beautiful city, and by 1954 only the most dangerous or obstructive war damage had been cleared, resulting in a kind of higgledy-piggledy redevelopment of bomb sites in favoured locations, seemingly without an overall concept or plan. But the city was full of life. Theatres, concert halls and cinemas were full, the streets and restaurants were crowded with people. But, most important of all, the population had retained its own brand of rough humour, encapsuled in a phlegmatic manner. It is the spirit of the place which makes it so special.

Glyndebourne had not performed *Cenerentola* for a whole year, so it needed to be brought back to its original polish, musically and dramatically. Luckily the almost all-Mediterranean cast who had first performed the work at Glyndebourne in 1952 was available. Unfortunately, my father succumbed to a flu virus and had to stay in bed. It fell to me to run the rehearsals.

Came the first performance. The theatre was packed. Everybody in the company was nervous but confident. After the Overture, the curtain rose on the antics of the deliciously scatty 'ugly sisters' of Alda Noni and Fernanda Cadoni. The Glyndebourne audiences had always reacted with a few giggles, but the German public (there must have been some foreigners among them?) were too well-brought-up, or thought they were witnessing 'culture', to react aloud. For about 20 minutes there was a church-like hush in the auditorium. We, backstage, were nonplussed, tried to analyse what could possibly be wrong, and became a little depressed. The singers said afterwards they had found it hard work to make contact with the audience. Ian Wallace, an experienced comedian, played the father, 'Don Magnifico'. At the end of his long aria, addressed to his daughters and containing fanciful analogies, there was an extraordinary, enormous noise. For a split second I thought something had crashed down on to the stage, and I believe Ian Wallace looked up at the proscenium arch for a moment. It was the audience, yelling and clapping and stamping their feet. They had suddenly grasped, and approved of, a style of performance which they had not experienced before. A sense of fun in social caricature, the charm of dottiness were features mostly missing in German comedy, which had always been a little beer-heavy, pointedly underlining every detail. It may sound harsh, but natural charm, as opposed to the put-on variety, is what the Germans admire in other people and find it so hard to produce themselves. The audience had decided to embrace the 'new' style, and there was no holding them. At the end of the performance the applause went on for a good half hour, and the last enthusiasts only left when the house lights were turned off, except for the single-bulb emergency light in the ceiling of the auditorium.

My father had a telephone by his bed to receive interim reports during the performance. I called him at the end from the stage manager's corner, to send him greetings and 'get well soon' messages from the artists and all the staff and to let him hear the tremendous applause.

The situation at the opera house which Carl took over in 1954 was somewhat similar to the conditions he found in 1931. Heinz Tietjen had again been his immediate predecessor. Tietjen, the astute tightrope-walker, had flourished during the Nazi years and had managed to survive the de-Nazification process as well. The opera house was, however, in urgent need of spiritual rejuvenation. There was no real sense of ensemble; the forces at the disposal of the house were used in a haphazard instead of an organised way, which caused loss of morale. And a lot of guests were used as singers, conductors and producers when there was no need for them. In fact, the malaise of the *Städtische Oper* was symptomatic for the change within the traditional German repertory system which was beginning to make itself felt. While all the medium-sized and smaller German opera houses were perforce (through budgetary constraint) continuing to practise the well-tried ensemble system, the larger and very large houses were aspiring to enter the club of international players: the New York Metropolitan, La Scala, Milan, Grand Opera, Paris, Vienna State Opera etc. Post-war Covent Garden was a new boy in this circle, beginning to play the same stakes. These theatres mainly used international stars in the pit and on stage – on short-term or guest contracts, a system which was made possible by the improvement in air travel.

The result of these emerging changes was two-fold: through the great demand for the services of a relatively small number of stars, rehearsal periods became shorter and shorter, and because the small band of stars performed in all the theatres of the international circuit, all productions of a particular work tended to look the same, wherever it was mounted. This situation came to such a pitch that a serious study was begun to assess the advantages or otherwise of creating a cooperative ring of super-houses. Instead

210

of multiplying the cost and work-load of mounting similar productions in each individual theatre, the proposal was to allocate an agreed list of new productions among the members of the clan. Subsequently all these productions would be made available to all the other theatres belonging to the ring. If there were, say, five members of this cooperative, capital costs on productions would be reduced by 80 per cent at a stroke. Such accounting is, as the German saying goes, 'milkmaid reckoning', capital costs of productions (sets, costumes, etc.) amount to only a small proportion of the annual budget of a modern opera house. Personnel costs eat up the lion's share of the available finance. In all attempts at rationalisation of production costs by joint financing, the burden of safe transport of scenery and costumes together with 'hidden' items incurred in liaising between two or more opera houses are usually underestimated. The idea was abandoned.

Carl continued to believe in the theatre family. The benevolent dictator, the *Intendant*, as head of the family, would choose the people whom he considered to have the right qualities as artists and human beings to realise the programme of productions which he had set himself as a goal for the next few years. There was room in the given budget to engage guest artists for specific tasks, but his chief aim was to create a homogeneous force of diverse talents tied to the *Städtische Oper* for the major part of the year. He was well aware of the growing star cult. But instead of buying artists off the shelf in the marketplace, so to speak, he hoped to make stars of the members of his own ensemble, and to a large extent he succeeded. He tried to achieve the synthesis of representative repertory and modern music-theatre. It was not an easy task. Audiences were

'longing for good theatre after the void of the last war years, but they really wanted to hear and see the beloved classics and hoped that beautiful voices and melodies would make them forget the drabness of the daily struggle,'

as one critic put it, who accused the audience of 'cultural impotence'. Another critic found:

'The repertories of the opera houses of our large cities show

211

an astonishing sameness... No other sector of the arts has suffered a similar degree of ossification.'

Having been a reformer all his life, Carl relished the situation. He decided to start on renewing the neglected standard works and to introduce a wider repertory. He chose for his first production Verdi's *Nabucco*, which had never been performed at the *Städtische Oper* before. It was a good choice, because it is a highly political piece about the brutality of power struggles, and has little to do with long beards and long robes. Although Carl desisted from updating the opera, the audience understood only too well its relevance to recent German history. The impact of the production was astonishing: *Nabucco* had to be given 100 times within a few years, and the famous 'concentration camp' chorus had to be repeated *in toto* at every performance.

Carl bound a very modern choreographer to the house, Tatjana Gsovsky, who brought a new shine to the ballet group and presented a demanding repertory from a wide range of living composers. The opera repertory was enriched by rarely heard works, like Busoni's *Doktor Faust*, Weber's *Oberon*, Mozart's *Idomeneo*, Dallapiccola's *Night Flight*. etc, etc. For *The Saint of Bleeker Street* he invited the composer, Gian Carlo Menotti, to produce. In his own productions Carl concentrated at first on the standard repertory, particularly works which were close to his heart and which were in urgent need of renewal, e.g. *Cosi fan Tutte*, *Nozze di Figaro*, *Otello*, *Carmen*, *Falstaff et al*. Carl also added a new branch to the *Städtische Oper*, an opera studio, which performed in various modern venues and enabled the public to get acquainted with contemporary or experimental works, and gave young people a chance to experience opera without having to cross the threshold of the temple of music. This is a common fear called 'Schwellenangst' in German.

It was perhaps a pity that he allowed himself to be persuaded to mount new productions of works which had had sensational successes in his first term as *Intendant* of the *Städtische Oper* in 1931–33, such as Verdi's *Masked Ball* and Kurt Weill's *Die Bürgschaft*. Not that the new productions were less good or less successful, but if, for example, Carl had decided to produce the world premiere of Werner Henze's *Re Corvo* [King Stag] himself, it might have set a signal to the public that opera must forever search for new horizons, or it will inevitably descend to museum status. He must have felt that his work load did not allow him the amount of time on which he had always insisted for preparing a new production. He engaged a guest producer.

Re Corvo is a fascinating mixture of romantic fairytale and Commedia del'Arte. During the course of rehearsals it was edited to a certain extent, with the help, or rather, in discussions with the composer. It was felt to be too long and too complicated in the interplay of the different elements. Leonard Steckel, one of the most experienced drama producers in Germany, was put in charge of the production. I thought it a stimulating, exciting performance, which made considerable demands on the attention span of the audience and its willingness to explore. That was exactly what the customers in the gallery, of all places, rejected. There were wild scenes of booing, shouting and whistling during the premiere, and a storm of protest at the end.

My father was shocked – and extremely angry. During the first two years of his *Intendantship* the changing attitude of some sections of the public had begun to manifest itself. Occasionally there were critical articles and letters in the papers, saying the *Städtische Oper* had become too addicted to modern music. Now, the pent-up feeling had exploded, and Carl decided to take on what he called the 'Mafia' of the gallery. That the portion of the audience which is generally regarded as the most enlightened and knowledgeable part, should protest against the quantity of modern music offered by the theatre, seemed quite bizarre to Carl. He confronted the opposition straight away; in his fury he called them 'irresponsible rowdies' and lectured them on the theatre's task of furthering contemporary art. All this was, of course, widely reported. Professor Tiburtius, senator for Education and Cultural Affairs, persuaded my reluctant father to invite the 'Mafia' to a serious discussion. He, who normally thrived on such occasions, found the exercise dispiriting and distasteful. The organised galleryites turned out to be old-fashioned in their thinking and incapable of understanding what the meaning of this consummate art form 'opera' really is. They were only interested in delectable eighteenth- and nineteenth-century music performed by stars.

The lack of 'guest stars' was the second major issue. Carl clung to the idea of a star-status ensemble tied to the house for, at least, large parts of the year. He had people like Dietrich Fischer-Dieskau, Pilar Lorengar and Elisabeth Grümmer under contract, to mention just three international artists. They were available for all the rehearsals required to achieve a thoroughly prepared production. On the other hand, the travelling stars just jetted in and out, ruining any cohesive performance, by, necessarily, 'doing their own thing'. Pilar Lorengar, for example, had been the darling of the Berliners. Her popularity waned when she refused to rush about 'guesting'. She wanted to do what she called 'real' work in an ensemble. But to prove her status she accepted an engagement at the Metropolitan Opera, and she was feted there. After her return to Berlin, nothing more was said about Lorengar lacking international renown. While opera had its origin in elitist (court) entertainment, it is sad to reflect that, even in our democratic and enlightened age, there is still an element of snobbery or elitism in opera-going in some places. In Berlin the 'guest star' problem simply would not go away in the 1950s.

A year and a half after the *Re Corvo eclat*, Carl produced a new *Carmen* at the *Städtische Oper*. For the lead role he had engaged a talented young coloured American, Vera Little. At the end of the performance there were loud boos from the gallery. To prove to the shocked ensemble that the protest was directed at him, he asked them to let him go out by himself for a solo curtain call. He was right. The vociferous gallery wanted to hear one of the star Carmens of the moment, and not a young artist, however talented. Carl was deeply hurt by this mindless chauvinistic demonstration. Only a year before, the whole opera company had celebrated his seventieth birthday with a comprehensive show of music known to be dear to his heart. The full company, including orchestra, chorus and soloists was ranged on the stage. The auditorium was full of prominent members of Berlin's cultural life and company relatives, plus two large thrones from the theatre stores, decked with flowers, for Carl and Gertie. It was a beautiful and moving occasion, and the city of Berlin honoured my father with the award of the Ernst Reuter medal.

There was yet another issue waiting to be resolved by Carl on his Berlin take-over in 1954, this time not an extraneous distraction by the obstreperous gallery. But this problem was right at the heart of the artistic potential of the institute. It was the question of finding the best possible music director for the opera house. When Tietjen departed, he bequeathed to Carl a theatre without a distinctive musical profile. There were three extremely competent conductors, but not the outstanding musical personality that a house of the rank of the *Städtische Oper* demanded. Carl made the search for a worthy partner to head the music side of the theatre his first priority – and faced difficulties which he found hard to comprehend. He had to remind himself that Berlin was an enclave in 'enemy' territory; it was cumbersome to travel in or out (except by air, passports required), and for some people impossible to travel, full stop. There was no chance to drive out into the country to relax – because there was no country, except on the wrong side of the barbed wire and watchtowers surrounding the whole city. The Russians had tried to starve Berlin into submission with their blockade, worthy of a mediaeval siege. Although that attempt was defeated, it had an aftertaste; it made people wonder whether it would be wise to be stuck in the city in such an uncertain climate. One after another Carl's candidates for the post of music director declined – with regret. They all belonged to the first rank older generation. He then examined the group of younger music directors in the provinces. The outstanding career had been made by Wolfgang Sawallisch – after he had given himself a number of years to 'learn the repertory' in the small house of Aachen. Detailed negotiations dragged on, while Carl opted for personal experience of cooperation by inviting Sawallisch to conduct a new production of Verdi's *Masked Ball* which he produced.

All went well, even though Sawallisch was temperamentally worlds removed from Carl's personality: cool and calculating, but precise and just as demanding. In the end, negotiations collapsed over unjustifiable demands by Sawallisch. He wanted exclusive powers over choice of repertory, casting and engagement of singers, etc. etc: a list of powers which were not available to any music director in any German theatre, and which would have reduced the scope of the *Intendant*'s role to that of an administrator under the music director. Strange demands to make of an *Intendant* of Carl's standing and career. It was perhaps a rather awkward way of saying 'No thank you', but avoiding doing just that. But Carl was blamed for letting Sawallisch slip out of his grasp. There were voices in the papers criticising him for not making enough concessions in order to land a special talent – written by people who were not aware of the exact details of the negotiations and had no inkling of the dangers of a 'wrong' solution. For Carl, it was not a question of hanging on to certain strands of '*Intendant*-power', but of the responsibility of the office vis-à-vis the providers of the subsidy, State and Municipality. It is clearly impossible to have one person making the decisions and another person bearing the responsibility.

The adverse publicity in the Sawallisch case could have been avoided, I am sure, had Carl set out the facts in a simple, straightforward statement to all the papers, leaving it to them whether they wanted to use it or not. Although Carl had a generous quantum of charisma and no problems with personal relationships, he was incapable, throughout his life, of promoting his own interests. While fighting for the needs of his theatre, for instance in committee meetings of the subsidising authority, he enjoyed running rings round his adversaries among the politicians. But he would not spend time on contacting useful people in the right places at the right moment to do a little propaganda on his own account. He would have found it deadly boring. He never used a personal representative, agent or PR person.

By coincidence, I had earlier decided to try to get a job as producer in Germany, to learn the repertory more quickly and to experience the continental system of subsidised theatre at firsthand. I called on several *Intendants* and told my story of what I wanted and what little experience I had. The *Intendant* in Hannover reacted differently from the others when I introduced myself. He smiled as he asked me to sit down and begin my spiel – and he kept smiling all the way through. I wondered whether there was anything wrong. When I had finished, he said: 'I knew you as a baby.' He had been a devoted student of my father's in Frankfurt, and frequently came to the apartment for private lessons. My father could never tear himself away from the lesson he was giving, which often resulted in students being kept waiting or, if the weather was fine, being asked to take the children for a walk in the park opposite. My prospective *Intendant* said: 'I hated you and your sister. But that is not enough reason to give you a job now. As it happens, our chief producer this morning gave notice for the end of the season. We were debating whom we might approach when you rang. Are you prepared to do a guest production with a view to a contract?' Six weeks later was the premiere of Cimarosa's *The Secret Marriage* which I had not come across before. *Intendant* Kurt Ehrhardt came to me in the interval and said: 'Will you accept a three-year contract?' I started my appointment in Hannover in August of 1954, at the same time as my father took up his new/old post in Berlin.

His work at Glyndebourne had meanwhile expanded into longer and more arduous seasons. The number of performances increased from 14 in 1950 to 68 in 1959, two productions against six. Beginning with the 1954 season experienced assistants, e.g. Anthony Besch and myself, were given the task of rehearsing one or the other of my father's existing productions, to lighten the burden on him. In 1955 he did a new production of *Le Nozze di Figaro* with beautiful designs by Oliver Messel. For the Edinburgh Festival that year, Verdi's *Falstaff* was added to the Glyndebourne repertory for the first time, conducted by Carlo Maria Giulini and designed by Osbert Lancaster. Giulini, a sensitive and honest musician, excused himself from all later invitations to return to Glyndebourne – which was much regretted by everybody, because the collaboration among the production team appeared to be so smooth and inspired.

The 1955 cast were astonishingly well-balanced vocally and as characters, and Lancaster had created sets and costumes which were theatrically 'in period', with a delightful Lancastrian streak of irony. But the last scene in the Forest of Windsor was, as it should be, sheer magic. Although it employs large forces, *Falstaff* is really an intimate work, well suited to smaller theatres like Glyndebourne or, in this first instance, the King's Theatre, Edinburgh. That applies only if Verdi's unique filigree score receives the kind of meticulous care in preparation which had become synonymous with the name of Glyndebourne. It had a great success.

217

Glyndebourne was becoming ever more adept at attracting sponsorship in terms of cash or materials, made additional revenue through a glossy (and interesting!) Festival programme, and – most important of all – began to be sold out for every performance. That was an amazing turnround financially in a span of five years.

With the complex situations entailed in his Berlin position and the expanding Glyndebourne Festival, Carl had to deal with increasing responsibilities. Even so, the work ethos at Glyndebourne retained that unique quality of a dedicated, hardworking family. This feeling was undoubtedly mainly due to the personality and artistic integrity of Carl. It was as if the artists were working for him, to match his sincerity, instead of looking only to their personal gain. At the same time it seemed that Carl, at the age of 65, had entered into a particularly powerful phase in his work, a kind of artistic apotheosis. All his productions were of the highest standard, *quasi* a distillation of his credo and his craft, developed over almost 50 years of intense work in the theatre. Probably the end of the period of bitty bouts of guesting and teaching, and the formidable challenges of his Berlin appointment in a period of massive changes in attitude and expression in society, had something to do with this final burst of energy in his life.

The Glyndebourne management did not always see it in this light. My father's inability regularly to match the pace of correspondence which John Christie and Moran Caplat desired, led occasionally to some tension and also encouraged the tendency of Caplat to try and usurp some artistic decisions. This trend had already manifested itself in Rudi Bing's last years at Glyndebourne (after the end of the war), but at that time it was almost inevitable through the horrendous difficulties of communication.

The 1956 season had been planned to include new productions of *Die Zauberflöte* and *Die Entführung aus dem Serail*. Carl was keen to achieve a new approach to the *Magic Flute*. He did some preliminary work with Sir Hugh Casson, in whom he had found a stimulating partner on *Alceste* three years earlier. Sir Hugh and his costume designer Miss Evans produced interesting ideas with a strong Japanese influence. The *Magic Flute* is, after all, an oriental fairy tale. It was a great pity that Carl could not quite bring himself to pursue this line of thought. It offered him what he was looking

218

for, a more modern look at the work. Glyndebourne pressurised Carl into accepting Oliver Messel as designer, pleading dangerously close deadlines for making of scenery and costumes. Messel had provided excellent designs for *Idomeneo*, *Cenerentola*, *Figaro* and *Comte Ory*. He and Carl had worked well together. Messel's designs for the *Magic Flute* were beautiful, but close to a museum piece: Viennese Baroque, with the typical stock images of broken columns of the Romantic period. The young and convincing cast included Geraint Evans, a perfect Papageno, Joan Sutherland as the First Lady, the just-discovered Pilar Lorengar as a touching Pamina, Mattiwilda Dobbs – who sailed through the testing Queen of the Night music as if she had no idea how difficult it was – and Ernst Häfliger, a manly Tamino.

A little backstage incident illuminates the family feeling at Glyndebourne. A young German soprano, singing Donna Elvira in *Giovanni*, was terribly nervous and consequently suffered from lack of sleep. The kind Yugoslav Sarastro heard about this, and approached her at the end of her evening rehearsal and said: 'I 'ave Slibovitch, come to me forr sleepingk.' However, there were quite a few genuine romances too – inevitably.

Seraglio was the first full-length production at Glyndebourne entrusted to me. I had no problem in working with Oliver Messel on this work, as it suited his style perfectly. Paul Sacher conducted with delicacy and firmness, two supremely important ingredients of Mozart's score, so often underrated. He also cleansed the work of all sentimentality and made it human. The cast was as near-perfect as one could only dream about, and the production was well received. (Through the unforgivable mistake in the production index of Spike Hughes' book, Bernard Levin, in his excellent obituary of my father in *The Times*, unfortunately singled out my production as one of his best achievements.)

In 1957 Geraint Evans sang his first Falstaff, a role which he relished and made very much his own. He mastered all the facets of the character to perfection, the bluffness, philosophy, slyness, charm, cowardice and, underlying it all, a great natural nobility. A few years later, in an interview, he said how he had enjoyed forging the role with Carl and finished with: 'I believe the Professor thought he had invented me.'

The 1958 season consisted mainly of current productions, but was preceded by a slice of cheek on the part of Glyndebourne. An invitation had come from Paris to present two productions at the Spring Festival called *Theatre des Nations*. Glyndebourne opted for *Falstaff* and *Le Comte Ory* (in French). Our nervousness was not justified; the reception was magnificent. John Christie, although not a Francophile, came to Paris to share in the glow of the company's success with the public and critics. There is a wonderful photograph of him attending a reception in honour of Glyndebourne at the British Embassy. It reveals the epitome of a British upper-class landowner of a fading age come to town in style – comfortable loose-cut clothes, a hat called a square bowler. His stance is confident, rock-solid, certain of his position and his mission in life, warm and kind, not arrogant.

John had had to be a little more careful of his health in recent years; heart trouble had sent an advance warning. But otherwise he remained the same, he still turned out the dressing room lights before everybody had left, tried to convince some patrons that one of the orchestra players on the croquet lawn was in fact Sir Thomas Beecham. But he had very few opportunities to bring people into the theatre to watch one of my father's awesome outbursts of fury during rehearsals. Carl had become more mellow, but his rehearsals were just as intense as before. I heard later that John and Audrey had wanted to terminate my engagement at Glyndebourne, fearing that my influence on Carl's work was too calming. I doubt it. John's sense of fun never left him, not even during illness. One day, when he was supposed to be accompanied by a nurse every moment of the day, Carl and I met him wandering about between the theatre and the canteen. Carl asked anxiously: 'John, are you all right? Where is your nurse?' He came closer: 'I've locked her in the cupboard.'

The 1959 season was the twenty-fifth anniversary of the first Festival at Glyndebourne. It was decided to open on the same day, 28 May, with a work which nobody would have thought suitable for the small theatre only 10 years earlier, *Der Rosenkavalier* by Richard Strauss. It is in fact an intimate opera, except for three brief scenes, but it employs large orchestral forces. The quadrumvirate had indeed considered the possibility of doing

220

Rosenkavalier before and after the war, because Fritz Busch thought that Strauss' own reduced orchestral version would make it possible. In the meantime the auditorium had been enlarged in volume (under the same roof) as well as seating, which had risen to just under 800.

Carl had been responsible for the artistic direction of the Glyndebourne Festival – together with Fritz Busch, when he was there – since the first season in 1934. 1959 was to become his farewell. One day in late 1958 Carl had a letter from John Christie, saying that he was retiring and handing over the reins to his son George, who had already become Chairman of the Board a few years earlier. He said he thought perhaps it was time for Carl to retire as well. He sent best wishes, mentioning that the dog was well. Carl was incredibly hurt, not so much by the fact as the manner of his dismissal. It read to him as if he had only been in charge of the vegetable garden – one of 'my men'. It seemed such a long way from the touching letter he received, shut away in Turkey in 1941, from Rudi Bing describing his and John Christie's lonely life in wartime Glyndebourne, when John suddenly said:'If only Charles would walk through the door now.'

So *Rosenkavalier* became his farewell gift to his 'favourite baby', as he called Glyndebourne. Leopold Ludwig, from Hamburg, was called in to conduct. He had the reputation of being a Strauss specialist. The eighteenth-century Vienna of the plot was the ideal vehicle for Oliver Messel's marvellous scenery and costumes down to the smallest detail. The only thing he did not quite manage to convey, perhaps, was the *nouveau riche* character of the upstart Faninal's house in Act 2, compared to the 'real' thing in the first Act. But then I have never seen this subtle difference brought out in any other production. The cast was also nothing short of ideal: Elisabeth Söderström as a vulnerable, ardent, romantic aristocrat with a cheeky sense of humour, Regine Crespin noble to her fingertips, with a smile in her resignation and so intensely human as the *Feldmarschallin*, Oscar Czerwenka for once a boorish, overbearing Baron Ochs in whom one could feel his aristocratic core, and Anneliese Rothenberger's fragile, shy Sophie. All the smaller parts kept pace with this outstanding quartet. It was one of Glyndebourne's most perfect achievements to date, the critics acknowledged it as such, and the audience were carried away. At the end of the performance John Christie and my father came on stage. Christie made one of his famous, rather muddled, speeches, talking about all his likes and dislikes but forgetting to say anything at all about the purpose of the exercise, namely to say 'Goodbye' or possibly '*Au revoir*' to the artistic Director of Glyndebourne's first 25 years – until Moran Caplat reminded him, and then he handed over an exquisite rose bowl, designed and inscribed for the occasion.

As a relatively new citizen of the USA, Carl had to have a special law passed through Congress which would allow him to stay abroad longer without losing the citizenship. The time drew near when this would not be possible any more; in fact, the summer of 1961 was the deadline. Since he had taken over the *Städtische Oper* in 1954, Carl had spent a great deal of time on the planning for the new opera house to be built on the site of the one destroyed in the war. He concerned himself with all the minute details of the technical provisions behind the curtain, as well as the layout and facilities of the auditorium and in the foyers. He liked this work particularly, because he had once been engaged with his architect friend Clemens Holzmeister in devising plans for 'the ideal theatre', while they were both working in Turkey. Holzmeister subsequently built the new *Grosse Festspielhaus* in Salzburg. No theatre site is ever perfect, of course – in Berlin, the size and shape of the plot was given through the existing road layout, while in Salzburg Holzmeister had to hollow out the Mönchsberg, in the middle of town, to accommodate the enormous theatre he was commissioned to design. Theatres (and hospitals?) probably have to be counted the most complicated buildings. In Berlin and Salzburg, the results were good for the audience as well as the 'workers'. A determined effort was made to complete the new building in Berlin in time for the introduction of a new *Intendant*. Against all precedents, the deadline was achieved.

Senator Professor Tiburtius also asked for Carl's advice in the delicate task of finding the right successor. The shortlist was narrowed to two candidates: the first was Wieland Wagner, Richard's grandson, who had revolutionised the Bayreuth Festival. Formerly the temple of unquestioning tradition, Bayreuth was transformed by Wieland's – and his brother Wolfgang's – modern interpretation of the great Wagner masterpieces. Their treatment made the Wagner operas interesting once more. The other candidate was Gustav Rudolf Sellner, *Intendant* in Darmstadt. Carl invited both of them to do a production in the soon-to-be-phased-out old house in Berlin. Wagner produced an interesting, slightly controversial *Aida*; Sellner was given Schoenberg's fiendishly difficult *Moses and Aaron*. The idea was that the whole theatre personnel and the audience should have a chance to gain an impression of the two main contenders. The Senator finally came to the conclusion that the future would be better served under Sellner.

Carl, in the meantime, continued his final flourish of successes with *Comte Ory*, *Falstaff* (he had to work hard to persuade Fischer-Dieskau to take the title role, in which he could not see himself at all), and a rarely performed work by Cherubini, *Medea*, plus a new *Rosenkavalier*. He had carefully worked out a plan to hand over to the new *Intendant* a polished array of productions for transfer to the new house. The last season in the old theatre was almost exclusively devoted to this task. In Germany over 30 opera houses had to be rebuilt/newly built after the war. Every time, one of the main problems on moving into a new theatre proved to be how to provide a balanced and interesting repertory from existing productions until enough new operas have been produced by the new management. Carl could be pleased that he had done everything in his power to ease the problems of his successor – something that is fairly rare.

My father had always been fond of the sea. He decided the journey into his new life as a pensioner in the US should be a treat – he wanted to go by boat. Silvia and I met him and Gertie in Rotterdam, where they embarked on a Dutch liner for New York. It was June, and the weather was gorgeous. While Gertie settled into their cabin right under the bridge, looking out over the bows, my father showed Silvia and me the whole ship, including the children's playroom. He was as pleased as if he had designed and owned the whole thing. The trip was only a qualified success, unfortunately. As soon as they had left the Continental Shelf behind a violent storm blew up, which tied the parents to their beds for four days and nights. The storm abated, but they immediately ran into a dense fog bank which enveloped the boat for the next two-and-a-half days, all the way to New York. The foghorn was right above their cabin.

Why the parents wanted to retire to the States, and particularly Los Angeles or vicinity, was a mystery for us at first. Carl had been so scathing about the cultural desert of Southern California. And he was so essentially European, although he did enjoy discovering the States and observing the people. The reasons for their decision must have been that all three younger children lived in the US – though a few thousand miles away in the East.

Carl and Gertie soon found a comfortable bungalow with an enormous garage and small garden in Pacific Palisades, at the western end of Los Angeles, several hundred feet up, with a lovely view over the Pacific and into the almost uninhabited hills. At the age of 74, my father signed a 20-year mortgage and became what is now known as a first-time buyer. Although he had no talent for practical work, he decided to learn and set to creating a garden out of their strip of land, which the Americans call a back yard. His methods were unorthodox – such as picking aphids off his roses with tweezers and putting them to death in a ceremonial *auto-da-fe*, but all his carefully positioned planting of shrubs and small trees soon made a charming, and in part exotic, frame to their lawn. The benign climate made everything grow incredibly fast by European standards.

I don't think the sudden change from supercharged working schedules to a pensioner's life proved a problem for Carl. Apart from making the house lived-in and his garden established, he had time at last to catch up with reading. The parents also renewed contact with their friends from earlier times – although they had never indulged in much socialising. Carl did, however, lack intellectual stimulus. He hated the jargon and style of American magazines and newspapers. He helped to initiate the setting-up of a group of men, who met in each others' houses once a month. They were middle-aged or elderly and represented a wide range of professions: diplomats, nuclear physicists, writers, film makers and doctors. The idea was to discuss topical or general problems of a political, social or environmental nature, for instance. Carl

224

enjoyed the range of company and subjects, although he was not a typical 'club' man at all. Occasionally he had to call his group to order, reminding them that they were not meeting just to enjoy the hostess' food and tell anecdotes. That kind of socialising was of no interest to him.

Carl continued with the odd opera production in New York, and he had to return to Berlin quite soon to do the opening production in the new house. It was a generous gesture of the new *Intendant* to invite his predecessor, and, one could say, the doyen of German *Intendants*, to open the first season with a new *Don Giovanni*. It turned out a mixed blessing. He was happy, of course, to work with the ensemble again, which now included some new members, but he was obliged to accept a designer who represented the fashionable trend of overblown, overintrusive, overcomplicated scenery and costumes. It was the beginning of the new style of representational, not to say ostentatious, opera policy, the very thing Carl had fought against. Perhaps it was the right time for him to have left the stage. Or at least he had taken the first step. A few years later he was invited back to Berlin to produce the *Rake's Progress* – his third production including the world premiere of the work in Venice and Glyndebourne. The Berlin production was a kind of eightieth birthday celebration for him and the audience.

One more production was important to him, to seal his relationship with Glyndebourne. In 1962 he went back to Sussex to produce, for the first time in his life, Debussy's *Pelleas et Melisande*. Again the designer turned out to be a problem, a very talented young man, Beni Montresor, who brought limited stagecraft experience to an elusive and complicated work. The atmosphere of set and costume designs was marvellous for this extraordinary, mystic, romantic and, at times, brutal opera. The problem lay in translating the designs into workable – and lightable – stage sets, particularly since the music is continuous within each act and requires some hazardously quick set changes. In the end, all these difficulties were overcome successfully. It was a happy occasion for Carl to renew his long-standing partnership with the conductor, Vittorio Gui. He brought out all the subtleties of the strangely modern score of Debussy's only opera. It became obvious to me early on into rehearsals how productive it was for Carl to be confronted with a work he had not done before. The cast were good, without being individually outstanding. Carl made a seemingly ideal whole out of the components he was working with. In tandem with their reaction to *Rosenkavalier*, three years earlier, some of the critics thought this was the best thing Carl had ever done at Glyndebourne. A satisfactory exit.

He did not go back to Glyndebourne after *Pelleas*. He could not picture himself sitting in the auditorium and watching a performance. He preferred to live with the vivid memories of the excitement and worries of building something unique and leading it to an unprecedented success within a quarter of a century. He could also have reflected on the fact that he, more than anybody else, had brought about a new appraisal of opera production in Britain and had, therefore, been the principal source of opera renaissance which had developed after the war, through his own work and that of the assistants he had trained, to be followed by a whole new generation of new producers. Perhaps he reflected on it, but not once did he lay claim to the achievement.

In 1951 a festival was launched in the small port of Wexford in South-East Ireland. It was conceived under unusual circumstances. Sir Compton Mackenzie told a group of friends in Wexford if they disliked the opera performances available in Dublin so much, they should start their own festival. And so it came about that four ardent music-lovers: two doctors, one hotel owner and a postman, set up a committee under the chairmanship of Dr Tom Walsh to establish a new festival. They were richly rewarded for the enormous amount of energy they expended on this project: Wexford is firmly established on the festival calendar of the cognoscenti.

From the start Wexford had a particularly happy working – and social – atmosphere. The whole population, at first sceptical, became besotted with opera before long. Dr Walsh and his team scanned the airwaves for opera performances on their high-powered radios and displayed an uncanny capacity for spotting good voices. As a result Wexford experienced a stream of talented artists from around the world, including almost every rising star. The people of Wexford took the artists to their hearts and worked round the clock to make every one welcome and to make the festival a success. The festival specialised in lesser-known works and I did 12 productions starting with *L'Elisir d'Amore* in 1952 and including *La Gioconda!*

For 1965 Dr Walsh had the idea of inviting my father to produce Massenet's *Don Quichotte*, myself to produce *Traviata* and Mozart's *Finta Giardiniera* and Judith, my eldest daughter of my first marriage, to design the Mozart production and to build the good horse *Rosinante* for the Massenet opera. It was a very happy family occasion.

In Los Angeles Carl continued his amateur efforts in his garden – with some spectacular successes, such as his tubs with hundreds of beautiful orchids. He started to box them carefully and send them to his children. He liked it even better if we came to see him and Gertie in their new home, which gloried in the mixed-metaphor address of Enchanted Way, Pacific Palisades. Los Angeles is really a horrible place, but has a number of redeeming features, such as the Farmers' Market – where Carl liked to take people to eat – the beaches, the hills, the empty canyons, Easter Sunrise Service in the Hollywood Bowl, the desert. Even Disneyland and Marineland are fascinating in their own way – ignoring the razmatazz, they are highly professional.

Soon Carl found that he felt deprived without breathing the air of Europe occasionally. Luckily, he was still a member of various international bodies, like the International Theatre Institute. Their meetings gave him a welcome excuse for a trip to Europe – and sometimes even paid his travelling expenses. My father was financially better off in retirement than he had ever been – no obligations and a secure income. In his last years in Berlin he had made a point of negotiating a higher pension, rather than a higher salary. When he approached his nineties he used to say: 'Poor, poor Berlin. Having to pay me that pension for so many years'.

Two things were really important to him on the long-haul trips to Europe via the Eastern States: the theatre, and seeing his children and grandchildren. As a teenager, he had been told by the head of the Potulicky family not to hanker after his father's name, but to go out and start a new family tree. As the number of his own children increased and then the grandchildren started to arrive, he developed a strong patriarchal pride. My brother and younger sisters had two children each. Silvia and I had eight children – and I had two more from a previous marriage. That made 16 in all. His joy was only tempered by his worry how Silvia and I could manage financially. Silvia made the announcement of the happy news later and later each time. I think it was her letter saying that the arrival of number six was imminent, which prompted the telegraphic response from my father: 'Suggest name: Basta.'

When he came to visit us in Britain or in Germany he wanted to go to the theatre every night, especially in the places where I was *Intendant*. He would go to anything and everything, even operettas and musicals. I don't think it was just the pride of the patriarch sitting in the box of the *Intendant*. He was actually feeling the drought of worthwhile theatrical experiences in Los Angeles. There were, of course, quite a number of modern and also experimental groups working in the city, always in an *ad-hoc*, haphazard way, and usually without sufficient resources. What he disliked intensely about the American drama scene of the time was the fetish of being 'modern' by speaking 'naturally', which was the equivalent of being largely inaudible. He realised clearly enough that the theatre has to develop continually, but he had been brought up to believe that the use of the human voice is the most important and effective instrument at the disposal of an actor. When my brother was forming his theatrical career, Carl could not resist giving him advice and warning him about false gods. In the end, they fell out over the problem of modern presentation. My sister Christa was very keen to train to be a singer once she had settled in the States. My father was so obsessed with the fear that she might increase the 'theatrical proletariat' that he put every obstacle in her way, without having given her the benefit of a proper test or trial period. Eventually she gave up her plan. She felt quite bitter about it – she concentrated on her other passion, writing, and produced remarkable, haunting poetry.

With his large tribe of children, grandchildren and great-grand-children around him, Carl felt he had got on level terms with the Potulicky family. And yet he would have liked to have something personal, a physical tie to his father's memory. He wrote to his stepmother, if that is the word, Countess Potulicky, in Warsaw, saying that it would be his dearest wish to have some small personal souvenir of his father. He received a very nice, kind reply, saying that she had nothing she could give him. Her husband had died suddenly and had left many debts, life had been difficult – and the war had destroyed the rest. Was her warm, but guarded language meant to frustrate any possible claim by Carl?

A few years later, Carl received a letter from a Stanislaus Potulicky, explaining that he was the eldest son of Count Anton's marriage, his only living relative. He was in New York with his wife. My father, at the age of 75, was very excited indeed to have found his own brother. It was almost a religious act for him to embrace Stash, as he was called for short, and his wife Mary, and thus close the family circle. They came to love each other and met often, particularly when Stash and Mary moved out to California. Stash had my father's forehead and his lively, searching eyes, and a warm, kind nature. He never ceased to wonder about their completely different upbringing and their careers. He had not learnt anything other than running an estate, and had fled from the Russians by stowing away on a boat to Sweden. His brother's life in the theatre was a miracle to him. Whenever I went out to California I visited my uncle Stash. He still drove down to the beach at the age of 92 and had a dip in the Pacific under supervision of his nurse.

Carl could not cope at all with the onset of infirmity round about his ninetieth birthday. What he really needed was a Zimmer frame, to allow him to move about the house without falling over and injuring himself. He sneakily tried to avoid using it – and of course he did fall over. When we prevailed on him to use the Zimmer, he treated it jauntily, almost like a walking stick. That was not ideal either. We teased him about being too proud. A good friend of the family's (Carl had known him for 70 years), John Brahm, a film director, lived fairly close and came to visit regularly. He had had a stroke which left one leg paralysed, but he surmounted the problem through his philosophical equilibrium. Even this excellent example did not make my father mend his ways.

He and John Brahm remained passionately interested in the arts to the end. One day Silvia and I took the two old men to see the brand new musical *A Chorus Line*, which was the rage of the moment. At that time there was no provision for wheelchair users. It proved ridiculously difficult to get them to a good vantage point in the Circle. At the end they were both enthusiastic, as Carl thought the production was brilliant and the whole idea and structure riveting. I asked him whether he had understood the heavily-accented American which the actors used. 'Not a word,' he said with a sly smile.

However, he still enjoyed putting on an act, as on the occasion of his birthday when we children jointly gave him an armchair with a motor for lifting and tilting the occupant of the seat, very gently, into the upright position – like a mini-dumper truck. After a couple of lessons, Carl was to operate the system himself. The astonishment and wonder in his eyes and body language as he was stood upright by the chair was an effective bit of stagecraft.

I went out to Los Angeles every year, to continue the productions of operas for schoolchildren which Carl had started. Every time I came laden with messages from acquaintances and friends wanting to be remembered to him and wishing him well. It made me sad to see how pleased he was to hear from so many people with whom he had no contact by correspondence. It seemed quite unnatural that he should feel so lonely and forgotten – when obviously he was not. He kept saying: 'Really? Such and such has not forgotten me?' It even annoyed me, because everybody connected with or interested in the theatre remembered him at that time.

It was probably the distance from Europe and living in that unloved desert of Los Angeles which made him feel so isolated. On the other hand, there were always dozens of newspaper articles and radio programmes whenever he reached another milestone of age, and people came, sometimes a long way, to interview him. Most of these tributes charted his outstanding career, influenced by political events which Carl had managed to turn to advantage through his eagerness to learn from experiencing different cultures. The tributes pointed to the innovation which he brought about on his arrival to the opera scene in the 1920s; the thoroughness with which he rid productions of the old pomposity and posturing; the way his work concentrated on the human element; his ability to distil from the music and text the most subtle variations of human emotions, whether the source was Rossini, Stravinsky, a contemporary composer, or Verdi and Mozart. His genius for teaching was often written about, e.g. as witnessed in the BBC Masterclasses, and his uncommon ability to handle people and inspire them. The most respected theatre people and critics combined to analyse and describe his powers. He was very pleased, but felt too far away from it all. It was not that he craved more official acknowledgement. He had several Honorary Doctorates, the CBE (his most prized honour), and similar orders from Germany, Italy, Austria and Denmark. Perhaps he simply suffered from the natural feeling that, even in his over-full life, he had not accomplished everything he had wished to do.

Carl's feeling of isolation became suddenly worse when he, or Gertie, decided he should give up his trips to Europe. At that time it had become fashionable in America to sue doctors for anything and everything. His own doctor had merely said one day: 'I can no longer take responsibility for your trip to Europe' – just to protect himself, of course, but panic set in and the trip was cancelled. My father began to fade rapidly. He felt imprisoned. About two years later he said to me:

'I should not have allowed the doctor's remark to frighten me. And if I had had a stroke on the trip to Europe – what matter? I have had a good life.'

And then, at the age of 92, the one thing happened which he had not even considered, his wife Gertie, 12 years his junior, died. It was a great shock to him. For many years he had worried about what would happen to Gertie when he was no more, until I told him quite firmly that we four children had every intention of making her life as pleasant and interesting as we could. My sisters Renata and Christa took it in turn to be with Carl as much as they could after Gertie's death, even though they had to neglect their own families all the while, thousands of miles away. For the rest of the time, Carl had to rely mostly on South American illegal immigrants as housekeepers. It was hard for him, as he found it very difficult to communicate with them.

My own mother had been widowed for many years, my stepfather Hans Oppenheim having succumbed to an untreatable leukaemia. Although they had felt it necessary to separate many decades before, I believe my mother had always remained in love with my father. For her ninetieth birthday he sent her a present with this note :

'I saw this necklace and was touched by the thought: how much I would have liked to put it round your neck, my first great love. Please accept it from me, as a small expression of our young, beautiful love. May God protect you and grant you years of enjoyment still in remembering the past.'

In May 1980 my father had to go into hospital. When I arrived in Los Angeles, my sisters were at his bedside. He was connected to two or three tubes and was under sedation, dozing most of the time, but had no problem in recognising and remembering everything. He was very happy to have us with him. Every half hour or hour, a nurse would come into his room with a trolley, looked at the name on the bed and at his/her clipboard, sorted out the prescribed drugs and put them in his mouth. Renata had to return to New York that evening; Christa and I stayed at the bedside. After a few hours the medicine routine made me nervous. Christa and I decided to talk to the doctor. I told him that we were wondering what was going on. If the purpose of the drugs was simply to keep the body machine running, we were not in favour of it, because it hardly represented any recognisable form of life for Carl. The doctor explained that he had continued the drugs which our father had already been prescribed before, and had added one or two. We said that we did not want the kind of treatment which had kept Marshal Tito artificially alive for weeks if not months, a while before.

When we returned next morning Carl was wide awake, greeting us with great joy. We talked and laughed, he had a little nap from time to time; occasionally he would fall silent and an intense look of searching for something in the far distance came into his eyes. It was quite strange. Then, suddenly, he threw back his bedclothes and made as if to get out of bed. We stopped him just in time – he was still attached to his tubes. We talked about present-day problems and reminisced some more. Finally he grew tired and wanted to go to sleep. It had been such an animated and lovely day, Christa and I were quite tired too. We decided to go home to my father's house, have a shower and something to eat and then return. We had not been home long when the telephone rang: our father had died peacefully in his sleep. It had been a good life and a long one. He had given immeasurable joy to his family, and to so many other people.

In a memorial service in Berlin, the then *Intendant* of the *Städtische Oper*, and the most prominent of modern opera producers, spoke a comprehensive epitaph for my father's professional career:

'Carl Ebert was the father of all our endeavours.'

INDEX

235